# Why I was born in
# Africa

# Why I was born in
# Africa

The previously unrecorded history of
Elysium and the Lion Kingdom

JUDITH KÜSEL

Published by Judith Küsel

http://www.judithkusel.com

info@judithkusel.com

First edition 2017

**Why I Was Born in Africa**

ISBN 978-0-620-72114-1

Editor: Janet Hayward Vollmer

Proofreader: Michelle Bovey-Wood

Photography: Judith Küsel

Book design: Vanessa Wilson

Production assistant: Jill Charlotte

Typesetting and production: Quickfox Publishing

Printed by Creda Communications, Cape Town, South Africa

# Dedication

This book is dedicated to those beautiful and precious souls who kept faith in me. No matter how much I was being challenged, they loved me unconditionally.

First and foremost, this is for my sister, Barbara, and my brother-in-law, Braam Botha and their family, who were there through thick and thin. They helped me enormously through the darkest period of my life, giving me a home and shelter when I needed it most. I cannot thank them enough.

This is also for my brother, Peter, who supported me, kept faith in me and taught me to never, ever give up. When he saw my journey coming together, he thanked me for keeping the family tradition alive and for cleaving open new pathways for humanity.

Grateful thanks to the rest of my family: My parents, brothers and sister, for teaching me so many valuable lessons about life. Most of all, thank you for never giving up on my visions and dreams. That pioneering spirit and perseverance, and the inner strength springing from my profound connection to the Divine, have stood the test of time.

I thank Jill Charlotte for her unfailing support, and for always being there for me when I needed encouragement and someone to cheer me on. Also,

thank you for her immense work in editing and putting together this book.

I thank Janet Hayward Vollmer, who volunteered to do the editing over a time period of about three years, in addition to her own work as an English teacher in France. Thank you, Janet, for believing in me and my vision, and for all the work you put in.

I thank Susan Kerr and Jill Charlotte for being there when I needed crystal-clear information and guidance from Cosmic sources, and the reassurance that I was indeed on track.

Thank you also to those beautiful souls who have supported my work via Facebook, Twitter, my website, and my WordPress site, and who have had Soul readings from me and bought my first book, *Soul Empowerment*.

More than anything, I thank the Divine, my Higher Guides, the Archangels, the Elohim and Elohim Councils, the Ancient Ones, the Lion King and the Lion People, and all those who guided me, opened up my transmitter channels, activated keys and codes, and were there for me so often when I had no one to turn to and nowhere to go to. You have been my anchor and my stay: The source of the greatest love in my life!

# Contents

# Foreword

My initial contact with Judith was in 2012, when I read an article she had written. Having been born and raised in Zimbabwe, I felt an instant connection and strong desire to have a Soul reading with her. In this reading, with uncanny accuracy, she was able to clarify many things I'd sensed but had been unable to fully express. It brought me great insight and confirmation. This was my first experience (in this life!) of her incredible ability to connect individuals with their deep Soul purpose, using her gift of clear seeing, and the capacity to put herself aside and transmit higher guidance and Divine keys and blueprints.

Since then, I've had the privilege of getting to know her better, both through editing this biographical account of her journey to discover our lost ancient history, and also through meeting her in person. We first met in her beloved Nature's Valley in South Africa, where I had a rejuvenating walk on her magical beach, and was warmly welcomed into her home. Later, I was a participant in her seminars in the Languedoc region of France, which was transformative on many levels.

Judith is a wise and loving woman who walks her talk and follows her inner guidance consistently and uncompromisingly, fully embodying her gifts and her higher Soul identity. Thus, she has been able to help,

inspire and educate many, both in this world and in the next.

On our inner and outer journey, during the seminars in France, we observed her profound connection to our planet and its energies, and her ability to read the landscape and traverse time and dimensions when mapping our collective history. She helped us to access our own heart wisdom, as well as the divine feminine energies of sacred France; the site of the ancient Mystery Schools. She showed us how to perceive deeper layers of truth, and other dimensions and realities...

She is following her path, step by step, helping to liberate both lands and people from suffering and historical pain over many generations, and doing her part to bring back the kingdom of heart and love. It is exciting to watch her journey unfold so precisely, in heavenly order and timing.

I am grateful for these precious opportunities for us all to unite and make our unique contributions at this incredible moment in the history of our planet, at the dawn of the New Golden Age... Thank you, Judith, for being a spiritual pioneer and a way-shower, and for shining your bright light on the path ahead.

**– Jan Hayward**

# Foreword (cont.)

I have had the pleasure of knowing Judith for many years. I first made her acquaintance when she was embarking on her path towards discovering who she really was and why her perceptions were so heightened, and becoming increasingly so. From the outset, she had an unprecedented depth and range of abilities to read and interpret the energy around her and that of other people, present in these bodies or not, and so to distil what was really going on. All the while, she is motivated by her innate, inherent sense of a greater purpose. She is fuelled by her extreme joy in her major contribution to the spiritual upliftment of this planet. She is a pioneer in the arts of restoring ancient wisdoms and practices to this sometimes sleepy planet.

Her story is unique, as it is based in the untold forgotten secrets of Africa, as she reveals these long-ago, old truths; dissembling their current relevance. She has visited sites of buried spiritual truths that were waiting for her to recognise and remember. This is not an academic book based on hope, but a dynamic, interactive play between the mundane now and the eternal truth.

From the outset, she largely carved her path out alone, leaning towards what really is – the full spectrum of this life and source energy. With her unique, finely-tuned ability to span the here-and-now with the over-there-and-then, she ushers in the bright future.

She is a beautiful visionary – a bridge between the worlds; a modern-day shaman who goes on ahead so we that may follow. Her other-worldly ways of perceiving things are what make her so different. She has walked and driven and climbed and explored southern Africa to unlock these secrets. There is a growing appreciation on all fronts for what she actually does say and how she has mastered the subtle art of living in both worlds at once to bring them together. She is tireless and absolutely dedicated to her mission to transform and uplift.

Judith is also a consummate artist in her own right, as witnessed by her expression in many mediums. She presents her visions and understandings in a growing number of ways: From the written word, to public speaking, counselling, and her artful choice of lifestyle. She has a rapidly-growing international following, as the world recognises her as a writer, speaker, photographer, artist and healer on all levels, as she radiates out in all directions. She shares her vision in every way she can and is about to launch into her next adventure in France, where she will uncover more secrets to share with us there. She is a light being extraordinaire!

**– Jill Charlotte**

# Introduction

## The Awakening

How does one start an inner Quest?

Mine started during an extremely difficult period of my life – when a dark night of the soul had descended upon me and everything that I held most dear was caving in on me – and I asked myself the question: "*Why was I born in Africa?*" Why not in Germany, for instance, from where my family originated?

Here I was, a fifth-generation German South African living on the African continent, wondering why my Soul had chosen Africa for its short sojourn on Earth!

The question arose when my carefully constructed, successful working life suddenly collapsed around me, and the proverbial carpet was pulled from under my feet. I was shocked and disheartened to find myself in what had become a rapidly snowballing political minefield.

I had been a librarian at the Natal Provincial and Public Library Services for 34 years, and I had enjoyed every minute of it. It had combined my deep love for both books and people. I loved inspiring the community to become involved with various library projects and community fundraising activities, since there was a dire shortage of funding for new books.

One day, after a morning off, I returned, and a junior staff member followed me into my office declaring: "If you do not vacate this office within two hours, it will be done for you!"

Not one of my superiors had even bothered to call me in and explain the reason for this sudden demotion. Rather, they had left the job to the junior staff members!

The affirmative action policy in South Africa

meant that, in an unmitigated political move, someone else could be instantly appointed head librarian – even someone completely unqualified for the position.

Amidst community outrage, with articles appearing in local newspapers, our trade union took the matter to court. The advocate won the case in my favor, but no one heeded this decision. Indeed, it became a quagmire, with death threats coming my way as a result.

The answer to my question, "Why was I born in Africa?" came in the middle of the night! I was asked to take out a map of Africa, to find my birth place and then to locate the 33° longitude line and the matching latitude line, and to mark them in red.

As I did this, I was told that my having been born in Africa was neither a fluke nor an accident, but it was indeed the only place on the planet where my Soul could have incarnated at this time! My hometown was deliberately small and hidden away, but it was located on one of the most sacred energy lines on Earth.

I was completely stunned by this revelation, and from that moment on, I began seeing energy fields and strange things started to occur.

In May 2008, I was given a vision that profoundly changed my life. I was standing on the edge of a cliff with my Higher Guides, and they were showing me the valley below, which was filled with thousands of people. They asked me: "How long are you going to stand at the edge of this cliff and not have the courage to step off it and find your wings to fly?"

I was then shown an eagle (which is my totem animal) and how it learns to fly when its mother kicks it out of the nest. It is forced to find its wings and fly. The next day, I handed in my resignation. It was as if a weight had been lifted off me!

In my wildest dreams, I had no idea where this simple question would lead me, nor what would happen next. All I knew was that I had to find an answer from somewhere deep inside, and I promised myself that no matter what happened, I would not die with my dream of writing a book still unfulfilled within me. I owed it to myself.

If I was to die at the end of my quest, at least I would have died following my dream, and not because of the actual death threats coming my way!

This book took shape from the answers I received. It records the subsequent journey that led me to discover something so profound that it truly is of global significance. Today, I am reaching thousands of people across the world with my writings, teachings and Soul readings.

The first chapters describe the beginning of this journey and the pieces of the puzzle, as they were revealed to me. I ask you to simply read this account as if you were journeying with me. As my travels unfold, Africa will start revealing her veiled face.

I have left my diary entries largely unedited, recording my experiences in the moment, for I wanted this book to be as authentic as possible – mostly because this journey is an extraordinary one, and it goes as deeply into the layers of the subconscious landscape as it does into the conscious, visible one. Through my journey, I finally learnt about the Super Consciousness Energy Field, and just how to tap into it.

This was an awakening, an opening up of my Soul on multiple levels, that enabled me to tap into something ancient, profound and previously unrecorded.

I am asking you, therefore, to accompany me on this journey, and, as it unfolds, to keep your heart and mind open, for it will trigger vast memory banks within your Soul, too.

# PART I

# JOURNEY TO KAAPSEHOOP

# CHAPTER 1

# My Quest…

All journeys first start with a vision that becomes a quest.

During the early 2000s, when my life was in a state of flux, I started to shift in many ways. Up until that time, my whole existence had been living and working among books. As I look back upon all those years as a librarian, I had always had a deep hunger within me to know about the extraordinary, the hidden and the mysterious. Those years had been but preparation for one day embarking on my sacred quest.

I was born in a small hamlet in the foothills of the massive Drakensberg Mountains[1] (the Dragon's mountains) in Natal[2], in the east of South Africa. I grew up as the youngest of a family of six. My parents loved exploring the hinterland of Natal and Zululand. Weekends often involved family outings with picnics and travelling long distances to faraway places with strange-sounding names, which were mostly Zulu or Swazi[3].

As both my parents came from German pioneering stock, these trips were filled with stories of what my ancestors had encountered when they came to live in the wilds of Africa. They originated from Lower Saxony and Hanover, in what was then a collection of small German states before the unification of

---

1   Drakensberg (Afrikaans: Drakensberge) is the name given to the eastern portion of the Great Escarpment which encloses the central Southern African Plateau. The Great Escarpment reaches its greatest elevation in this region – 2 000–3 000m (6 600–9 800ft) (*Atlas of Southern Africa* (1984). p. 13, 190-192. Readers Digest Association, Cape Town)

2   KwaZulu-Natal also referred to as KZN or Natal, meaning "Place of the Zulu". It is located in the south-east of the country and enjoys a long shoreline beside the Indian Ocean, sharing borders with three other provinces and Mozambique, Swaziland and Lesotho. Its capital is Pietermaritzburg and its largest city is Durban. (*Wikipedia*)

3   The Zulus of KwaZulu-Natal belong to the larger Nguni linguistic group, whose origin is lost in an oral tradition that precedes recorded history. The Zulu (Zulu: amaZulu) are a Bantu ethnic group of southern Africa and the largest ethnic group in South Africa. An estimated 10–11 million people live mainly in KwaZulu-Natal. The Swazis fled from their original home in Mozambique to the Pongola River Valley in KZN. (*Wikipedia*)

*The massive Amphitheatre in the KwaZulu-Natal Drakensberg. Our ancestral farms lie in the foothills of these imposing mountains. Some farms are in the Escort area, while others are on the border, further west, where the escarpment is in Paulpietersburg.*

*The imposing crests of Champagne Castle, flanked by Monk's Cowl, KwaZulu-Natal Drakensberg.*

Germany under Bismarck. My family arrived in Natal, South Africa, in 1857.

My paternal great-great-great grandfather had befriended both the Zulu and Swazi kings and built homesteads for them. My mother's grandfather had translated the Lutheran Bible into Zulu and had been Superintendent of the Hermannsburg Mission[4] in South Africa. Interlaced with all of this were the Anglo-Zulu as well as the two Anglo-Boer wars, which pierced deeply into the hearts and souls of my ancestors. They lost everything they owned during these two wars, and had to start again from scratch.

Our family lore always included stories of unusual events and collective encounters that were beyond the ordinary and mundane.

On one of our ancestral farms is a mountain named Table Mountain. Legend has it that the Zulus/Swazis rounded up cattle and would disappear into the cave and tunnel systems of this mountain. A few days later, the cattle would appear on the other side of the Hlobane Mountains, miles away from their place of departure. Somehow or other, the Zulus knew how to use an underground tunnel system.

Some pioneers tried to enter those tunnels, but got lost in the hidden mazes underground.

This used to fascinate me. Underground tunnel systems? How did they get there, and where did they lead to?

Other stories included those of sacred mountains and areas where one simply did not go, for strange things happened there! Certain places in Zululand existed where no white man or woman dared go, as these areas were strictly forbidden under tribal law. Those who had risked venturing there usually did not live to tell their tales, or simply disappeared. Even today, there are regions of Africa with no cellphone reception, where radio signals cannot connect, for mysterious reasons.

I remember my father showing us old gold mines in Zululand[5], which comprised deep holes in the ground. My brothers, who were much older than me, then went to explore them, but found that they just appeared to end up in an abyss. I always wished that I could have ventured down one, but somehow I knew that if I did, I would not have returned!

The whispers and the legends would one day come back to haunt me. With this came a remembering of my deep desire to explore the higher meaning of it all.

From 1994, things started happening in my life, which I now recognize as a soul-awakening. Deep down, I felt an immense yearning, along with a dawning understanding that there was something I had to complete, with which I had to gift the world. It was a growing, deep, internal restlessness, and I could not as yet understand where it came from or what it meant.

During this time, I was invited to go to the Drakensberg Mountains with a friend. While hiking up one of the gorges, I first came into contact with an energy that I could not understand, but I could feel very strongly.

I recall that my friend had gone off searching for a path (we had taken a wrong turn and were on some animal track, trying to figure out how to get back to the hotel). I sat down on a rock, as something seemed to be pulling me towards the waterfall and stream below.

As I sat down, something strange happened. I felt myself being lifted into what seemed like a swirling tunnel of light, and I could literally feel myself spanning the dimensions. I do not know how long I was in that altered state. All I remember is my friend tapping me on the shoulder a few times, bringing me back to reality.

---

4    Hermannsburg was established in 1854 as the first station of the Hermannsburg Missionary Society, which was based in Hermannsburg, Germany. (*Wikipedia*)

5    Zululand is one of the 11 district municipalities (districts) of KwaZulu-Natal province. (*Wikipedia*)

At that time, she could not understand what had happened, and somehow I could not find the words to describe it all. It was only much later, when we had managed to find our way back to the hotel, that I managed to share my story. During that moment, when I was in that tunnel, an ancient Bushman by the name of X-Ham! appeared to me. He said he wished to work with me, for there were secrets there I needed to understand or retrieve. His people had withdrawn from that location because they had been hunted down like animals.

Later, I had a conversation with a local gentleman, who told me there was a San cave just beneath the rock on which I had been sitting, and that he, too, had had strange experiences in that cave!

This story, as well as the strange way X-Ham! had appeared, prompted me to start reading up about the San. Most importantly, it helped me to start viewing the landscape of Africa with different eyes. What was

*The Bushmen/San people of southern Africa are the oldest known inhabitants of this region. Their DNA dates back 200 000 years. They were here long before the African tribes came to this region.*

*Remaining Bushmen still live in the Northern Cape and the Kalahari Desert in South Africa. Some are still found in Botswana and Namibia. This photo was taken in the Kalahari Desert.*

*An eland, one of the biggest antelopes of South Africa, only naturally occurs in small pockets; the Natal Drakensberg being one of them. The San had a deep respect for this animal, which led to more and more confrontations with the colonists, who hunted them down for sport.*

this energy I had experienced? Was it to be found only in that particular spot of the Drakensberg, or did it exist elsewhere?

Had the San known also known about and felt it? Is that the reason I saw the Bushman standing in front of me? The experience of that energy had such a profound effect on me that it seemed to haunt me. From then on, I started looking at the landscape around me from a fresh perspective.

I found that when I was travelling, I would be drawn to some places, and would then be prompted to go for a hike. During one such hike, I felt that energy again and I knew that I was going into an altered state. With it, I suddenly started to see the Earth energy lines. What is more, I started to see pyramids, or pyramidal shapes, in the landscape!

I was really puzzled by all of that was happening, and it consistently led me back to the San people. I started researching everything I could about them. To my utter amazement, I found that all of the known San sites where cave paintings and drawings had been found had something in common. Or, at least, I had found a common thread:

- The caves were sacred to the San and are normally found on high-energy spots, on or near mountains where there are natural forests, and near streams or flowing water.
- There always was a connection to the eland, which they believed was sacred and had been given to them by their god as a gift. Thus, all the place names in South Africa containing "eland" will always have some or other sacred spot pertaining to the San, in close proximity.
- The caves from which the shamans worked were known as the trance caves. The shamans could move between worlds, attaining a higher

*The grandeur of the Amphitheatre in the Drakensberg. The whole uKhahlamba Drakensberg Mountain System has been declared a World Heritage Site.*

*A typical overhanging cliff and cave. Note the natural forest and water resource.*

or altered state, and then bring back messages to their people and practise advanced healing. Interestingly, they were known to grow lions' manes during their trance states! They were also known for their sexual power during these sojourns or rites.

- Some of the caves had drawings or markings in them, which depicted a serpent-like energy.

They were known as the "rain-makers". When the earliest colonists in Natal pursued the Bushmen who stole their cattle, they found, to their frustration, that torrents of rain would descend upon them as soon as the shaman sounded the eland horn. The sound of the horn brought down the rain, and the colonists were forced to cease their pursuit and return home. It was recorded that the cattle and Bushmen would disappear into the mountains and caves, never to be seen again.

During this time of research and exploration, I began to notice that my own third eye was opening up. I felt that it was connected to this energy; allowing me, to my surprise, the sudden ability to read the landscape and energy lines.

## A Matter of Perception!

**JOURNAL ENTRY**

Moments arise on the journey through life in which your whole perception, the way you see the world, changes. In that moment, time as such does not exist. You realize that you are here on this planet for just a moment, and that infinity is but a breath away...

When you see the stars, the Cosmos, the constellations and galaxies, and realize just how small this planet really is in the greater cosmic whole, then you also realize that your lifetime here is but a tiny fraction of a second spent. In fact, your Soul moves on, and this planet will be here long after you have come and gone.

It is then that you start to walk lightly on this Earth!

With all that was happening around me at that time, I started noticing that my perceptions had changed. What I had perceived as real and solid had shifted to such an extent that I was seeing the countryside around me with completely different eyes.

In moments like these, I was led to see things that most people cannot see or sense with the naked eye. I don't quite know what triggered it all. It might have been that in the intense pain I was feeling, I was looking inside for help, and not outside.

While seeking solace in nature, taking joy in the first drops of summer rain after a long drought, I was drawn to drive to the top of a mountain overlooking the town in which I was staying. I was surrounded by masses of flowers that had sprung up overnight, and the beautiful smell of a cleansed and rejuvenated Earth.

As I stood there, overlooking the valleys and hills that stretched far into the distance, a herd of zebra[6] appeared as if from nowhere, and started galloping past. They were a magnificent sight of beauty in motion...

At that very same moment, I became aware that my inner sight had opened. Suddenly I was seeing the landscape before me in a different manner. I could actually tune into the ancient energy fields that were here long before I was born.

It was quite amazing: For the first time, I could see pyramids, and I could clearly see the ley lines – as if in gold stretching across the horizon.

I had never paid much attention to such ley lines, although I did know they existed. Then I was guided to open my vision and 'see' the landscape before me with my inner eye, which would, in turn, open my outer eye to clearly see where these lines were.

From then onwards, I was led to all of the sites connected to these lines. I could actually feel the

---

6    Zebra are several species of African equids (horse family) with distinctive black-and-white-striped coats. Their stripes come in varying patterns that are unique to each animal. (*Wikipedia*)

energy coursing through them, and they would lead me on to the next site.

I started making notes. I realized these lines followed a distinct pattern, with two triangles interlaced, like the Star of David, in a circle of Light forming a tetrahedron.

I started channeling messages from the Intergalactic Federation of the Great White Brotherhood. On numerous occasions, I was shown where these lines were and what they stood for. (I will go into more detail about the rest later. Suffice to say that this helped me a great deal with identifying these places.)

I had been shown that this African continent is, in fact, far older than anyone had even imagined. As my ancient memory banks were activated by the Federation, I remembered who my Soul really was and what I had been called to do here on this continent.

Yet, it was a gradual unfolding. It did not happen overnight.

As with all things: When the pupil is ready, the teacher will appear.

I was given only a little information at a time, so that I could assimilate it. My ever-seeking mind would then try to make sense of what I had been given. Working in a library enabled me to tap into a vast knowledge pool. I found that while searching the system for books, I was led to the correct ones. Every time, this would either confirm what I had been given, or help me gain further insight into what I was dealing with. I started realizing that I was not the only soul on the planet who had sensed or seen this, and that it was connected to ancient technology and memory banks that had been hidden on the African continent since the beginning of time.

Most importantly, I started reading up on the mythology of the African people. I was guided to read about the San shamans and also the work of Credo Mutwa[7], the Zulu High Sanusi, or high priest of the sangomas[8], the healers, or priesthood, of the African cultures.

While reading these books, I was intrigued by how their stories provided keys to greater understanding – but in ways that most would not comprehend. Yet, it was all there.

One of the most amazing pieces of information I came across while researching the San was in a work by Professor Lewis-Williams[9], an expert on San paintings. He describes the ancient rock paintings of the San people in the Drakensberg as images drawn by the shamans that depict the inner journeys they made to the Otherworld while in a trans state! What was even more interesting was the way he described (confirmed also by other researchers) that the San shamans in their trans state grew the lion's mane – a golden lion's mane!

The DNA of the San people is very intriguing, in that their genes go back 200 000 years in Africa, and they are not connected to any other race on the African continent! They are the oldest remaining people with a particular strain of DNA and are thus unique!

Another revelation and confirmation was the fact that the San always welcome the sight of the Pleiades on the horizon. They connect the Great Creator Source with the Pleiades constellation!

---

7   Vusamazulu Credo Mutwa is a Zulu sangoma from South Africa. He is an author of books on stories that mix traditional Zulu folklore, extraterrestrial encounters and his own personally created fables. (*Wikipedia*)

8   A sangoma performs a holistic and symbolic form of healing by drawing on the embedded beliefs of the black South African culture: That ancestors in the afterlife guide and protect the living. (Richter, Marlise, 'Traditional Medicines and Traditional Healers in South Africa', 2003)

9   James David Lewis-Williams is a South African archaeologist. He is best known for his research on southern African San rock art, of which it can be said that he found a 'Rosetta Stone'. He is the founder and previous director of the Rock Art Research Institute.

If you read their stories, one is initially confronted with a strange creation story, which I found reflected in many ways in the book by Ken Carey[10] on the Bird people of the Ancient Red Native American people.

The San did not believe in Bird people, however. They believed that the plant, insect and animal kingdoms reigned supreme *before* Man was created by God from the Pleiades! Interestingly, they always said that the insect, plant and animal kingdoms were sacred because they were the 'elder brothers'!

It is then of vital importance to note that one of their gods is the praying mantis[11]!

What was even more intriguing to me was the fact that the eland, one of the largest antelope of the African continent, was also considered sacred, as they believed the eland had come to them as a gift from their Creator God! Thus, the eland was revered by them.

This only made sense to me afterwards, when I started to understand the reason why: The eland is the only antelope in southern Africa that has a layer of fat around its heart. This provided the San with a crucial means of survival, as no human being can live without fat in some form or other in their daily diet.

The San eat mostly fruit and edible plants, which they gather from nature. As they were primarily a Stone-Age people, they simply had no means to slaughter animals on a grand scale, as the white hunters subsequently did – often just for sport.

When they were in need of meat in their diet, the shaman would first go into a trance-like state and connect with an eland, asking it to sacrifice itself for the sake of the people. Once the eland was killed, the fat was given first to the elderly, in order for them to be strengthened and survive.

Every single part of the eland was utilized. Even the blood was mixed with ochre and used for rock paintings.

Curiously, I was then led to start reading the writings of the first colonists who had settled in Natal. When comparing the data with impressions of modern-day archaeologists, I began to get a very clear picture of why I had been inspired to learn about these people. I realized that they held an important key to this part of the African continent!

My research led me to a map of southern Africa that showed the distribution of the eland. Amazingly, the eland is only found in certain parts of the region: Precisely on both the holiest sites of the San people and on the even more ancient energy grids and ley lines!

Here was a so-called primitive people who knew exactly where the energy centers were. They also acted as Guardians of such places. It was incredible indeed!

I began to pin-point the local sites where rock paintings could still be seen. Strangely enough, all of them were exactly where they should be. Most often, I began to look at the landscape. Sure enough, the pyramids were there, as well as the energy lines!

These sites had another feature in common: They were (in Natal, at least) in the high places in the mountains, and always near streams or rivers and natural forests.

I had simultaneously been doing research on the medieval history of the Languedoc area in southern France and northern Spain, and on the Pyrenees (which will be another book). I suddenly realized that the San and Druids[12] of the Celts[13] had one thing in common: Ancient forests and groves. The Druids always considered the oak groves as ancient

---

10  Ken Carey, *The Return of the Bird Tribes*, Harper Collins, 1991.

11  The praying mantis is named for its prominent front legs, which are bent and held together at an angle which suggests the position of prayer. (*Wikipedia*)

12  A Druid was a member of the educated, professional class among the Celtic peoples of Gaul, Britain, Ireland, and possibly elsewhere during the Iron Age. (*Wikipedia*)

13  The Celts were people in Iron Age and medieval Europe who spoke Celtic languages and had cultural similarities. (*Wikipedia*)

Keepers of wisdom and portals, and thus as holy!

What was even more amazing is that the ankh[14], or Egyptian cross, was known and used by the San long before the Egyptians used it. It was known for its very potent energy and used mostly for healing purposes!

It was not the only cross that I found: The four-sided cross was also found carved into rocks all over the Drakensberg and elsewhere...

I was stumbling into clues... little puzzle pieces all over the place...

This then lead me to the next step in my investigation, which was becoming a more and more fascinating journey.

I wanted to know what the other African cultures had to share. I have to note here that one has to understand something about southern Africa, which is vital when comprehending the greater whole:

When the original white settlers created their first settlement in Cape Town, the only people they encountered were the San and the Strandlopers[15], who were of the same race, but found mainly along the southern African coastline.

There were no other people inland.

When the white settlers started to expand their horizons, they were stopped in their tracks at the Kei River where, for the first time, they encountered other African people.

These were the Xhosa, who were a nomadic people, like the Nguni[16] and other tribes found in southern Africa. They came from the West Coast in the region of the Equator. They were mainly herdsmen who followed their herds of nguni cattle south, in search of better grazing. They were, therefore, a migratory people, and only settled here in the 1830s.

Interestingly, recent studies have shown that this is indeed true, as the DNA strains of both the nguni cattle and dog stem from much farther north – Egypt, in fact!

They eventually mixed with the San people. Traces of their language and features testify to this.

Credo Mutwa, the last sanusi, or High Priest Shaman of the Zulu People in Africa, relates in his books that the African people have always called themselves the Children of the Sun God, and that they believed that they came from the stars. They had a particular affinity with the Pleiades, Orion, the Dog Star and Sirius.

They share the same or similar stories about the feathered serpent with the Native American people. The serpent-like coil makes its way into African carvings on stones everywhere.

I will come back to Credo Mutwa at a later stage, because what I had read was not making any sense to me at this time. It would only make sense very much later on in my journey. I filed everything at the back of my mind.

The more I struggled to find answers, and the more I was shown of the inner planes, the more I realized that there was something unique about the African continent and landscape that no one had ever sensed or seen before.

It was about that time that I had contact with someone who was interested in ancient iron ore smelting sites in KwaZulu-Natal. Since he wanted information,

---

14  The ankh, also known as breath of life, the key of the Nile or *crux ansata* (Latin meaning 'cross with a handle'), was the ancient Egyptian hieroglyphic character that read 'life'. ("King Hezekiah in the Bible: Royal Seal of Hezekiah Comes to Light", Biblical Archaeology Society)

15  The Strandlopers were a San-derived people who lived by hunting and gathering food along the beaches of south-western Africa, from the Cape Colony to the Skeleton Coast. Most strandloper communities did not persist in the face of demographic and economic changes that occurred in southern and south-western Africa during the 19th and 20th centuries. They disappeared through assimilation. (Sydow, W.,1973, "Contributions to the history and protohistory of the Topnaar Strandloper settlement at the Kuiseb River Mouth near Walvis Bay", *South African Archaeological Bulletin 28* (111/112): 73–77. JSTOR 3888563)

16  Nguni people are pastoralist groups, part of the greater Bantu group occupying much of the east and Southern parts of Africa. (*Wikipedia*)

I asked around. I then had the most amazing conversation with a local geologist (who wishes not to be named) about the wilds of Zululand. There are still untamed and hostile places found in Zululand. Some of these places are so inaccessible (partly because of constant tribal wars) that few white people have ever dared venture there.

The Zulus were known for their superior spears, and their smelting sites can still be found along certain streams and places in north-western KwaZulu-Natal. I was shown one such place and was amazed.

The geologist told me that he was asked to do some surveying in one of the most inhospitable parts of Zululand. He found the richest deposits of the finest iron ore at a site that is considered holy by the Zulus. They said that it had been shown and given to them by the Sun God.

At the same time, I was told an interesting story about underground cities in the Lebombo Mountains[17] in Zululand. This confirmed what I had realized for myself: There was certainly far more there than the eye could see. It was both ancient and hidden and somehow, I was connected to it.

This, then, was the beginning of my quest to find the truth...

My working life, however, started to fall apart completely. A dark night of the soul truly descended upon me. I now understand that what transpired was part of my awakening and calling to follow my true quest, but at the time it was sheer hell to endure!

I was transferred from the library to a museum: One of the few situated on a battlefield. It was there that I had to finally acknowledge that, via my third eye, I could see things others could not. I knew then that I had to trust my perceptions.

I was working on a battlefield where both of my ancestral great-grandfathers had fought on the Boer side against the British forces in the Battle of Talana Hill[18] – the first battle of the Anglo-Boer War[19]. To my utter astonishment, I found that I could see the British soldiers who had fallen in this battle 100 years before, but I went into total denial about it all!

During a ghost tour on the commemorative night of the battle, when BBC cameras and microphones were attached to me, I experienced the whole battle in graphic technicolor detail. I relayed what I was seeing via the microphone! (I was told that I was 100% accurate by other psychics on the scene.) So I finally had to confront the incorrect, conditioned beliefs with which I had been indoctrinated, and I had to reconnect to the core 'inner me', which knew and saw from very deep within. However, it took me nearly two years to even acknowledge that I had this gift and to make peace with it.

When one's deeper knowing is awakened, synchronicity sets in. As I was forced to delve deeper into the history of this part of the world, I was reminded of the caves and tunnel systems – this time by the caretaker at the museum, who shared his own experiences with me.

I started delving deeper.

I was now once more being confronted with

---

17   The Lebombo Mountains are an 800km long, narrow range of mountains in southern Africa. They stretch from Hluhluwe in KwaZulu-Natal in the south, to Punda Maria in the Limpopo Province in the north. (*Wikipedia*)

18   The Battle of Talana Hill, also known as the Battle of Glencoe, was the first major clash of the Second Boer War. A frontal attack by British infantry, supported by artillery, drove Boers from a hilltop position, but the British suffered heavy casualties in the process. (*Wikipedia*)

19   Boer War. This refer either of the two conflicts between Britain and the South African Boers. The first (1880-1881) happened when the Boers sought to regain the independence given up for British aid against the Zulus. The second (1899-1902) took place when the Orange Free State and Transvaal declared war on Britain. (*Wikipedia*)

energy lines; with landscapes that I could suddenly 'read'; and recalling these old stories of tunnels and strange things happening. One evening, before going to bed, I again asked the urgent question: "**Why was I born in Africa? Please tell me!**"

The next day, I found myself pouring over a map of Africa. Holding a pencil, I looked at the exact location where I was born. My inner guidance told me to draw lines on this map. At first I was told to look for the 25° and 33°–36° longitude lines and to mark them in red. Then I was asked to look up the longitude line nearest to the place I was born. I found it. I was instructed to mark this in red, too.

I then had to find the latitude lines between 20° and 36°. I was told that because of the very high frequency of my Soul, I could only have incarnated on this planet in the particular place I was born. I had especially chosen my mother, as she carried the correct DNA and genes that enabled my Soul to incarnate, and because of the mutual karmic debt we had to discharge.

For days, I searched high and low in the library for answers.

I started researching the 33° longitude line, and found that in ancient times, this was the 0° longitude line. It was Isaac Newton who had modified the

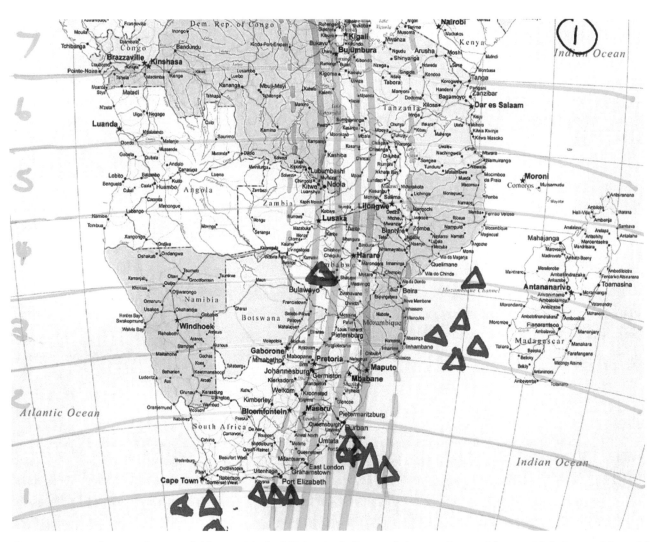

*Drawing energy lines on the map of Africa, with the 33° longitude line, and the crystal pyramids, as guided. I was told to add 10° to the right and left of the 33° longitude line, because Earth had shifted on its axis a few times.*

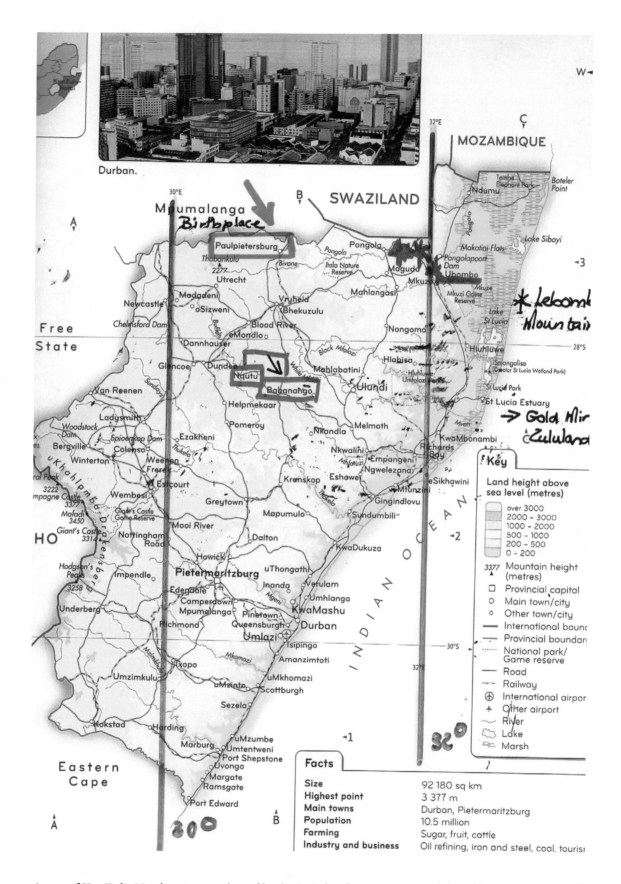

*A map of KwaZulu-Natal noting my place of birth; the Lebombo Mountains; and the gold mines in Zululand.*

world maps and made Greenwich the new 0° line, thus changing the longitude lines of the entire Earth.

At least I now had confirmation that there was something unusual, or extraordinary about the 33° longitude line. I asked why I was given leeway for my calculations on either side of this line, and was told that Earth had shifted five times on its axis, thus the lines had also shifted, so this was necessary. The same principle applied to the latitude lines.

A few weeks later, I was standing with my brothers on the mountain peak of my birthplace, knee-deep in fields of wild gladioli, looking down on my ancestral land, with Table Mountain in the distance.

To my utter amazement, my vision started shifting, and I saw the landscape change before my eyes. This massive mountain of my childhood, where we had been forbidden to explore, shifted into an enormous Sphinx, with energy lines everywhere, as far as I could see. I searched for pyramids, and sure enough, there in the distance, I saw one. The odd, cone-shaped mountain my father always pointed out was, in fact, a type of a honing station.

That night I could not sleep. As I jotted down my vision, I finally understood that I was discovering some of the unrecorded, forgotten history of this African continent that had been buried in the mists of time. Africa was not at all primitive, as the European settlers have always believed it to be! Indeed, what I had seen was highly developed and reminiscent of Egypt, but even more advanced.

At that moment, there arose a deep and profound yearning within me to find out more about what I had seen and discovered, and to record the untold and unexplored true history of Africa. My quest had begun!

During this time, I was invited to go to the Drakensberg, Monk's Cowl region once more. One day, sitting on a rock, just drinking in the fresh mountain air and the magnificent scenery, insight dawned on me about my vision. I understood that not only was my own Soul intricately linked with this continent, but I had something very important to retrieve and return to humanity. It would be completely new and utterly different, yet ancient. It would act as a catalyst deep in the souls of people, and help to anchor in the higher states of consciousness whatsoever they were.

They were not in the Pyramids of Giza, nor in the Hall of Records or the Akashic Records[20] – for these only existed much later – but they were from the very beginning of life on Earth. Whatever needed to be retrieved also had to be reactivated, and somehow, I was the one who would have to do it! At this time, how to even start doing this was beyond my imagination!

That night, I had a profound vision: I saw myself standing in front of a huge, shining, white pyramid that emitted an intense, blinding, white light. Indeed, it seemed to consist of clear-white crystal. I saw myself dressed in a long, white, almost transparent, shimmering garment. I knew that this was where I had worked. Looking around, I saw that this pyramid appeared to form the middle of a much larger complex, which was circular in form, and divided equally into four parts. Each section had a huge building dominating it, but in the middle of this whole stood a massive Crystal Pyramid. I was given the name: *The Crystal Pyramid of the White Flame*.

I was then taken inside this enormous structure, where there were vast halls filled with beautiful flowers and hanging gardens, and elevators that transported you to multiple levels.

I was told that this pyramid housed the Super Consciousness Matrix Energy Fields, which recorded all of the wisdom, higher knowledge, teaching, and healing. It was here that all the records of everything

---

20  The Akashic records (Akasha is a Sanskrit word meaning "sky", "space" or "aether") are collectively understood to be a collection of mystical knowledge that is encoded in the aether: i.e. on a non-physical plane of existence. (*Wikipedia*)

that had ever happened on the planet pertaining to the 12 Master Galaxies and the Central Suns were kept for safekeeping.

I was told that in the beginning, in my true Soul form, I had worked here as the High Priestess in charge of the Temple of the White Flame. I found myself in a vast space that looked almost like the massive library I had worked in. The only difference was that the space was empty. I saw myself sitting on a chair and tapping into the records, which were housed as pure fragments of energy rays, and I moved into an altered state. These records were then beamed into me as an energy form that I could then transmit.

A voice said: "*You are a transmitter channel and this is how you have access to all the ancient keys and codes.*"

The next day, I poured over the map of Africa again. Was this temple that I had seen, and which was obviously not the Pyramids of Giza, for real? If so, where could it have been?

I found myself sitting and drawing pyramids on the map of Africa. They seemed to be close to the Giza line, but slightly east. I was told that this is again due to the Earth's axis shifting. To my amazement, I began drawing 7 pyramids, being told that these 7 components formed one single unit, the largest being the Crystal Pyramid of the White Flame.

I looked at the map again. The pyramids began in the sea, and ended somewhere in Zimbabwe[21]. Some seemed to be in the straits between Mozambique[22] and Madagascar[23]. I then realized that Madagascar had formed part of the African continent at some stage. With its breaking away, these pyramids might well have sunk underneath the sea.

At that stage, I had visions of myself working at this pyramid temple with Thoth[24] and another High Priest. All the land masses were sinking, and a huge spacecraft was hovering over the scene. I clearly saw the three of us gathering all the temple records for safeguarding and being beamed up into this craft.

At the same moment, another huge spacecraft arrived. It, in turn, beamed up the white flame of the temple. I was told that this flame had gone to Andromeda for safekeeping until the planet was ready to receive it once more, along with the knowledge contained therein.

Thoth, the other High Priest and I then deposited part of the records into the massive chambers underneath the Sphinx in Egypt, where the remnants of the records in energetic form are housed. These records, however, were stored in a different form and format – and deliberately so – to be kept safe until humanity was ready to retrieve this information.

I subsequently discovered that in the Emerald Tablets of Thoth[25], it is recorded that he flew the records to Egypt for safekeeping. To my utter astonishment, I also found out that Thoth had laid down the energy lines and grids on the planet. I knew, at last, that I was not imagining things. I was merely retrieving what I had witnessed and been part of thousands of years before!

---

21  Zimbabwe is a landlocked country in southern Africa, known for its dramatic landscape and diverse wildlife. (*Wikipedia*)

22  Mozambique is a southern African nation whose long Indian Ocean coastline is dotted with popular beaches. (*Wikipedia*)

23  Madagascar, a huge island nation off the south-east coast of Africa. It is home to thousands of animal species – like lemurs – which are found nowhere else, plus rainforests, beaches and reefs. (*Wikipedia*)

24  Thoth was the god of writing and knowledge. The ancient Egyptians believed that Thoth gave them the gift of hieroglyphic writing. He was also connected to the Moon. (*Wikipedia*)

25  The Emerald Tablet, also known as the Smaragdine Tablet, or Tabula Smaragdina, is a compact and cryptic piece of the Hermetica which is reputed to contain the secret of the prima materia and its transmutation. It was highly regarded by European alchemists as the foundation of their art and its Hermetic tradition. (*Wikipedia*)

# CHAPTER 2

# The Journey Begins

May 2008 saw me resigning from my position as a librarian. In August 2009, I decided to finally follow my higher calling, as I could no longer postpone my fool's journey.

All I had was a map of Africa with red lines drawn on it; my inner seeing and hearing; the visions of the Pyramid Temple of the White Flame; and such a deep and intense desire to find this temple, to be reunited with it, and to retrieve whatever was needed. I knew that, somehow, all of this was linked to the 33° longitude and latitude lines marked in red on my map of Africa.

Where should I start? Again, I poured over my map and asked for guidance. My pencil landed not where I'd imagined, but rather on the east coast of Africa, much further down than where I had originally thought I should go. I had always thought that it would be Durban, but my pencil had landed at a place called Harkerville, between Knysna and Plettenberg Bay in the Western Cape[1].

Why so far down? My gut instinct told me that maybe I was being led to something very important and that I needed to follow my intuition. In the past, that had proved to be my best compass. I set out, my car packed with only my most important pieces of clothing, a new camera, my journals, and myself! I had no idea what would happen, or where I would end up, and I didn't care.

Whatever money I had left was now going to be invested in this journey. If that meant the end of everything else, so be it. At least I would not one day die with my vision, my quest and my dream still within me, never having had the courage to follow the inner promptings and yearning of my Soul…

I felt a sense of freedom, wildness, and excitement that I had not experienced for years. Something deep and profound had been awakened within me, and I loved that feeling!

---

1    The Western Cape is a South African province with coasts bordering the Indian and Atlantic oceans. It's known for the port city of Cape Town. It is set beneath Table Mountain, part of a national park by the same name (*Wikipedia*)

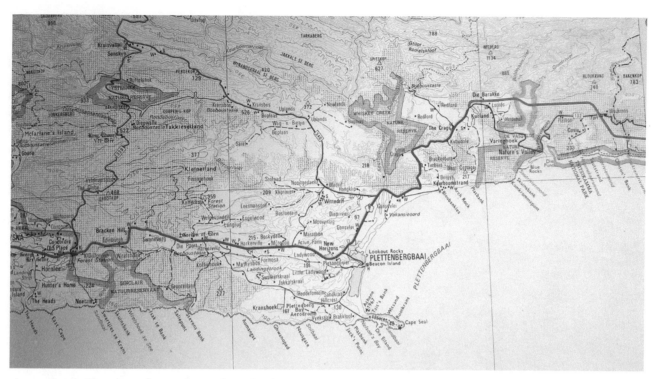

*A map showing key areas of my early travels on the Western Cape coast of South Africa.*

## JOURNAL ENTRY

### Journey started officially August 17, 2009

At one stage, just before Reddersburg, I was suddenly transported back in time to millions of years ago, and with my 'inward eye' I saw the Karoo[2] as it had been then: Islands, islands, and more islands. Some had pyramids on them! There were tremendous expanses of water, and only the tips of the mountains stood out at the time. It was a jungle with lush, green vegetation and palm trees. So truly tropical!

Then I 'saw' huge dinosaurs towering above the vegetation and was told that this had been a part of the Elysian[3] civilization. When they attempted to blow up the dinosaurs because they had become pests, the entire ocean floor shook with volcanic outbursts. One

*Graaff-Reinet and a typical Karoo koppie – a small hill rising up from the African veld.*

---

2   The Karoo, from a Khoikhoi word, possibly "garo", meaning "desert"), is a semi-desert natural region of South Africa. There is no exact definition of what constitutes the Karoo, and therefore its extent is also not precisely defined. (*Standard Encyclopaedia of Southern Africa*, Potgieter, D.J. & du Plessis, T.C, Vol. 6. pp. 306-307, 1972, Nasou, Cape Town)

3   Elysian: Relating to, or characteristic of Heaven, or Paradise. (*Wikipedia*)

*The Karoo is dry, arid and desolate in places.*

can still see the pebbles, sand, and the purple cliffs where the mountain passes were hacked out. Thus, the Karoo was laid bare as a wasteland. As the water dried up, new land masses were formed and others sank under the sea.

Here, where once lush tropical trees and plants had thrived, there was now desert wilderness owing to the volcanic ash and residual radiation. Living became unsustainable on this arid land mass. This happened more than 400 000 million years ago.

I saw that the subterranean bases still exist, as they are clearly defined by the pyramids that are still visible here. From the exterior, they have taken on the appearance of mountains or rock-like koppies, which

no one notices unless their inner vision is open and they can 'see'.

I clearly saw the light vortex, which allows one to enter…

My perceptions about the transformation of this area from lush vegetation into desert land were confirmed the next day when the owner of the B&B in which I stayed gave me a geological survey of this whole area!

In the Camdeboo National Park[4], there's a place where these strange rock formations exemplify this entire violent history: The Valley of Desolation! I was touched. It meant that what I was seeing with my inner eye was being confirmed once again!

---

4   The Camdeboo National Park is located in the Karoo and almost completely surrounds the Eastern Cape town of Graaff-Reinet. (*Wikipedia*)

*The Karoo's vast expanse.*

*The Outeniqua Mountains twirl and whirl as one starts climbing towards the final barrier before reaching George.*

*The spectacular Outeniqua Pass.*

*Kranshoek, near Harperville, halfway between Plettenberg Bay and Knysna where my journey started.*

*My sketch of what the Karoo used to look like: Tropical islands.*

Driving through the aridness of the Karoo became like a journey through space and time into what used to be a tropical, fertile place, buzzing with life. Gradually the landscape changed and the fynbos started to emerge alongside the road in beautiful lavender hues.

Strange mountains appeared, twisted and turned as if a giant hand had twirled and bent them into shape. It spoke of turbulence, and magnitude.

As I started climbing upward from the Karoo plains, in the distance, and to my utmost delight, pyramids started appearing once more!

The spectacular Outeniqua[5] Pass, the gateway to George, had me totally overawed. This must be one of the most beautiful passes in South Africa.

The magnificent drive along the Garden Route[6], betwixt and between mountains and sea, took my breath away. As I arrived at my destination, Coral Tree Cottages at Harkerville, halfway between Knysna and Plettenberg Bay, I felt a profound sense of home-coming, of finally returning home to something so meaningful within.

Driving along, I had the impression that the Great Crystal Pyramid Temple I was searching for off the east coast of Africa had to be somewhere here. I felt the presence of an energy pool, almost contained, and growing stronger. I was starting to tap into the energy fields.

---

5   The Outeniqua Mountains are located along the Garden Route of South Africa. They run parallel to the coast and form a continuous range with the Langeberg to the west and the Tsitsikamma Mountains to the east. (*Wikipedia*)

6   The Garden Route is a stretch of South Africa's south-eastern coast that extends from Mossel Bay in the Western Cape to the Storms River in the Eastern Cape. (*Wikipedia*)

I sometimes had glimpses of it, ridged between two massive boulders, overgrown with seaweed and coral. With the rising sea beds and earthquakes, the Pyramid Temple was in the process of rising again!

## When Does a Quest Become a Journey, and a Journey Become a Quest?

During the weeks I spent in that area, amazing things manifested. I had a growing sense of getting closer to where I was meant to be. Interestingly, though, it was not as much on the land, but more under the sea.

I was starting to define it as an immeasurable vortex energy field, and I felt myself pushed more and more to find the *source* of this field. I wanted to identify it and understand its higher meaning and what had happened there, now that its source was lying under the sea.

As I started to consciously tap into this energy field, I found that my own inner hearing and seeing increased. I was told that my frequencies and vibrations were being lifted unconsciously. I certainly felt more energized, but at the time I put it down to the fact that I was close to the sea. I always seem to feel more uplifted and rejuvenated when I am surrounded by water and mountains. That certainly was the case then.

During that time, I received the following message:

*There is a great need now to activate the Crystal Temple, and we are trying to convey this message to you as clearly as possible. You need to be here now to drink in this ambience, but also to tune into the Cosmic Light forces present. We are thus now activating your energy field to be the highest it can be. This is needed so that you can activate the keys and be guided to the other Keepers. Understand this is a metaphor. The keys at this moment exist on another plane or dimension, yet are still real. This means that your faculties and psychic abilities will*

*again be reactivated to their absolute highest potential, enabling you to tap into energy fields at will.*

*This will in turn assist us to use you as the means to activate the remaining energy grids. This is the most important phase of your whole journey and will lead you to all corners of the Earth; to travel the highways and by-ways to find all that is and should be. This is the most beautiful way to experience life – as a journey – a way of life!*

*You will be able to identify and simultaneously activate all the grids, and we will bring all those who once chose to be on the same path and were involved in the final struggles in Elysium, Mu and Atlantis together as One!*

*In this Oneness, old scenes will be re-enacted once again, as previous choices resurface and, with it, the ancient struggle between Light and Dark, as all reach for a state of balance, Oneness.*

*You will be called upon to act as the catalyst to bring the true history of the world into the open once more. It will be a time when you notice most clearly how people are drawn to you: Especially those who were directly involved. You will have to bring all the missing keys and pieces together, as only when united into Oneness, as part of the greater whole, can the dimensional shift happen.*

*When united, all the rest will fall into place and you will be happy to function in this manner again as the "true you". This is why you incarnated – to find what went awry and why; to write; to teach; and to inspire others to bring wholeness to the world again. It is only when this unity is rediscovered, with adherence to a world of One, that the entire planet can ascend and move to the Higher Planes of consciousness.*

*This will lead to the birth of the New World, the birth of the Golden Age, the dying of the old, of what had been, being transformed into the new. It has come and it will be!*

*Now is a time of rediscovery, of activating that which has been lost. When you view this, you will discover that this has been your role all along. First you had to help build everything up. Then followed the destruction. In your attempt to restore this balance, you lost your life. Now it is a time to heal and unite all those different components. Something new will be birthed, and with it comes the return of wholeness, comfort and knowledge, as you spread your true Light into the world, which you have always done, but will now do 100 000-fold more.*

*As everything comes together, it is renewed. As everything springs forth, it is reborn. In this process, you will witness beauty unfolding, like a butterfly emerging from the cocoon, becoming and growing into its full potential. This is the entering into what exists eternally, but now is emerging as something new and unique, in this total "beingness", that always has been and that always will be.*

*Elysium, Atlantis and Lemuria are rising again, and you are the agent or catalyst, as you were born in Africa and enabled to be what you need to be – to bring the missing pieces together.*

*As you tune into the higher vibrations and frequencies, you become a more potent conduit of this energy; and the more you concentrate on it, the more it will accelerate.*

*The world will feel a pull towards Africa such as has never been felt before, and suddenly all will want to know what Africa embodies, as that which they no longer have access to. It is truly a time when everyone will sit up and take notice, and as all else crumbles, the pull towards the Light emitted from Africa will be such that people will flock to its shores to ask for wisdom from its people.*

*As this process happens, it will encompass a struggle that has always existed. In the end, there is a need for balance, and when balance is reached, conflict will dissolve.*

*Understand that for each step you take to lift off the ground and learn to fly, you will encounter resistance, since you have to overcome the forces of gravity.*

*Once done, a great healing will take place at all other levels. Ultimately, you always attract the opposite, so that in the act of being challenged, the moment is reached when you must take a stand and either defend your position, or be overcome by the opposing force.*

*When you stand your ground and refuse to be frightened or overwhelmed, you suddenly become what you, in truth, always were, and in tune with who you are capable of being.*

*You then step into your highest power, of total beingness. It has been there. You've just never used it.*

At the time, receiving messages like this never made sense. I had to dig deeper and deeper into myself, and the ancient meaning of the Hermetic principle, "As above, so below," took on a whole new meaning.

First of all, I had to trust where I was being led, and then let the 'why' reveal itself as it willed. I decided then and there to stop where prompted to stop, and to literally go where my nose led me.

During that time, I experienced amazing and interesting things – mostly states of being I had not known before. I was being led to explore the greater areas of Knysna[7], Kranshoek and Plettenberg Bay. I found myself climbing into my car and ending up wherever I found another link or clue, or where I encountered energy in a new form.

I discovered that in some areas, energy was more potent and very strong, and in other places, it was depleted. In several places, like Thesen Island in Knysna, I even felt a type of bitter-cold, almost dark and threatening energy.

I was becoming more and more like a finely-tuned instrument, feeling and feeding the information that I was retrieving, and tapping into some giant computer (which I would recognize much later as the colossal

---

7   Knysna probably from a Khoikhoi word meaning "ferns", is a town on the Route. It lies 34° south of the equator. It is 72km east from the town of George, and 25km west of Plettenberg Bay. (*Chronological order of town establishment in South Africa based on Floyd*, 1960:20-26)

*What remains of of the Rainbow Crystal Temple at Coney Beach, Knysna.*

Super Consciousness Field), and then absorbing and transmitting what was coming through me. However, it took me another four years to really start understanding this. At the time, I was just 'allowing' whatever wanted to come through me.

In a higher sense, I was being awakened. Something within me was triggering Soul memory banks, as I was brought higher and higher into increased awareness, merging with my higher Soul self.

When I was at The Heads in Knysna, I realized that a part of an ancient pyramid structure was hidden there: Eroded and very much worn and torn, but a pyramid alright. Its energies, however, were not what I was seeking. It was but an empty shell. I felt that whatever I was searching for must be beyond that, and somehow further from the shore.

What was so noteworthy was that the Knysna harbor was closed, mainly due to dangerous sea conditions, so there was a real danger of me landing up on the huge rocks on either side of The Heads if I was to explore this area. I received confirmation that this area was part of a larger vortex energy originating from the sea, not the land.

I made a sketch in my notebook, based on my inner musings and questions, and identified the possible location of the Crystal Temple halfway to Plettenberg Bay. This would change as a result of what happened later.

I clearly saw the pyramid in sacred geometrical form. The energy was very high, and I sensed the temple was buried under the sea. It has an extraordinary high frequency and was transmitting electromagnetic fields. There was a complex attached to it, which was also buried. But where could this be?

My explorations took me to Plettenberg Bay next. Upon entering this town, I immediately saw what I

*The Heads, Coney Beach, Knysna, where I first started tuning into the Crystal Pyramid Temples under the sea.*

*The pyramid mountains (Tsitsikamma) frame the spectacular snow-white beaches of Plettenberg Bay.*

had been searching for all along – pyramids! There they were, towering upwards and flanking the entire bay, dominating the scene. My heart sang! I knew I would find my answers, not only in Knysna, but here in Plettenberg Bay and then wherever else those huge giants were located.

Robberg instantly reminded me of a sphinx with its head missing. Years later, confirmation of this first impression came! I felt the energies here, more so than I had in Knysna, and I was drawn to the Keurbooms Beach[8], in an effort to get nearer to those pyramids. As soon as I arrived at Keurbooms, I sensed that I was entering some kind of magical place. It was vibrating with this vortex energy. (It was only when I returned to that area and lived in Nature's Valley[9] that I finally had accurate confirmation of this. There is, indeed, magic happening there. It is vortex energy magic).

It was here that I found myself sitting between certain rocks to which I had been drawn. They formed a circled in which I was compelled to sit. I stopped there because of the rising tide and did not explore beyond that point until a few years later. I felt I had to be there and meditate.

In those moments of reflection, I entered an even higher vibrational energy field. It was not only the strongest I had ever experienced, but I seemed to dissolve… the ego 'I'… and I felt myself becoming someone else. I was one with Mother Earth, the rocks, the sea, and all of life. I recorded this incident in the following excerpts from my writing:

### JOURNAL ENTRY

I sat down and started my meditation… when to my amazement, a beautiful mermaid appeared. At first I thought I was imagining things, but then realized she was real enough, with glossy locks of red-copper hair and stunning green eyes. Because I was switching frequencies, I was able to see and speak with her, while others may not have been able to share my perceptions.

She introduced herself as the Queen of the Mermaids. She said she and the Angel Dolphins were in charge of the Crystal Pyramid Temple of the White Flame, which had sunk offshore from where I was sitting. They ensured that the temple had remained intact, and only those authorized to do so could enter. She said I had lived as a High Priestess there, and had been called back to bring about the return of the White Flame to Earth, as this temple and the others were rising from the seabed in preparation for the shift in consciousness that would happen here.

She said that deep within me I held important information that I had to retrieve, along with codes and keys that were to be used with the energy that this temple represented. It held control of the most vital keys.

I was stunned, to say the least. She then asked me if I had any wishes she could grant me, so that I would remember this as being real and not just the product of my imagination. I asked for three things:

1. That the MTN (my local internet service provider) connection on my laptop be sorted out, as I had had difficulties connecting to the internet.
2. That I would see dolphins. I had not yet seen one, and I so yearned to see a whole school of dolphins!
3. That I would be given, or find, a pansy shell.

I decided to go out to eat at the restaurant overlooking the rocks and the beach. I noticed a bus-load of British tourists had arrived. I was sitting waiting, when they started shouting: "Dolphins! Dolphins!" We all rushed to the railing, and sure enough, there was a school of dolphins swimming quite near to the huge rocks.

---

8    The Keurbooms River runs in the Western Cape Province of South Africa. (*Wikipedia*)

9    Nature's Valley is a holiday resort and small village on the Garden Route, along the southern Cape coast. It lies between the Soutrivier, the foothills of the Tsitsikamma Mountains, the Indian Ocean and the Groot River lagoon. (*Wikipedia*)

*The Queen of the Mermaids, as I sketched her.*

The restaurant owner ran out and said she could not believe it as: "The dolphins never swam there because it was too close to the rocks!" I smiled, for I knew that my first wish had been granted!

From there, I went back to Plettenberg Bay and was directed to an MTN shop, where they managed to sort out my connection problems in an instant. My second wish had also been fulfilled!

Next to the MTN shop was a small shop that sold items like beach towels, jewellery etc. I wandered in, and there, and to my amazement, some pansy shells sat among the jewellery in a glass case. The lady behind the counter was busy, so I browsed around. I noticed her looking at me time and again.

As soon as the other customer had paid, she came to me and said: "I saw you looking at the pansy shells?" I said: "Yes," and asked if they were real. She confirmed that they were and then, to my surprise, said: "When you came through that door, I had a very strange feeling. I saw light all around you, and then I knew that I had to give you a pansy shell!"

*A pansy shell. When it breaks, a dove appears from inside it. It is considered a blessing to find one of these on the snow white beaches of Plettenberg Bay – the only place in South Africa where you can find them.*

*One of the Guardians at Keurboomstrand.*

Tears were running down my cheeks… My third wish was being granted and I did not know how to tell this lady that a miracle had just happened.

Driving back to the chalet in the late afternoon, I felt like I was floating. All my wishes had been fulfilled within a few hours of seeing the mermaid, and I had been reconnected to the Temple of the White Flame. Confirmation had come!

I returned the next day to retrieve my pansy shell. To my utter delight, instead of one, I was given three!

## "My Cup Runneth Over!"

I had no words to express my gratitude for the confirmation I had received from the queen. I now knew for sure that my fool's journey had commenced in earnest and that it all was linking up to the Crystal Pyramid Temple under the sea and to the keys and codes. More than this, it was the ancient history of this part of Africa that I had to unearth… the truth of who these first people were, and then to reconnect with the heart and soul of Africa!

* * * * *

At that time, this miracle sustained me, in the sense that I knew I had to continue my journey to find the source of this energy. Although I knew it was linked to the Crystal Pyramid under the sea, I also knew I would be led to some source, or information, that had to be retrieved. I had no idea what it was. I simply had to trust that I would be led to wherever it was.

I felt one day that I would return to Keurbooms to restore something very significant there. First, though, I had to find information elsewhere. In this, my gut feeling would be proven absolutely correct,

for only a few years later the full import and higher meaning of all this came to me. By then, I had recovered immensely significant puzzle pieces that would enable me to finally understand what was happening in this area, and why.

About two nights later, I was pouring over the map of Africa again, asking for guidance. When I had set off on my journey to find the pyramids marked on my map, I thought that the true Temple of the White Flame may be offshore on the east coast of Africa.

I had found an extensive vortex energy there, and I knew that it was connected to the Crystal Pyramid under the sea, but was this the pyramid I was looking for, or was it something else? And how would I know the difference?

I also knew that all of this was linked in some way to the 33° longitude line, and that the vortex energy formed part of the whole. But how?

The pyramid mountains in the Tsitsikamma[10] seemed to be pulling me further north, in some way. So I had the notion there must be something there that would give me the keys to everything else.

What was it that I needed to find or retrieve? I found myself thinking of the fool going on a journey to goodness knows where! I was being pulled back home to the Drakensberg. I felt intuitively that this was all linked up.

As I approached the mountains, my heart and soul sang. The nearer I drove to these pyramid mountains, the more I realized that the energy was still present there, but in a different form.

I suddenly saw a sign saying "Elandsberg" and was immediately reminded of the San. Where eland were found, there were sacred places, so something must be going on there. I had just stopped at the Bloukrans River San Centre, but had felt myself being drawn still further north.

---

10   The Tsitsikamma National Park is a protected area on the Garden Route, Western Cape. It is a coastal reserve well known for its indigenous forests and dramatic coastline. (*Wikipedia*)

*Storms River Mouth.*

I was prompted to turn off to visit the Tsitsikamma Nature Reserve. When I arrived, I knew that this was just where I was meant to be. I drank in the splendor, the sheer majesty of the scenery, where the waters whirled and swirled in huge vortex energy patterns, and the mountains and rocks formed spectacular images that spanned time and space!

Before I knew it, I had a chalet just where I wanted it to be – on the rocks, overlooking the churning vortex sea. I felt like I had just won a jackpot in Heaven!

I ate dinner that evening while sitting and drink-ing it all in. I knew I would find answers here. Again, I had that sense of having been there before, and of a familiar knowing…

The next morning, I was jumping from rock to rock, absolutely enchanted and fascinated by that wonderland. In the process of exploring, I was marveling at the strange rock formations and wonder-ing how the sea could have carved out such unusual formations. It reminded me of Machu Picchu[11], with the sheer magnificence of the mountains and the superb energy.

---

11  Machu Picchu is an Incan citadel set high in the Andes Mountains in Peru. Built in the 15th century and later abandoned, it's renowned for its sophisticated dry-stone walls that fuse huge blocks without the use of mortar, intriguing buildings that play on astronomical alignments, and panoramic views. (*Wikipedia*)

*The rock on which I was sitting.*

In between the chalets there were fields of white arum lilies blossoming in profusion, much as they do in Natal. I was greatly intrigued by the stones and rocks. They looked as if they were hand-hewn, like the ones at the Giza Pyramids[12]. The stones are in a straight line, which fascinated me.

As I continued, following a part of the famous

*Perfect fits – and there were more of them.*

---

12 The Great Pyramid of Giza is the oldest and largest of the three pyramids in the Giza pyramid complex bordering what is now El Giza, Egypt. It is the oldest of the Seven Wonders of the Ancient World, and is the only one to remain largely intact. (*Wikipedia*)

*The rocks are hewn and in perfect alignment.*

Otter Trail[13] and just wandering about, pictures started emerging as I honed into the energies and lost records of the area.

While pondering the information I was being given, I sat down on a huge rock ledge. The next minute, I was told to rise and examine the rock. It took a few promptings, but when I did get up, I saw what looked like a wall! The rocks were perfectly hewn in exact squares and fitted so snugly into one

*Strange inscriptions on this rock and others at Storms River Mouth.*

another that you could not even slide a knife between them!

It is then that I understood why I had been reminded of Machu Picchu. In the next instant, I had an extensive download of information about what had happened here and about the rock walls.

\* \* \* \* \*

*"When the city that stood here disappeared under the surf and sea, there was a temple with a certain crystal that could be used to bring great energy into being — an electromagnetic spiraling energy. When correctly utilized, it could light up huge cities and enable travel at great speed on transport discs. If misused, however, it could become a potent weapon of mass destruction.*

*This is the story of what actually happened in the battle for control of this power:*

*The Black Magi wanted to use this vortex energy to attack the Temple of the White Flame, for whoever gained the power base of that Temple would rule the entire planet. They therefore gathered around them the best scientists in this city to formulate ways to control this energy form, and to condense it into a type of laser beam or laser-like energy.*

---

13    The Otter Trail is a hiking trail along the Garden Route coast of South Africa. It is named for the Cape clawless otter that occurs in this region. (*Wikipedia*)

*They wanted to design it to penetrate the protective shield around the Temple, to gain access, although they could not destroy it, as it was an essential power base. They planned to infiltrate the island and kill the High Priesthood to control this base.*

*Then the Black Magi took command of the entire city that once stood there, via devious means, such as using mind control on the scientists to ensure their plan succeeded. The High Priest and Priestess in charge of the Temple were warned of the attack, and they placed everyone on red alert, so to utilize their collective minds to activate the shield already in place around the temple and island.*

*So, with the help of the Intergalactic Fleet, they deflected the missile and sent it back from whence it came. However this destroyed the city, which was the size of Johannesburg[14]. It sank instantly into the sea, simultaneously draining the whole inland region of the Karoo, leaving it as a wasteland, as radiation settled in, and molten rock and lava were created by this intense heat. As the laser missile remains active and has formed a vortex on land and off the coast, ships still cannot come near this coastline and a large number have been wrecked there.*

I have the impression of huge underground buildings and temples covered with coral and seaweed, which would now be seen as rocks, when in fact they are underground structures.

*The entire city was wiped out instantaneously as gigantic tidal waves erupted. The same energy is still here, with its potent force still creating the swirling waters and vortex.*

\* \* \* \* \*

Slowly, but surely, a picture was emerging of the origin of Earth at the very beginning – of a type of Garden of Eden, a Utopia, that existed but was then destroyed. Additionally, I saw vast land masses being torn away, disappearing into the sea, with other land flooded, as new land masses emerged.

I started to understand that I could not be looking at the records of Atlantis or those of Lemuria, but instead of some earlier civilization that was millions of years older!

It was apparent to me that this was an accurate vision of the emerging history of our planet. The primal energies present from the very beginning had somehow been obscured in the mists of time.

## JOURNAL ENTRY

Pivotal moments… those moments when you realize that your calling is greater than the sum total of who and what you are…

Now that I had figured out what had happened here, I was called to go back to where I started my journey… Little did I know what I would find, for when I finally got back home, I was pulled further north to retrieve a tremendously important piece of the self-same memory bank.

---

14   Johannesburg, South Africa's biggest city and capital of its inland Gauteng province, began as a 19th-century gold-mining settlement. (*Wikipedia*)

# CHAPTER 3

# Research and Revelations…

My journey now continued as I travelled up the coast, leaving the pyramid mountains of Tsitsikamma behind me. As I headed towards Port Elizabeth[1], the landscape started flattening out and the energies became depleted.

I felt as if this part existed on newly-formed land that had emerged as the other land masses sank into the sea.

Port Elizabeth itself was a disappointment, and I found it energetically unremarkable. Soon I was again surrounded by bushveld[2], shrub and thorn trees, between Port Elizabeth and East London[3].

Travelling through these areas, I was reminded of Zululand, which has the same kind of hills covered with thorn trees, but this area was wild, and desolate.

Empty shells of the homes of the 1820 settlers peeked forlornly through the shrub, long forgotten and abandoned. The Fish River wound its way along the deep crevices between the mountains. The road felt longer and longer, with no towns in between where I could stop and stretch my legs. It was with great relief that I finally arrived in King Williamstown[4] and could have a very late lunch.

East London came as pleasant surprise after Port Elizabeth, as it meandered along. Interestingly, my hosts came from the same area in Natal that I did. I wanted to travel up the coast to Port St Johns to find the elusive Crystal Pyramids, but was cautioned by them not to go there, for it would not be safe for me to travel alone. They suggested that I take another route,

---

1  Port Elizabeth, known as the Windy City, or *iBhayi* ('the bay' in isiXhosa), is a coastal hub in the Eastern Cape and one of the largest cities in South Africa. It lies 770km east of Cape Town.

2  Bushveld: A terrain of thick, scrubby trees and bush in dense thickets, with grassy groundcover in between. (*http:www.yourdictionary.com*)

3  East London is a city on the south-east coast of South Africa, in the Eastern Cape. The city lies on the Indian Ocean coast, largely between the Buffalo River and the Nahoon River. It has the country's only river port. (*Wikipedia*)

4  King William's Town is a town in the Eastern Cape province along the banks of the Buffalo River.

along the Maluti Mountains, right into Southern Drakensberg, before heading to Pietermaritzburg.

It was an incredibly beautiful stretch of road that wound its way along the Maluti Mountains[5] and Lesotho border, and then into Griqualand East, Matatiele and Kokstad. I then took the familiar coastal road from there, via Durban to Pietermaritzburg[6], where I met with my dear friend, Jill.

While travelling through Natal, I was again reminded of the Crystal Pyramids and their connection to my beloved Drakensberg Mountains. Sure enough, I saw the craft of the Intergalactic Fleet accompanying me on this journey, and I felt the call to go to Monk's Cowl and Cathedral Peak for a few days.

It was here, in my beloved familiar places again, that I had time to reflect on the journey behind me. I was starting to draw the energy lines together, and to understand that somehow I was being led to discover something really vast and as yet undefined.

I meandered my way through the Midlands before venturing further afield, through my mother's ancestral lands and then deeper into the Drakensberg. I had booked into the Champagne Castle Hotel and, as soon as I could, I dressed in my hiking gear and started climbing uphill.

I was sitting on a rock in spellbound wonder, in perfect solitude, watching the water gushing from a beautiful waterfall high up in the mountains, when I became aware that I was not actually alone. I felt and saw Light beings all around me as I connected with Mother Earth. It was as if everything was flowing together in one, single, massive stream of light, like a rainbow bridge. I saw how Heaven and Earth became as one. It was one of those moments when I merged with everything and ceased to be on Earth, flowing in the Cosmic River of Life!

I was again given the visions of the Crystal Pyramids, and the Temple of the White Flame. Somehow, I knew that one day I would understand, and everything would become clear.

Not yet, though!

Three days later, I was travelling north-east again, and this time I was prompted to go to the eastern escarpment of the Drakensberg Mountains. I first did a detour to visit friends and family in my old home grounds of Dundee and Glencoe, before travelling into Mpumalanga[7].

My next destination was Waterval Boven[8] and the area around it. I had booked into a guest house on the farm next to the main road and wanted to explore, as I was being drawn here.

When travelling in the region of Dullstroom, the strange rock formations immediately caught my eye, as did the endless stone circles. They were without entrances and strewn everywhere. They reminded me of similar stone circles I had seen on my cousins' farm on the border between Natal and Zululand, where the Buffalo River meets the Tugela River. It was also in that area that my father had shown us the gold mines that had shafts going straight down into the ground.

---

5    The Maluti Mountains are a mountain range in the highlands of the Kingdom of Lesotho. They extend about 100km into the Free State. The Maloti Range is part of the Drakensberg system, which includes ranges across large areas of South Africa. (*https://www.britannica.com*)

6    Pietermaritzburg is the capital and second-largest city in the province of KwaZulu-Natal, South Africa. It was founded in 1838. (*Wikipedia*)

7    Mpumalanga (Zulu for "the place where the Sun rises") is a province in eastern South Africa, bordering the nations of Swaziland and Mozambique. (*Wikipedia*)

8    Waterval Boven is a small town situated on the edge of the escarpment, on the banks of the Elands River, above the 75m Elands Falls, on the railway line from Pretoria to Maputo in Mpumalanga. (*Wikipedia*)

I had the impression of great cities that had suffered some kind of disaster; a huge upheaval of some sort, and possibly a nuclear explosion, or an explosion from the immense impact of an asteroid or comet that had resulted in this crater.

The stones were again precision-cut and stacked one upon the other in neat circles. Others appeared to be randomly scattered about. Of course, the farmers had used these stones as building material, so some appeared to have been dismantled, but others had been left intact.

What came to mind was a consecutive city complex, or series of circular cities with round temples crowned with pyramids. These were the honing centers for the energy grids. So, when looking at the landscape and even the hills here, I always found that the energy felt stronger in some spots than others. I sensed the contours of the landscape had energy flowing in straight lines in some places, and in a spiraling manner elsewhere.

Everything here seemed to come from time immemorial!

This must have been part of a very ancient civilization where gold was mined. My vision expanded, and I saw tall people with a reddish skin hue who had been the ruling priesthood and royalty.

Then they faded away, with others taking their place, who looked different. I saw this expanding over many millions of years. A coming and going! The landscape changed, and at times it was entirely destroyed and buried before the next people built over what had been there before.

*My sketch of the mounds at Nelspruit.*

This is where it all began: Those underground civilizations and space stations still exist, and their people are living here unnoticed and unseen!

They live in the underground cities and prefer to stay hidden, although they are human. They exist in the 5th dimensional state and, therefore, one has to tune into them, for they cannot be seen with the naked eye.

I found some hidden pyramids and got the impression of other huge ones underground. When travelling to Nelspruit I saw 7 mounds, which seemed to have been melded together as a result of intense heat. I had the impression that they were man-made and not naturally occurring. They were remnants of control centers for aircraft traffic. I again felt that an immense catastrophe had occurred, which had released extreme heat that had melted these buildings.

When I was in Nelspruit, I intuited that this entire area had once been an ancient metropolis – even larger than that of the modern-day Johannesburg/ Pretoria metropolitan area, with spacecraft and multiple buildings teeming with life. There was a diverse mix of people: Some giants; several of those mythological creatures; half-man, half-beasts; and other even stranger-looking ones!

I felt that the first civilization here had been a few million years old. It had worked with the elementals in the rocks. They could literally dissolve them and transform them into feather-light energy masses that could then, using their minds, be teleported and placed precisely where they were needed. The rocks would then materialize again into their original forms! This is how the ancient pyramids were constructed, as well as the massive megalithic ones found all over the world.

In Nelspruit, there are huge megalithic rocks everywhere – often randomly planted in municipal gardens and used as decoration. I sensed a significant connection here with Avebury, Stonehenge and the Celts.

The pyramids here formed a pattern that created an energy grid. This in turn formed a massive energy conduit, or energy substation, for the spiraling energy used by the Ancients.

The words "Central Command Center" came to me repeatedly, and I felt that this used to be a central hub in ancient times.

While having lunch at a restaurant, I had an astonishing encounter with a total stranger who approached me saying that she had an important message for me. She said that she had to give me a code, which was 777.

To say that I was amazed was an understatement, but in the subsequent events of the next few weeks, this encoded number would prove to be of vital importance.

My next stop was Waterval Boven, where I found even more of these stone circles. They appeared to be scattered up and downhill in circular patterns.

From there, I was led to Kaapsehoop and the oldest stone circle in the world, which is called Adam's Calendar.

Despite the estimated age of this calendar being 250 000 years, I immediately felt that this place was even more ancient. Walking along, I saw a massive Crystal Pyramid hovering over the plateau – actually, two. One was pointed upwards and the other downwards. One moved clockwise and the other counterclockwise.

Standing on the edge of the cliff, I immediately honed into the 7 pyramids in the valley below and felt all of them move into one single energy field.

I also sensed the grave of a giant there, who was way over 13ft tall, with red hair and reddish skin.

The stone circle itself was interesting enough, but it did not hold my attention as the pyramids did. I could not even touch the rocks, as I felt their powerful energy and I knew that they were not of this world.

There were two rocks that I later understood to be the Horus portals. I instinctively knew that if I had

*The whole vast area, from Dullstroom and Waterval Boven, up to Nelspruit and then also up into the north, is strewn with stone circle upon stone circle. This is an example.*

*The stones in the circles are neatly stacked, and they emit a ringing sound when struck. One finds exactly the same structures strewn all over Zululand and Natal.*

stepped between them, I would have been teleported into space.

It was here that the wild horses appeared to greet me for the first time. During the events of the next few weeks, they would become my guardians, my guides and my helpers.

The next day, I booked myself into a guesthouse at Kaapsehoop. The most amazing adventures were awaiting me.

# CHAPTER 4

# The Inner and Outer Quest: Incredible Discoveries and Deep Confirmation

I was sitting deep in contemplation in my more-than-comfortable hotel room. Outside the mist was swirling and twirling, and it reminded me of the mists of Avalon[1]. Interestingly, quite a few people had commented on my soul-connection to Avalon over the past few months. I had just taken it in my stride.

I was in a new 'becoming-and-growing' process in my life, and on a quest that might have resembled one of those of the Knights of the Round Table[2] and their ladies who went in search for the Holy Grail[3]. Only, my grail was something more than a cup, and infinitely more than I could ever express in words.

I was looking for something vast and intimately connected to the African continent, but at that time, I had no idea how it would unfold. All I knew was that I was finding my puzzle pieces, and that one day, they would slot together and on to the map of Africa. This would complete something incredibly ancient and groundbreaking.

I poured over the maps of Africa again, and noted that the 7 pyramids I had found in this area were exactly on the 33° line. (I have noted since then that with the Earth's shifts, some of these sacred places were also a little out of alignment, as the Earth's axis and plates have also moved.) This meant that my search had led me to exactly the right spot.

The pyramids were down below, and the stone circle was on the plateau of the same mountain I

---

1  Avalon: In Arthurian legend, this is an island paradise in the western seas to which King Arthur was taken after he was mortally wounded in battle. (*Wikipedia*)

2  The Knights of the Round Table were characters in the legends about King Arthur. They were the best knights in King Arthur's kingdom and lived in his castle, Camelot. (*Wikipedia*)

3  Holy Grail: This is a dish, plate, stone or cup that is part of an important theme of Arthurian literature. According to legend, it has special powers and is designed to provide happiness, eternal youth and food in infinite abundance. (*Wikipedia*)

stood on, where towering grey boulders were strewn all over. In the dense mist, they looked like ancient ghosts wandering around…

Wearing my raincoat and hiking shoes, I took my walking stick and off I went into the rolling mists, hardly able to see 2ft ahead of me. The receptionist was rather concerned. She warned me about the ancient gold mine shafts, which were huge holes in the ground of goodness-knows how deep! These shafts are man-made and look like holes, but they go directly into the Earth. They were created and are unlike what we now know as mine shafts. Apparently, some people had fallen into them and disappeared, as no one knew just how deep they were. There were also contemporary gold mines in the valley below, but they had conventional shafts.

When she mentioned these cavities, I was reminded of the gold mines I had seen in Zululand. The links were there!

I found myself in this misty, twirling, surreal wonderland… It was one of the most amazing journeys of my life. The deeper I wandered among these ancient stones, the more fascinating the excursion became. The rocks appeared and formed, or rather reformed, into the strangest shapes and sizes I have ever seen. They were the same grey hue as the stones at Adam's Calendar. They clearly came from the same source, and were arranged in bizarre formations. Some seemed to have been thrown upside down; some were hanging in mid-air; and others were lying at incredible angles. Some had tortoise-like faces, and others reminded me of serpents. Indeed, some even looked like mini-sphinxes!

Sometimes the paths just circled. At other times, I was stopped dead in my tracks and forced to retrace my steps. Then, from out of the mist, the wild horses appeared, as if from nowhere! I felt that they were my appointed guardian Angles, as they always seemed to somehow sense my presence, and I, theirs. Whenever I wandered, or felt a little lost, the horses would lead me back home!

### JOURNAL ENTRY

I looked at the stones in utter amazement... Gradually the stones, the horses, the mist and I seemed to merge into one... I find that I am lost in a wonderland where time is non-existent and where I can simply forget all and be...

For in the swirling mist, nobody goes near the stones. Just me and the horses. From faraway, I sometimes heard voices, but then asked the horses to guide me, and I was already enfolded in the protection of the Angels all around.

My attention was suddenly caught by the Eye of Horus[4] appearing out of the blue as an almost sphinx-like statue. The staring eyes seemed to be looking into the distance, showing me the way.

Something changed. I felt the energy transforming. The vibration and the frequencies shifted, and some-

*Strange figures and shapes in the mist.*

---

4   The Eye of Horus is an ancient Egyptian symbol of protection, royal power and good health. (*Wikipedia*)

*Horus appearing...*

thing was there that I had not noticed before. I clambered over some rocks and overgrowth and saw steps clearly etched in the stone. I climbed up to a type of platform, feeling a deep sense of standing on holy ground.... consecrated ground!

I paused, remembering that there were Guardians at such places, and you first had to ask permission before access would be granted.

I called in my Guardian Angles, spirit guides, my Archangels and Ascended Masters, in particular Serapis Bey, as he is the Ascended Master with the overall responsibility for the well-being of the African continent, specifically the Giza line, the pyramids and all that is visible and invisible in Africa.

I asked them to please contact the Guardians here to ask them to give me permission to enter.

There was a moment of complete silence. Time was of no essence. I felt the mist growing thicker and moisture drops wetting my hair. I had my jersey cap over my head, but was asked to even put the hood of my raincoat up.

Suddenly I felt the presence of other Beings and saw the 12 gathered there, forming a circle, with me in the middle. Silently they were welcoming me in and asking me to step forward.

Without having been given the instruction, I gave the "Namaste" greeting 7 times, in all 4 directions, and was then allowed to enter that portal. I felt I was being blessed and shown the way.

For one moment, the mist lifted and then I saw it: A beautiful place, with the most amazing natural garden and a waterway. I sensed that once there must have been an exquisite waterfall here. The plants seemed to belong to this cliff, with faces carved into the sides; the mist making them appear surreal. I saw lion-type faces that reminded me of the Sphinx, and then noticed that Horus was guarding the area far and wide. Something was directing my attention upwards... I looked over Horus's statue and the platform, and caught sight of a huge face behind it.

For a moment, I thought this was the carving of a sphinx, as the hair reminded me of a lion's mane. Then, I realized this was so, but it was a human being! He was sitting on an enormous stone throne, dominating the surroundings. His nose was prominent, as were his other features, and his hair fell over his shoulders. It was amazing. I could make out his arms held loosely on his lap, as well as his legs, as he sat like a king on this massive throne.

I asked the Guardians of this place who this was. They said this was a shrine dedicated to a king, and that these stones are the ruins of his beloved city. And sure enough, the statue was of a giant, with facial features that conveyed a calm tranquillity.

I was deeply moved, sensing this was a holy place with a timelessness about it that was not easy to describe. I couldn't find words. I stood there for a long time and just drank it in. I asked permission to sit, and then she appeared in front of me: The Great Mother! I felt a connection there that was deeply moving and realized that she, too, was intimately connected to this place.

She told me how much she loved this location; how they had created the new race to help; and how much they loved them. I eventually rose, thanking the Guardians and all of my other helpers. I was then led to a place to which I could return whenever necessary. Suddenly, out of the mist seven horses appeared, and

I knew that they had been silently guarding me all of this time.

When I eventually surfaced from the mist and found my way back to the village, to my utter amazement I realized that I had been there the entire day, yet it had seemed like only a few minutes. Another incredible fact was that I had done a complete circle in the mist, without consciously trying to do so.

The next morning, I wandered off again, but this time further afield. The more I roamed, the more I realized I was in the splendid remains of a huge palace that had once stood here.

I recognized the Sphinx and the familiar faces of a certain type of gargoyle[5] everywhere. But, things were strewn about. I clearly saw a looming doorway across the path. It was here amongst the ferns and the rocks that I sat and meditated.

*The Ancient Ones, as sketched by me.*

---

5    In architecture, a gargoyle is a carved or formed grotesque figure with a spout designed to convey water from a roof and away from the side of a building. (Wikipedia)

*The figure of a lion-type man sitting on a huge throne appeared on the other side of the platform, through the mist.*

*The gigantic figure: A sphinx-like lion man sitting.*

*A hole in the rock.*

The Guardians of the area appeared and spoke of the splendor of this location. It was a sprawling, lofty palace with tall pillars, like a modern-day apartment block, with hanging gardens and waterfalls.

It had been the jewel in the crown – a beloved city and a teeming metropolis. It had been a happy place in the sense that everyone had worked together and it had been peaceful and well administered.

I then looked at the stones and structures and asked myself: "So, what happened here?"

In response, the Mother wept as she told me how two brothers had fought, and how their weapons had melted everything in sight, thus destroying the entire

*Strange figures and molten rocks, all that remains of a gigantic palace complex. The tortoise-like, reptilian figures are found everywhere, as well as what was once a Sphinx.*

area. Finally, she told me how the great palace was bombarded and destroyed with one horrendous explosion. The whole structure imploded and erupted, until these pillars and foundation stones were the only reminder of what had been.

"Don't ever let this happen again. My heart is bleeding. There should be no more wars between brothers, but rather, there must be peace. That is why you are being called here now – why we allowed the Guardians to let this be discovered and made known to Earth after all this time. We want the wounds to be healed so people learn to move pride and ego out of the way and to rather work as one and reign in peace."

Then they all took their leave of me and I was left with a profound sense of something indescribable, and my tears felt so close.

I finally found my way back to my room, once again sopping wet and cold. I put the heater on, pulled on some warm clothes, and lay down to sleep.

I had walked and climbed for two days and been

*Giant tortoise-like figures appear everywhere.*

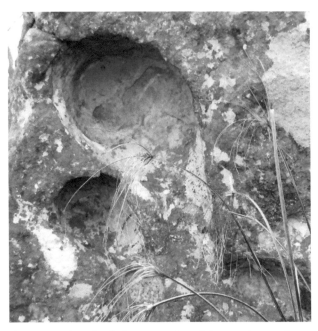

*Strange and perfect holes in another of those molten rocks..*

lost in the mists of time. I'd had an intensely emotional experience and I felt confused.

My sense of my destiny here was stronger than ever before.

It was at Kaapsehoop that I first connected to my very own unicorn, called Elysium. The fact that my unicorn and the first civilization shared the same name felt to me to be by design, not accident.

It was only later that I heard about the unicorn link to Kaapsehoop and the white lions[6] of the Timbavati Game Reserve. Indeed, Linda Tucker[7], who wrote the book on the white lions of Timbavati, visited here with a group of tourists, looking for a white horse linked to the white lions. If they could do a ceremony with this horse, then the white lions in Africa would be saved.

At that time, there was an old, white horse who was practically blind. The ladies at the crystal shop made a marigold ointment to smear around his eyes to partially alleviate his discomfort. This horse grazed in the meadow in front of the shop every day. Linda Tucker and her group blessed him and invoked the spirit of the unicorns of Africa to assist the white lions.

Within a few months, a lion cub was born in Timbavati, and the white lions of Africa were saved!

So, meeting with my unicorn in that spot was something I feel was destined. Subsequent events illustrated the reason why.

That morning, for the first time since arriving, the entire area was clear of mist. It was still overcast and cold, but I could now actually see just how beautiful it really was on top of the Drakensberg escarpment, with forests and, of course, massive stones.

Yet, from my own private balcony, I could see how the mountains here formed a type of koppie (or kopje), as the stones were covered by the forest. I was immediately drawn there, with the clear intention of connecting with Elysium and what I sensed was a massive portal.

I knew I needed to do this. I had learnt to listen to my inner promptings. They merely told me it was because the portal and energy grids here had to be cleared and reactivated. I was the only one who could do this.

So, I set out with my hiking gear and camera, and immediately tried to find the wild horses. I started off on a trail, only to find that I could not go further. I had missed the horses, and so started to connect with them telepathically. I found myself retracing my steps.

I instantly felt myself being nudged towards the place where I had begun my journey the previous time, only, a little further away. Sure enough, three of the wild horses were waiting there!

The two adult horses, a stallion and mare, had a young filly. I had connected with the trio before, especially the filly. Now as I moved towards them, the adults ignored me, but the filly, golden-brown with a

6    The white lion is a rare color mutation of the Timbavati area. They are not a separate subspecies and are thought to be indigenous to the Timbavati region of South Africa for centuries. (Wikipedia)

7    Linda Tucker, *Mystery of the White Lions, Children of the Sun God*, Npenvu, 2010.

white star on her forehead, immediately approached me. I sent her deeply loving thoughts and she instantly responded, coming forward. I first extended my hand to stroke her face, but then she kissed me! I was profoundly touched by this. After all, these were wild horses and there was a bond between us that lasted throughout my stay there.

I telepathically asked her to please connect me to the Unicorn portal and to Elysium.

I then got permission from the group to move forward. She stepped ahead to show me the slightly hidden path, with a sheer rock-face on the right and dense thicket on the left. There, around a bend, was a steep, very narrow pathway. As I rounded the steep corner, pressed against the face of the rock, to my utter surprise I found my path completely blocked by a huge, brown stallion with a long, black mane and a white star on his forehead. A beautiful horse!

I sensed that he was the guardian of this place and that I needed his permission to step into the sacred place – the portal. I silently communicated love and light to him, explaining why I was here and what I had come to do.

Time stood still as we stood looking at each other, communicating silently. All of a sudden, he started to move up the path. I stepped out of the way so he could pass me and then, to my wonderment, I found my unicorn, Elysium, there – clearly visible now – asking me to follow him!

I can't remember much. I appeared to wind my way through the rocks, as the mist had descended all of a sudden. I was enveloped in a silvery-white veil as I simply followed him. Everything seemed surreal, as the rocks, shrubs and overgrowth mingled with what appeared to be a path. At one stage, I was taken off this path and onto another side path and told that I had taken a wrong turn, as that way led to an old mine shaft.

I continued following Elysium, even though there simply was no path at this stage. Then we came to a sudden clearing: A perfect circle with a huge stone in the middle. On the right was a large rock, and

protruding from it was another rock that looked almost like a seat or a throne.

I was told to go and stand there. It was too high to sit on, so I leaned against this sheer rock that was towering over me and held my walking stick between my legs, with the backpack against the stone, and sat (or half-sat) on the throne.

I felt like I was entering a kind of time warp. I was wrapped in the center of a cocoon of light swirling around me, with the impression of stepping out of my body into a different dimension and vibration – another frequency.

My walking stick transformed itself into a wand. With my feet firmly planted on the Earth, I immediately did a grounding meditation, connecting to the great obsidian crystal in the middle of the Earth. Then a miracle occurred!

At that moment I became my Soul self, the Shining One!

I felt the tremendous power of true Soul-self and realized that I was the Great Mother Goddess – the immortal one, who illuminated all! I found myself surrounded by the Guardians of this location, whom I had previously met, in long, white robes with blonde-white hair resting on their shoulders. They had huge purple-blue eyes and finely-chiselled faces of radiant beauty. They appeared androgynous, although some seemed to be predominantly male and others more female. They were ageless, reminding me of the drawings of the Ascended Masters. I felt them to be a part of this group, although they simply introduced themselves as Guardians or Keepers of this portal.

I then called in all those souls originally connected to this place: Those who had built it, then destroyed it, and worked within or with it. I called in those who had erected the structures and cities. I called in those who had created the slave species, and thus had fragments of their own souls scattered in their creations.

I called in the stuck souls: Those who never left this Earthly plane due to the war between the two brothers. I called in the tree and plant Guardians; the elementals; the fairies; the powers of the east, west, south, and north; as well as the four elements of fire, water, earth, air; and the ethers.

I called in the Guardians of the Animal Kingdom and all other living creatures connected to this place.

I called in the unicorns and the Guardians of this portal, Adam's Calendar, and the pyramids and energy centers.

By this time, I had a whole collection of souls gathered in a massive semi-circle all around me. I would estimate this number to be a thousand, if not more! Some were the most grotesque creatures I had ever seen. They were half-man, half-beast. Some certainly defied description, and others were completely hairless and humanoid. I stood/sat on the throne, with my feather-light wand now in my hands.

Then suddenly I began speaking: The "I am" that I have always been since time immemorial!

I reminded them of the very birth of this planet and then called in the Great Earth Mother Angel Gaia, and in she came.

I told them how they had wronged this planet and place, and how much suffering they had inflicted on all of life.

I affirmed that I had been sent to release and transmute all negative energies and karma with the White-Gold-Silver-Violet Flame of Transmutation, and that this would mean all who were trapped and blocking the energy grids, the pyramids and the portal, would be transmuted and rescinded here in the ethers.

It was amazing! I felt a huge power surging through me, nearly lifting me off the ground, as a blinding, white light beamed down from the great Mothership of the Ashtar High Command, which appeared above us. This light swirled down, enveloping everything with an unearthly brightness, blinding like the Sun! It was vast vortex energy, and somehow I knew that it was coming not only from the craft, but from the pyramid inside the Earth: The one in the etheric, and the ones below.

With each decree I made to release bad karma, pain, suffering, Soul memory banks and also stuck souls, I would tap the wand 7 times with great authority, so releasing all Angels who were imprisoned here by the ceremonies, pacts, and curses that had transpired. I also had the distinct feeling that human and animal sacrifices had been made.

The most powerful event occurred as I released all stuck soul energies, the emotional memory banks, and the pain and suffering blocking the port. At that moment, I recalled the woman I met at midday before the equinox tour and the number she had given me – 777 – saying that I should remember this, as I would need it!

I had to invoke all my helpers, the Archangels, the Ascended Masters, The Intergalactic Fleet, the Ashtar High Command, the unicorns, and the silver-gold-violet flame, and to tap the staff 7 times again and repeat this cleansing ritual of: 3 times 7 = 777 – in the eternal spheres as well as in the higher dimensions, right up to the Council of 12 who sit before the Divine Source!

As I stepped into my highest power and communicated telepathically with these Beings, I had my eyes closed. But at precisely that moment, the whole place lit up even more radiantly than before, with an immensely powerful gold-silver-violet light – so much so that when I opened my eyes for a second, I was blinded!

I then realized that there were 12 unicorns encircling us, and that I now stood in the center!

There was a rush of wind and a huge sucking motion. I felt it lifting my hair and stroking my face, and then sensed a huge vortex-like energy stretching over all the mountains and valleys, as all negative energies were cleared away, rescinded and removed!

Adam's Calendar's portals were also cleansed and reactivated, and all destructive energies there were removed!

I asked the Intergalactic Fleet, the Ashtar High Command (Ashtar is my husband and stems from Andromeda, as do I) that the huge Crystal Pyramid that had once guarded and energized the portals be replaced and reactivated. This was done.

When everything was completed, all the Beings

were kneeling in front of me, thanking their great beloved Mother for returning to this planet to heal them.

I then motioned them all to listen as I spoke to them with great love and compassion. I spoke about their souls now being released and cleansed; about the all-embracing love that is the Divine Source; and that they were now free to pursue their soul growth in other galaxies and Solar Systems, and to be reunited with their Soul-selves.

I thanked those who had remained here: The plant; bird; flower and animal kingdoms; the elementals; fairies; gnomes; rock people; the air; water; fire; earth; and ether powers; and Mother Gaia for the great love and devotion she gives to help keep this planet alive – often bearing the most suffering herself.

It felt like holy ground. And then I said the great prayer of Invocation of Oneness and the connection to the Divine Source. We were all united as one!

There they were, Beings kneeling all around me, and I could see many Light workers, my Soul custodians, Archangels, Angels, Ascended Masters and unicorns, gathering around rejoicing.

Finally, I asked if there were any questions before I left. The Keepers of the Place stood and thanked me and the Great Beloved Mother for helping them. I thanked them and released them to rejoice in this moment.

Archangel Azrael[8] and the hosts of Angels who help with the transition of souls then appeared and were asked to travel with these Angels so that the portal could be unblocked. Indeed, the decree I had delivered moments before had said just that. They would now be requested to vacate this place so that the final cleansing could occur, and the portal could be reactivated and opened.

Then a terrific surge of white, blinding mist surrounded everything with an even greater intensity. Swirling, ever swirling, the souls were gathered up and helped by the Angels to make the transition. The whole area was illuminated by this light, until all were helped to cross over, and things returned to normal. In a sense, it felt 'abnormal', as there was an unearthly feeling remaining. It was as if we had been transported into another time and space!

Then they left, and suddenly I was surrounded by the fairy folk and elementals. The birds started singing, and it appeared as if all of Nature had woken up after the complete and utter silence to dance and sing!

In a daze, I walked away with the strong knowing that the energy centers and portals were reopened and activated, and that this signified Africa rising up again. Here was the Key to the Crystal Temple, to usher in the return of the Golden Age to Earth!

I finished up with some quiet time at a look-out place. There I stood on the edge of a cliff on an enormous mountain peak, gazing down at the pyramids in the valley below, as far as the eye could see. I was profoundly moved, for I had often imagined myself doing just this in visions and dreams!

I was standing there, all alone. Around me was majestic beauty and stillness. Nothing and nobody else.

I was then told to sing the great invocation, the Aah-song that belonged to my people and my Soul. I stood there singing on the top of that cliff, repeating the invocation 7 times.

I know now in my Soul-self that I AM a goddess and immensely powerful. I needed to feel this that day, as it has empowered me and has, for some reason, filled me with the courage, strength and the true conviction that I am being called to do my supreme duty.

All else is secondary.

---

8    Azrael's name means "whom God helps". His role is primarily to help people cross over to Heaven at the time of physical death. (*Wikipedia*)

*It is here that the Ancient Ones appeared to me to thank me for opening the portal.*

I was in an altered state for some time afterwards and just sat on a rock on the ledge of the krans[9], overlooking the pyramids in the valley for a long time. It was late evening by the time I finally got back to the hotel.

Too much had happened, and I first had to absorb the immensity of it all.

---

It was here at Kaapsehoop that I again became aware of underground tunnels and cave systems, and the linking up of this network with the huge underground cities. It was only a few years later that I finally understood more about this African continent and what had truly happened here. That, however, is recorded elsewhere.

In this place, I met a woman and her 'crystal children', who were planting crystals in the ground to clear the energies to realign the whole area to the Earth grid. They were doing a sterling job, and I could see how they also simultaneously carried out rescue work. It was here, too, that I encountered a

witch called Mimi. She was something of an enigma and the first person I've ever met, who, on seeing me, immediately asked about the Crystal Skulls.

I had told no-one about the Crystal Skulls, which were part of my recall (recorded elsewhere in this book). So, I was surprised that Mimi had picked that up. She was adamant that I assist her to retrieve the Emerald Crystal Skull in the pyramids down in the valley.

However, I knew that until the planet and the collective body had raised its frequency and vibration, it must remain where it was for the time being, guarded by those in the underground city.

I had encountered these beings the day after I opened the portal, when they thanked me. Now they could open the ventilation shafts, which had been blocked for ages. They were very tall and reddish-blonde people, and I believe that they were a remnant of those once living above the ground, now transcended into a higher dimensional state of being.

It only dawned upon me much later that at Adam's Calendar there were multi-dimensional states

---

9  A krans is a rocky ridge or scar. (*Wikipedia*)

of being existing in parallel states of consciousness. If you switched frequency bands, you could tune into the higher or lower states of consciousness, and thus into the different dimensions that exist simultaneously.

This phenomenon has to do with the rivers of gold running through the two rivers. In addition to this, another important factor is that they are connected to the pyramids and the 33° longitude line.

To me, this area seemed to hold parallel existences, and so must be viewed through multidimensional glasses.

On my final day there, to my utter delight, there was a neighing from the wild horses as they galloped into the village, close to where I was packing my bags into my car. The filly came to greet me, and the rest of the horses waited for me. I walked up to them to say my goodbyes, my heart saddened to leave these beautiful creatures behind. They had guarded and watched over me.

The other villagers came out, as they had never seen anything like that happen before, and to all of our joy, the whole herd suddenly appeared and ran through the village neighing. The hotel receptionist shook her head in amazement, and said: "They did that especially for you!"

*The filly came to greet me: My best friend who helped me to communicate with the wild horses, as and when they guarded me. They were now saying their farewells by galloping through the village.*

As I drove away, they were waiting for me near the boom gate, and there I waved them goodbye.

Something of me will forever remain in that little village with the temples, palaces and Adam's Calendar, at Kaapsehoop!

# CHAPTER 5

# The Quest Continues: The Lion People Make Themselves Known

Meanwhile, the puzzle of the 33° longitude line, the Crystal Pyramid Temples, and the vortex energy would continue to haunt me.

In December 2009, I returned to Knysna for six months to try to solve this riddle. I retrieved more information during that time about the temples and the ancient history. At that time, I was starting to record it.

In August 2010, I left Africa and went to teach English at an Arabic school in Qatar, Middle East. I had been told that I would be leaving the shores of Africa for some time.

In 2011, I returned to South Africa and started writing and recording my travels. In 2012, I was called back to Nature's Valley to complete this book.

It was during that time that I had visions about the energy centers in Australia being severely obstructed. I then drew a sketch of the congested area and sent it to Australian friends, who set about clearing these lines.

I finally understood that Uluru[1] and Australia were linked to what I was recording in Africa, and that Australia was in great danger of earthquakes. The central part of it was actually breaking up. By mobilising the Light workers for assistance, a massive earthquake was prevented.

My attention would later be brought back to Australia in a profound way that would reveal its connection to the African continent.

However, back in South Africa, for the first time I started noticing the circles on the mountains, and how the same patterns continually repeated themselves: I had seen those same patterns in Waterval Boven and surrounds.

My experience of the vortex energy and the opening up of the portal had equipped me with vital

---

1   Uluru, or Ayer's Rock, is a massive sandstone monolith in the heart of the Northern Territory's Red Centre desert, 450km from Alice Springs. It is sacred to indigenous Australians and is believed to be about 700 million years old. (*Wikipedia*)

*Uluru is very ancient. Remains of pyramids are hidden underneath it.*

tools to understand the essence of what humanity has lost.

I began pouring over the maps of Africa again. To my astonishment, I was shown that the original Crystal Pyramid Temple of the Sun was in Zimbabwe. It fitted into the original arrangement of pyramids that I had randomly drawn.

On my return to Keurbooms Beach, I found Arch Rock and finally understood that I was standing right in the middle of the eye of the vortex energy. Looking at Google maps later, I confirmed this. What is so amazing about Keurbooms is that every day, between 11am and 1pm, that activated energy becomes palpable.

*Right: The energy lines I drew on a map of Australia, which all link up to Uluru and extremely ancient song lines, hidden pyramids, and tunnel systems, which all link up to Africa.*

*Arch Rock and the remains of three pyramids, as well as a massive vortex energy source that forms from land and sea, from Plettenberg Bay (Robberg) to Nature's Valley.*

into the mouth. Then, there, right in front of me, I saw three pyramids!

As the tide was coming in, towards 11am, I knew I had to return to the other side of the rocks. Any later and I would not be able to get beyond the high-water line. I reached the other side and was told to sit at a place with an overhanging rock where water was seeping out of the krans. It was incredible. I was sitting on pure crystal rocks, and I could feel myself connecting profoundly to the Earth. Then, at 11am, something very special happened. I easily moved into a meditative state and began shaking all over, energy coursing through me, like massive electric shocks.

In addition, it felt like I was in a sound chamber, as the sea was now churning and swirling in a vortex-like fashion. Before, it had been reasonably calm. I could feel the energy entering my crown chakra and then working itself through my whole body, as the sound became surreal, cosmic and somehow amplified. I cannot describe this.

I was then told to move into the Sun (I was wet through). Sitting there, I immediately experienced surges of energy wrenching my whole body. I was shifting consciousness and could see quite clearly that a massive Crystal Pyramid hung over the entire area. I was sitting directly under its apex! It was still there

## JOURNAL ENTRY

### Keurbooms, October 25, 2012

Today I arrived about 9.30am, which proved to be ideal, for the tide was coming in and was just low enough for me to go further than I had ever ventured before… I had seen people coming from that side, so knew there had to be a path somewhere. When I found it, I was intrigued. There was a huge door in the rocks, carved out by the sea. There, I saw faces in the rocks everywhere, with the two perfect circles just beyond, which I had previously noticed.

I could not get enough of this amazing hidden spot, with the one side where the river was flowing

*The door in the rocks.*

in the etheric plane. There were three pyramids on the other side, and the remains of this one. Then I saw another one pointing upwards, and the two formed a vast and powerful combined energy that was actually churning up the whole sea and working in incredible ways.

I had a vision of my future life. Then I more or less returned to my physical body, but moved and sat

*The overhanging cliff and the start of the stone circle at Keurbooms.*

*A stone circle offshore, where the vortex energy forms in the sea.*

on a rock as close as I could to this portal. If I had not sat down, I would have been lifted off my feet by the powerful energy. It was astonishing. At one stage I could feel myself being pulled up and up by the incredible force generated.

I knew I had to return home then, for I was working that afternoon. It was a difficult return journey. Because of the rising sea levels, I had to clamber over the massive rocks. I noticed that the further I went from the spot, the less powerful the energies were, so I knew that I had not been imagining it.

I will go back there for three hours next time, when I have the opportunity.

What is so astonishing is that this energy shift began precisely at 11am and was tremendously potent! There are faces on the rocks everywhere, reminding me of the Egyptian heads you see carved in their stone temples. This energy is so strong that it immediately took me into an altered state of consciousness and into other dimensions. It reminded me of Storms River Mouth and what I had experienced there.

I was shown today, when I shifted dimensions, that this links up with the pyramids under the sea. This all aligns 100 percent to the Pyramids of Giza. This is truly amazing.

I have only experienced this in one other place in South Africa: At Kaapsehoop and Adam's Calendar!

---

I have tested this time and again. Before 11am and after 13pm, the energy is depleted, but between 11am and 1pm, one can literally span dimensions there!

JOURNAL ENTRY

---

One day I was sitting with my back against a huge rock of an overhanging krans – once again in the middle of the stone circle there. Then, at about 11.15am, I had one of the most stunning experiences of my life! I was literally pulled up by this spiraling vortex energy into higher dimensions. It felt as if I was in a huge sound chamber, with the sounds of the sea and some higher frequency sounds coming from both the rock behind me, and the circle in front of me. I experienced the same endless sense of at-oneness and the feeling of stepping into my higher Soul-self that I had felt at Kaapsehoop.

This is, in fact, a portal leading into different levels of consciousness and communication, as the vortex energy pulls you into the Super Consciousness Fields.

It was here at Keurbooms that I first met the Keeper of the Place, a giant of a man, with a reddish-hued skin and long, dark hair. Walking beside him were two leopards! Two nights later, I heard the strangest sound outside my bedroom window. I knew that it was a leopard calling! The next day, a Nature's Valley resident and his wife saw a leopard walking past their home – in broad daylight! Leopards had not been seen there in many years. To me, this was just another confirmation of the validity of the information given to me.

I knew for certain then that I had made contact with the Lion People. The leopards were a sign that they were helping me to retrieve the ancient history of a long-forgotten people, as well as their highly sophisticated technology that had been lost in the mists of time.

## The Lion People

The Lion People came from Lyra at the time when Elysium was established to assist with the planning of cities, the design of the Crystal Pyramids, and the Crystal Pyramid Crystalline Grids.

They are famous for their incredible architecture and engineering technologies, and are known as the Master Architects, Engineers and Builders of the Cosmos.

Lyra was once a huge galaxy that formed part of a spiraling galaxy system, which included Andromeda and Sirius. It was more developed than any others conjured up elsewhere in the Cosmos.

Their hydraulic engineering feats were so highly advanced, and worked synergistically with both water and energy to literally create water features that hung suspended in mid-air

*My sketch of the leopard man who appeared to me at Keurbooms with a leopard at each side. He introduced me to the Lion People.*

*My sketch of the Lion King.*

They are a very tall race of giants, with reddish-blonde to reddish-copper hair that grew like a mane from their high foreheads. Their eyes are slanted and feline-looking. Some are liquid-gold to a deeper hazel, while others are green or brilliant-blue. Others have eyes that are almost black. Their facial features appear to be human, but seem to, at times, shape-shift into those of a lion, leopard or any other cat.

Some like to grow their beards, which adds to the leonine look. A few of the males will only grow a moustache and a "Henri Quatre" beard. The females have very lively eyes and the same mane of hair.

The Lion People are immensely powerful, but this power is carefully harnessed and used to uplift, create and expand the Cosmos. They are known for their intricate use of sacred geometry and alchemy within their designs. Their architectural and engineering feats, as well as the general layout of their cities, all use sacred geometry in order to accelerate the energies and fields. All of their constructions exist within a single energy field.

They first came to Earth at the time of Elysium, when their own home galaxy was still intact. However, with the subsequent Wars of the Heavens, their own galaxy was severely damaged, like that of Andromeda.

They sought refuge on Sirius and with the Andromedans. They then moved to new galaxies in order to start a new life there. Both Lyra and Andromeda formed part of the 7th Central Sun's Galaxies. They, therefore, work with the encodements of the 777.

They were the ones to bring the Sun Discs to this planet, and they activated and encoded them.

Their greatest engineering feats at the time of Elysium were the Temple of the Sun and the Temple of the White Flame. The latter was one of the Cosmic wonders: An architectural and engineering feat that stunned the rest of the Cosmos. They truly had surpassed themselves with this creation, by making significant use of sacred geometry; pyramid structures and energies; as well as hanging gardens and water features. It was a hydraulic, spiraling energy and sound frequency device that paved the way for a totally new technology that was later adopted for general use throughout the Cosmos.

Afterwards, following the demise of Elysium, the Lion People returned to Earth and then re-established a second civilization, which I will call the Lion Kingdom, with the remnants of what had been left of Elysium.

Their kingdom spanned the whole of the African continent. In the north, they built immense pyramids and huge structures. Most of that has now been covered by the Saharan sand and the Mediterranean Sea.

They were the true builders of the Giza Pyramids and the Sphinx: The Atlanteans later repaired the pyramids and used the foundations of the buildings that the Lion People had built to colonize Egypt. That was a million years later.

The Sphinx itself has 72 stories underground. I visit there regularly for initiations and suchlike. My next book will go into more detail about this.

The Lyran people form part of the Intergalactic Federation. They are, therefore, back in full force to assist with our planet's massive shifts.

Interestingly, all the features of San's sacred sites

*Another of those entrances. The other side of it has the giant face of the Guardian and Keeper of the vortex energy.*

are present at the Keurbooms location. There is a San cave higher up the same mountain, and a river flowing into the sea. There are the remains of three pyramids, and of one massive pyramid, too.

I first saw the pyramids when I arrived at Keurbooms. It was only recently, when boys were climbing Arch Rock, that I found out that my theory was correct. There is, indeed, a cave and hidden chamber in the rock (or what remains of the rock pyramid).

It resembles the Giza Pyramids in fascinating ways. I saw this in the visions I received, when I saw it still intact, as it used to be. Furthermore, it is perfectly aligned on the north-south axis, with the Sun passing through the hole on the top at noon.

It was first in Knysna, and in and around Nature's Valley, that I found extraordinary patterns on the mountains and very high energy. I was first alerted to the circles – the same circles and patterns I had noticed and observed before.

These circles remind me of beehive patterns, and particularly of the patterns made by sound harmonics. The rocks on the mountains in this area, as far as Storm's River, reflect Kaapsehoop to a tee. They have the same huge monoliths; the same color, with distinct faces in the rock; and most importantly, the same building blocks.

When I visited Coney Beach in Knysna recently, I noticed again how the remains of that massive rock, just before The Heads, has building blocks similar to those found in Egypt, Peru and elsewhere. Now they are very weathered and eroded from the constant pounding of the waves. It is indeed here where the vortex energy begins.

The more I started to explore this area, the more surprises popped up: Vast quarries; round holes in the mountains; and tools and implements that are so sophisticated that archaeologists have closed the sites to the public. These tools did not fit into their neat theories of the San Stone-Age people who were supposed to have made them.

*A strange gargoyle guarding the top of Arch Rock.*

*There are faces in the rocks everywhere. They act not only as Guardians of the portal here, but they also hold the energies steady.*

*Churning seas reflect the vortex energies at Keurbooms.*

There are caves with holes in them that remain in utter darkness, until 12 noon, when the Sun shines in... There are massive faces in stone that mark sacred sites... Huge stone gongs which, when sounded, can be heard for miles... There are also underground sound caves containing rock gongs. Some of these huge stones are perfectly aligned to the star systems, like Pleiades.

I will write more about Keurbooms and the vortex energy later in my book. It proved to be a very important piece in the puzzle. After I had experienced the incredible dimensional shift here, the remaining pieces started to fall into place.

I relooked at aerial photos of Keurbooms and, to my utter astonishment, I found a massive face staring out at me from just offshore, where the eye of the vortex energy center is situated! I could not believe my eyes. The face perfectly mirrored the huge stone face of the Keeper and Guardian that I had seen elsewhere!

I had tears of recognition running down my cheeks, for this was confirmation that this area, from Knysna to Storm's River, once formed part of buzzing metropolis before the land mass tore off and disappeared under the sea.

Geologists claim that as this happened, the Earth's crust broke in two, with one part moving underneath the other, thus pushing the part where the land mass had ripped off, upwards. So, the mountains in this region were born. This would explain why one finds pebbles cemented in sand on the top of the Robberg peninsula and elsewhere.

*More ancient rock formations.*

Crystals are found in the Tsitsikamma Forest, and even some of the roads are literally paved with them.

I now knew not only why I had been born in Africa, but why it had been in the south-eastern region specifically. I finally understood the great importance of Africa and its hidden secrets, which have never been fully understood and often completely overlooked.

Most significantly, all my journeys lead me back here. The information I had gathered and been given proved to be correct. For indeed, vast land masses had been ripped off here and sunk beneath the sea.

I will share my discoveries with you later in the book, but first we must go back to the very beginning, to when this planet was first created: The rising of Elysium.

*The massive face at the eye of the vortex at Keurbooms, staring out from the Google Earth Map!*

# PART 2


# HISTORY OF ELUSIUM
# AND THE
# WHITE FLAME

# CHAPTER 6

# And in the Beginning…

JOURNAL ENTRY

**October 2009, I recorded the following in my diary:**
I had a profoundly significant vision upon awakening: I was seeing coils and coils of enfolding serpent (vortex) energy being beamed down from the Cosmos, galaxies and constellations on to this planet. I was being touched by and enclosed within this same energy, and I felt this intensely within my heart center.

Then I saw how this serpent energy was inside and outside the Earth, until it became an all-encompassing flame – a vortex flame that was burning in and around the whole planet – cleansing and purifying everything on and within it.

The Sphinx was guarding the portal to the Ancient Secret Keys and Codes of Mankind, which had been forgotten back in the mists of time, as Earth fell from a 7$^{th}$ dimensional state into the 3$^{rd}$. It also guards an enormous portal, or energy grid, which is a lightning rod, a gigantic tuning fork that is being reactivated now. It is having a far-reaching effect on all of life here now!

Dimensions are basic frequency bands, and life exists on the frequency of the planet it forms a part of, and on which it sustains life. In essence, this means that when we raise our level of consciousness and our conscious energy fields, we can begin to tap into that which we were unable to understand or assimilate before.

Herein then, lies vital keys to understanding the whole origin of humanity and, likewise, the origin of all life on this planet. Africa holds the keys and codes for the rest of the world – until such a time as humanity raises its vibrational frequency enough to be able to unlock them.

Yet, contrary to the belief that these codes are held in the Giza plateau, and underneath the Sphinx, it is elsewhere in Africa that we have to focus to decipher them. We must also pay attention to the unwritten, unrecorded history of humanity and this planet.

One can only understand the true history of humanity and Africa when one understands where this all began: In time immemorial. Each soul on this planet has its origin somewhere in the infinity of Creation. Most of the souls now incarnated have soul links with the first 12 Galaxies ever created. So, to understand the subsequent history of Earth, we have to return to the very beginning.

## Galactic Co-creation of the Inner Earth, Agartha, and Planet Earth

### The First Creation

All of Creation is constantly rebirthing and expanding upon itself. In the beginning of time, 12 Master Galaxies formed, and hence the first 12 Master races were born. The Divine Source gave birth to 12 Sons and 12 Daughters, who were then in charge of each galaxy. They were given the birthright to co-create with the Divine Source. They were highly evolved and reflected the God-force itself back to the Divine Source.

In the first burst of Creation, souls were born. With that outburst of life 144 000 Soul groups, or Monads, came into being. These, together with the 12 Sons and 12 Daughters of God, formed the first nucleus of all that was ever created.

These souls were born to assume life forms and to bring the experience of life in its myriad forms back to the Divine Source, so that its creation could be reflected back to itself.

In the beginning there were 12 Master Galaxies. From them, all other life and life forms in Creation issued forth. In a higher sense then, they were recreating and expanding upon themselves, as all other life and life forms do. In this way, new planets started forming from the gases, becoming Solar Systems and then Universes, as Creation is an eternal process.

These first 12 Master Galaxies are the most highly evolved of all forms of life. Some contain life forms that are unknown on Earth. Their inhabitants do not have a physical form that one would easily recognize, yet they are highly advanced and intelligent.

Others do have a physical form, just like ours (for we reflect both the first Creation and the Creator), but their forms vibrate at a considerably higher frequency and so they are composed of a much lighter substance than we are. In our current form, we could only see them with our third eyes. Our physical eyes would be unable to do so, unless they chose to lower their frequency bands. Then, we could interact with them without knowing that they were not of our own kind.

The first Beings created were much taller than we currently can conceive of. They were way over 12ft (3.65m) tall, and so are remembered as 'giants'.

In the lesser galaxies, where new life and life forms from the Master Galaxies were first introduced, they subsequently took on varied forms. Some became smaller and more condensed. Some took on contrasting colors and hues, while others acquired a completely different form in order to experience life in another manner. However, all these beings reflect life itself back to the Creator God.

When the first Master Galaxies saw that the Divine was creating new forms of life, with new planets being formed from the gases, as their own galaxies started expanding upon themselves; they asked the Divine if they could experiment with these life forms to see how they would adapt to the new types of creation emerging. Permission was granted to specific Soul groups from the 12 Master Galaxies to act as co-creators with the Divine Source, to create new planets from the gases and to settle life on to these planets. They would see how they would adjust to this new form of life. (This refers to planets in the stages of birthing being stabilized and then being populated by mineral, plant and animal life from these 12 Master Galaxies.)

In an effort to co-ordinate these matters, an Inter-galactic Federation was formed, called the Great White Brother and Sisterhood. White does not refer to skin color, but rather to the incorporation of the intense, pure, white blinding Light emitted from the Divine Source.

Massive motherships[1] were built. These were like giant cities on which huge laboratories were maintained. They would transport all existing life forms to the outer reaches of their galaxies to discover new planets. There were highly trained and evolved Master scientists aboard who worked as team co-creators to settle on a planet, design it, and then to introduce life forms from their own laboratories. These motherships later developed into vast space cities, perpetually travelling and traversing the cosmos.

Sometimes, certain galaxies felt the need to send additional life forms, or to experiment further with some specific kind that they had already settled elsewhere and which was changing and evolving in form. They wanted to know how this new life would react in a different star system and under different stratospheric conditions, so they developed strains and other species as they proceeded, which then became new forms of life elsewhere.

However, they all were operating under the strict guidelines known as the Divine Law. These Cosmic Laws were laid down after a long and careful deliberation between the Council of 24 Elders, who sat on the Advisory Board of the Divine Source. They were in overall charge of what happened in the rest of Creation. So, they were asked to format these Laws that had been inspired and overseen by the Divine Source. It was decided that anyone breaking these laws would have to bear the consequences. This essentially meant that if you created something, or did something to contravene these laws, the Law of Karma would come into operation. This was, in essence, the Law of Cause and Effect.

In those early days of the first Creation, there was peace and harmony, so the Law of One reigned supreme and there were no problems.

## Life on Board the Motherships

When approaching Earth from the outer reaches of this Universe, travelling in the great motherships of the Intergalactic Fleet, one passes the inner or outer planets of these Solar Systems with great speed. Think of brightly flashing spheres standing out from the Cosmic greatness – the most magnificent display of unimaginable beauty and expanses of galaxies, counter-galaxies and star systems that this planet is, as yet, largely unaware of.

The great motherships are space cities in their own right. Not only do they have a control center where there are trained pilots in charge of the navigational systems, but there are also huge laboratories on board. There are extensive gardens supporting the whole city, where plant life flourishes and there are green spaces to relax and wander about in.

Most of the crew on board are scientists who are joined by their families, if they so choose. The crew generally have partners who totally complement them. Often partners also live on board, and they are both part of the crew, and thus of the overall system of the ship. Their children are then naturally inclined to follow in their parents' footsteps. Sometimes, though, they do opt to go back to their home galaxies or constellations and work there.

There are schools on board, not in the way that we would understand them, though. All information is especially programmed for each individual child from their day of birth. The information is beamed directly into the child's mind via Sun Discs, which are crystalline in form and pulsate with very high frequency spiraling energy fields. By being beamed directly into the mind, the information cannot be distorted and is immediately assimilated by the child, who is then guided and carefully monitored by the teachers in the

---

1   A mothership is a large vehicle that leads, serves, or carries other smaller vehicles. A mothership may be a maritime ship, aircraft, or spacecraft. (*Wikipedia*)

use or application of the knowledge. All the children have Soul readings at birth, so the parents and teachers know their life's mission and purpose and they are carefully assisted to step into their own natural role or calling once they reach the age of maturity.

An individual will then serve a period of apprenticeship under a Master teacher in their chosen field and assume full responsibility for the work that they were born to do.

The crews of the ship are as follows: (Terms are used that we will relate to, although in essence, the work may differ. As we are working with highly advanced technology that uses the mind and brain in a way people can't yet relate to, simpler terms are given in order to facilitate understanding. Most work is done by just using the brain to give commands telepathically and then to control the outcome, using only the mind.)

First you have the commander of the mothership. He usually falls under the High Command of the Intergalactic Fleet of the Great White Brotherhood – a confederation of galaxies and star systems of highly-evolved beings who serve the Divine Source as co-creators. They also patrol and monitor the different galaxies and systems.

The overall command is with Lord Ashtar, who is not only an Ascended Master, but also one of the Sons of God. He is in command of the whole fleet, yet is still able to monitor any situation from wherever he happens to be. He has been involved with the Creation and the stabilization of Earth since its beginning. So, he is very interested in what is going on here at present and visits this Universe and star system on a regular basis. He originates from Andromeda where he holds the title of High Prince

He also represents the Fleet in all aspects at the Intergalactic Federation's meetings. In this Universe, this is mostly done on a satellite station called Melchior[2]. (It's coincidence that one of the wise men from the Bible, who presented gifts to Jesus, was called by this name!)

The commander of such a mothership is then not only in charge of the whole ship, but also the pilots.

They have big and smaller craft in huge hangers, which are used for surveillance work or for shuttling the scientists on board to planets they are working on and with. Some of the smaller craft have the "flying saucer" shape (often reported as having been seen in the sky). One can describe them as discs (almost like a DVD or CD). They are equipped with all the instruments needed, as well as eating and sleeping quarters. They sometimes remain on the planets, working for extended periods of time. On Earth, they dock in the underground bunkers that have been here since their beginnings.

The pilots and crew are also involved in scouting work, reporting on the state of the space; the developments of the planetary systems; as well as measuring the magnetic storms that sometimes wreak havoc in the stratosphere. They are highly trained scientists who are able to work independently, but are always under the overall direction of the Commander.

The engineers are in charge of the maintenance of the craft, as well as the ship itself.

There are others in charge of maintenance of the family units, the laboratories, the ventilation systems, and so one. In other words, they do the general functioning and upkeep of these great craft, which can only physically land in special underground space stations that are equipped to handle their size.

Highly evolved technology transcends all forms of matter and works on the principle that all matter is a form of energy, and so a form of vibration and frequency. They are able to switch frequencies at will,

---

2    Melchior, or Melichior, was purportedly one of the Biblical Magi, along with Caspar and Balthazar, who visited the infant Jesus after he was born. He was traditionally called the King of Persia and brought the gift of gold to Jesus. In the Christian church, he is regarded as a saint. (*Wikipedia*)

just as you would simply change TV stations by using the remote control, or by pushing a switch with a finger. However, this is done with the mind, and all communications are telepathic.

They use huge screens to portray or transport images, so they can view anything going on in the constellations and galaxies elsewhere. They are in constant communication.

They can manipulate the energy forms to such an extent that huge craft can literally be teleported within seconds from one end of Creation to the next. Spanning of the dimensions and systems is done in the wink of an eye.

It all comes back to the principle that **All is One and One is All. As Above, So Below!** This means that if you realize that you are part of all – all can be part of you. So, you can use your own energy and the collective energy of everything around you, setting the intent as one unified will and one command!

This is something the human brain still has to master: The capacity to use the entire brain and not just a fraction of it. If all faculties are used, and are trained to be used from birth, one is simply capable of doing or creating anything! You are able to change forms and to create something from nothing.

It then becomes a matter of using the energies, by making use of the various frequencies and vibrations, honing into these, and then rearranging them into the place and form that you want them to be in or at.

The more highly advanced your Soul is, and the more highly evolved the galaxy or star system that you stem from, the greater your capacity to do this.

It is a matter of using the inherent creative force – the same force that is the Divine Source, from whom all life sprung into being, and then working with it – never against it, but as one. Universal Law is the law of at-one-ness.

Only when you master these concepts, never using them for ego or self-gain, but only for the highest good of all Creation, are you allowed to do this. It is a matter of taking responsibility to create only that which enhances or expands the original Creation. You

act as co-creator then. This is the ultimate determining moment in the evolutionary stage of the soul. From then on, the soul has the choice to once again return to the Divine Source and reunite with it, or to carry on doing this work, while also continuing to expand. Nothing is ever static, and is always in the process of creating and being created.

All highly evolved Beings have mastered this stage, thus conquering death and disease. They may have bodies, but are not attached to them. They have physical form, yet vibrate at a very high frequency, and can therefore teleport themselves and manifest and demanifest their form. Their form is perfection. So, self-mastery leads to eternal or everlasting life.

The mind has the capacity to rejuvenate and reactivate the cells and to manipulate the DNA structure of the body. The body always functions as one with all other bodies: The spiritual, emotional, physical and mental bodies, as well as the soul and the over-soul, or over-lighting soul (some call it the Higher Self). All other parts of the soul, the Monad, then work as one!

The mothership is a great cosmopolitan unit. Beings come from all the galaxies and star systems affiliated to the Intergalactic Federation of the Great White Brotherhood, and thus you get beings with different forms. Although most look like us, they are perfection in motion, and are far taller – 10ft – and are almost shimmering and ethereal in appearance. There are also others who were created differently, especially as the cosmos expanded and new star systems and galaxies came into being.

There are also the red races, from whom the American First Nation descended. They are also known as the Bird people and have long, dark-to-auburn hair.

There are also darker races. All are reflected in one way or another in the different races here on Earth. Most descend from beings who decided to stay here, largely on a voluntary basis.

The leonine (Lion) people stem from Lyra and Sirius, and the fishlike people stem from the so-called Dog Star. Some come from the Bear constellation, and other distant constellations that the world is not even aware of. All have a form in one way or another, and are highly evolved Beings.

They are all peaceful, since they have managed to bring their whole being into perfect balance and harmony with the Divine Source and they adhere to the Law-of-One.

There are family units on board, and with this, the usual comforts of family life. Great emphasis is placed on keeping the unit closely knit and in having a tender, loving, supportive environment. When one partner is occupied, such as working elsewhere or volunteering to incarnate on other planets, the other partner steps in to take on the role of both parents. So, the children are always in a supportive, loving and tight family where there is guidance, loving tenderness and care.

Pets live in simulated environments that closely resemble the home galaxies of the crew and scientists. These may be visited at any time.

The highly-evolved races have the ability, through using their inherent powers, to simply teleport themselves to any constellation or Solar System of their choice, and to be there in an instant. The higher the frequency such Beings emit, the greater the ability to manifest and demanifest at will!

Within the laboratories, there are scientists who work in the medical, veterinary, plant and elemental units. There are also those who record the developments and histories of different planets. Some do measurements. Some work with the stabilization and creation of newborn planets. So, all work as one. In a sense, they almost resemble the proverbial Ark, as there is plant and animal life in abundance, contributing to the overall balance and work being done on a much larger scale.

## A New Planet Comes into Being

In the far outreaches of the Cosmos, a new Solar System was forming as part of the Milky Way Galaxy, and a new planet was coming into being. It caught the attention of scientists on board a vast mothership of the Intergalactic Fleet passing by, which had completed the creation of Saturn, Jupiter, Marduk and Mars, and so they reported news of this planet.

After some investigation, a decision was made to develop it as one of the substations for this fleet, for there was a great need for shelter from the vast Cosmic electromagnetic storms, and for somewhere to restock and replenish certain commodities, rather than having to wait to do this in their home galaxies.

At that time, this newly-developing planet was very near to certain of the Master Galaxies, bearing in mind that Creation has a massive vortex-like energy with coils within the vortex continually spiraling in and outwards – not operating in a linear manner, as perhaps imagined. So, one galaxy is not next to another galaxy, or vice versa. Rather, they are arranged in layers.

After a meeting with Melchior, the Galactic Logos, it was decided to give the task of creating this substation to certain Soul groups, or Monads, from particular galaxies who were the nearest match to the octaves of the vortex-like Cosmic energy structure

The Soul group involved had to report directly to the Divine Source; they were the Illumined Ones. The galaxies involved were Sirius, Lyra, Orion, Andromeda, Pleiades, Arcturus, and the Bear constellation. There were others from Pegasus, the Milky Way Galaxy, and from planets within this Solar System: Venus, Jupiter and Saturn. As Mars and Marduk were also in a developing state, they were considered to be satellite stations.

These Beings then formed the nucleus and command for this new venture.

One should note that, at that time, the hub of Creation was focused on Marduk, the planet between Jupiter and Mars, as it was considered the administrative headquarters of this Solar System. The new planet was the last to be formed, and this new planet-in-formation was Planet Earth!

A special mothership was then built and equipped with life forms gathered from the 12 Master Galaxies, with the finest Master scientists acting as co-creators with the Divine, under Cosmic Law, creating this new satellite station for the Intergalactic Federation of the Great White Brotherhood and the Divine.

At first, they were thinking only in terms of creating a substation, or a replenishing station, where ships could be repaired, or where the crew could do experiments. Earth was ideally situated between Venus and Marduk, so owing to its position, it was easy to bring in supplies from the galaxies closest to Earth, which were the Pleiades, Sirius and Orion. Thus, they decided to build a satellite station in the inner core. This became the first settlement inside the planet.

## The Birth of Agartha, the Inner Earth, as a Satellite Station of the Intergalactic Fleet

Once a planet has been identified by the Intergalactic Fleet as stable enough to begin Creation, the first step, then, begins with the gases that facilitate the creation of all else. This process is monitored, as gradually the other elements, such as air, water, fire, and then solid matter from which the land mass is formed, are introduced.

Once the gases settle, the next stages are monitored. Initially, Earth was gas, then water, then the land masses were formed. Then the most vital ingredient of all was also added – air – without which no life form can exist. Then the next element, fire, was introduced, as most land masses are formed by the elementals and devas, who then also help scientists to stabilize those planets still in the birthing process.

The land masses were formed from the volcanic eruptions of the inner crust. The first crust hardened as the mass formed. The Earth is hollow in the center, and within the Earth the first settlement was founded, as the outer crust was still settling into its form. This Inner Earth settlement was called Agartha.

It is to be noted that this planet was never meant to be an entity on its own. Since the very beginning, it was but an experimental planet and one of the first of its kind.

First, the Inner Sun was created, so that the Inner Earth had its own Sun and was completely lit up from within. Different forms of life were introduced, mostly from the laboratories of the motherships and from the

various species of life donated just for this purpose by other planets. Perhaps the word 'donated' should be substituted for 'volunteered', as all life is revered, and only those wanting to be part of this experiment were allowed to participate.

Note here that all life forms have intelligence and a life of their own; whether sea coral, rock, plant or animal: All have intelligence and life. You may not create anything without asking permission from these beings to use their inherent divine essence.

When all work together as one, miraculous Creations can occur, as this is in total harmony with the Law of One!

Lakes, rivers, mountains, and plains were created around the large cities that blossomed forth.

The climate was temperate and was artificially controlled. There was abundant plant and animal life, and the whole colony manning this satellite station were very happy and content, as this was indeed like the proverbial Garden of Eden; peaceful, serene and truly magnificent – a marvel to behold! This inner civilization is far more ancient than any of the upper ones. They have never warred with any other planet, unlike the upper regions, which came later.

The satellite station was held in a bubble of protective shields and was totally able to sustain life on its own, independent of the Intergalactic Fleet. There were two massive stargate entrances on both sides of the spherical satellite station, which they could open and close at will.

Large spaceports and inner bunkers were added, where the great motherships and smaller craft could be repaired. These vessels would also replenish supplies that could not be grown on board.

In those days, the vessels sometimes had difficulty navigating this Solar System because of the very unstable energy fields, the source of which they were still trying to determine. They later found the source of this disturbance in the counter Solar System and counter galaxy, and then managed to stabilize the fields. However, the unstable fields at the time led to fierce electromagnetic storms, forcing the fleet to seek shelter on such satellite stations as their craft were in danger of disintegrating, while the crew worked on the spiraling (coil) electromagnetic propulsion systems.

Agartha, then, was like a central hub, where the great motherships would come and go, transporting scientists and crew to their home galaxies from time to time, and replenishing their stocks and supplies.

These crew members would be immediately replaced by others from the fleet – all under the overall High Command of the Intergalactic Fleet of the Great White Brotherhood and Commander Lord Ashtar, who worked in close liaison with the Intergalactic Council of Masters, and the Council of 12, which sit on the Advisory Board of the Divine Source.

Interestingly, the first crew members who started the satellite station and Inner Earth civilization, Agartha, later decided to settle there, and they have indeed become the Elder Brothers and Sisters of humankind. Some of these Beings are the Ancient Ones, who work with humanity and who have vowed never to leave the planet until the original state of balance and harmony has been restored, and with it the 7th dimensional state.

They also appear in different physical forms – from a very tall, white-skinned race with almost white hair and very large blue to green and hazel eyes, to a smaller red-skinned and dark skin hue race.

They can shapeshift quite easily and will sometimes make themselves known as white animals when they wish to grab the attention of human beings.

They work with a lot of the souls on Earth as higher guides, or as Wisdom Keepers. Some of these great and ancient Beings guard certain portals and entrances into the Inner Earth, like tunnel systems and star portals.

The stargate portals on either side of Agartha have often been closed when there have been wars or great turmoil on the surface of Mother Earth.

The whole populace of Agartha is, in fact, highly evolved and they live in a 7th dimensional state. They do not wish to interact with the people on the surface, finding them too primitive, destructive and war-like. They have had no wars, and continue to live in peace and harmony.

The ancient Mystery Schools often had contact with these Inner Teachers and Guardians, for there had always been an interconnectedness: They trained the Druid High Priestesses and High Priests in Ancient times, not only in Avalon, but also before that, in the Lion Kingdom and Elysium. Later, they were also very much involved with the inner circles of the Cathars and the Alchemical Mystery Schools. This, however, will be dealt with in my next book about my journey to France.

## Planet Earth's Outer Crust is Formed and Elysium is Born

When Agartha was fully functional and operating as an entity on its own, the scientists from the motherships noticed that an outer shell was busy forming and decided that they would like to experiment to see if they could co-create an outer crust by themselves (before, they had only co-created with a planet already in the making, as happens all over the cosmos with new stars and planets being born every day).

They then formed teams to co-create the outer planet – first the gasses, then the water, and then the land mass. They formed one single and very large Super Continent, surrounded by oceans, with smaller inland lakes and islands. They formed massive mountain ranges, rivers and streams, and then slowly but surely started to introduce living organisms from the laboratories aboard the motherships.

The Pleiadians brought in plants, insects, trees and fungi from their own galaxy, while others brought in fruit trees, flowering shrubs and vegetables. As all of this prospered and grew in profusion, they decided to introduce animal life. First were dinosaurs and reptiles of large size – imported from hidden galaxies and star systems in the wormhole (unknown to mankind at this time) between Sirius and Orion. Dolphins, whales and elephants – and mammals of that ilk – came from Sirius; wild horses from Lukuma; and the cat species from Lyra. Gradually, other species were introduced from other star systems and galaxies.

At this time, the great Crystalline Pyramid Grid, or

energy grid, was put in place around the whole planet to artificially control the climatic conditions and to shield the planet against the rampant cosmic storms and upheavals. This shield also acted as a barrier to prevent hostile elements from being able to interfere with the experiment, or to land their own craft there.

The Crystalline Pyramid Grid was a series of portals through which spacecraft could come and go, as they wished, to the space stations underground. These Crystalline Grid lines were also amplified by the Crystal Pyramids connected to them. All of these, working together, helped maintain Earth's state of balance. So, not only were climatic conditions stable here, but the Grid also acted as a natural energy source that could be tapped into by all Beings. This helped the smaller craft operate more effectively, and scientists could travel from one end of the planet to the next within seconds. They could actually use these lines to fly on, and thus the mythological gods remembered in the collective human psyche could literally fly!

At that time, the Crystalline Grid also enabled the scientists to communicate with all the other galaxies and constellations at will, as well as with the Divine Source. All beings were at-one. So, everyone could communicate freely with their loved ones wherever they were, and could keep up to date with happenings elsewhere, via the interlinking motherships' own communication systems, which were connected to the energy systems of each of the constellations, Universes, and other planets in this Solar System.

In time, this would become part of an even more important scientific innovation and power supply, which we will examine later.

The scientists created massive underground tunnel systems that linked the inner world, Agartha, to the outer world. They also knitted the underground space stations and crystalline chambers together. These crystalline chambers were the fertile growing ground for crystals, which they imported, as most of their technology works with the crystalline energies and energy fields.

They laid down a vast Super-Conscious Energy Field Matrix in and around the planet, which worked like a giant computer hard drive, recording everything that was happening on and inside the Earth. It was tuned directly into the 7th Central Sun of Illumination.

It was created to work in tandem with the whole energy system, forming a planetary communication network and technological hub into which they could plug their craft and recharge them. They could also teleport and communicate instantaneously across star systems – even bilocate, if necessary. In fact, it was so sophisticated that they brought in a specialized team to put it all in place. This was a new experiment and the first time ever that it had been done, intergalactically.

There was an enormous lightning rod holding the whole grid steady, around which massive vortex energy formed. During this time, another intricate grid line was installed, before the land mass on the outer planet finally settled. This was designed concurrently to link the inner and outer worlds, which would form the spinal cord of the planet. Its whole body and all of life would be supported by this grid line!

The Pyramid Crystalline Energy Grid was attached to the spinal column. The energy grids and energy centers had to be:

- Self-sufficient and able to supply the upper Earth with free energy in a form that was easily accessible.
- In the form of a net, that is, a network spanning the whole planet that would be able to sustain and transmit energy by tapping into the energy fields of the Earth and the Milky Way Galaxy, and into the most vital energy centers (I will come to this at a later stage). Yet, it had to be independent from that of Inner Earth, in case of emergencies, so that the hatches on both sides (aligning to the poles) could be closed, and the inner world could function as the satellite it essentially was. The energy grid could sustain this activity for an extended period of time, as it could sustain life independently. This would make Inner Earth less vulnerable to the outside dangers of asteroids, comets, and so on.

- The Crystalline Energy Net was then placed inside the first layers of the Earth and hidden, as more layers formed. There was also an outside web in the etheric layer around the planet, matching that of the inside. Simultaneously, the most important aspect of this web was also laid down (we will deal with this later). This outer energy field initially formed a protective shield around the planet, and could only be penetrated by the Intergalactic Fleet craft.

- A further layer was created inside and outside the planet, in different forms, that acted as an antenna, downloading and transmitting Cosmic energy beamed from the 7th Central Sun of the 7th Galaxy, which at that stage was clearly visible from Earth, as the 7th Galaxy was the closest to Earth then, as Sirius is now.

- The lightning rod was in the center, consisting of 33 vortex energy cores. Each one was a mini-galaxy that created energy within its center, which then in turn ignited a vast central vortex flame. This flame fed the Web of Light and all other energy centers of the planet.

When everything was finally in place and settled, she was a beautiful planet, considered the jewel in the crown of Creation! They named her Terra (Earth), and from that time, the planet became a living and breathing entity in its own right. She was called Lady Gaia[3], and she took up her crown with pride and joy.

There was great celebration in all the galaxies affiliated to the Intergalactic Council. She was the pride and joy of all who had created her! In fact, more than that, she was a miracle, and all who visited her stood in awe and wonder, amazed at her natural beauty and the great Light she emitted. It could be seen and felt in all four corners of this Universe and beyond.

Lady Gaia was dancing in the midst of this Creation, rejoicing in the perfection and beauty of it all. She loved her creatures, and they loved her. Everything was perfect. All was well!

All life and life forms follow certain predictable patterns. When you act as a co-creator, as these first scientists did, you follow patterns, or blueprints, that recur everywhere. This planet's spinal cord held the rest of the Crystalline Pyramid Energy Grid, or Web of Light, in place. It was simultaneously used as an immense tuning fork, or transmitter, of Cosmic sounds, or the harmonic sounds of the planet.

As all higher Cosmic frequencies vibrate with certain sounds and certain harmonics, this allowed those scientists to fine-tune the planet. Their own abilities to tune into life and life forms allowed what they were creating to vibrate at whatever tune, sound or harmonic frequency they wished.

Each planet, Solar System, Universe and galaxy has its own tonal chord, as each individual soul does. Since Earth was a new planet, it was given its own tonal chord, and it emitted its unique sound frequencies and vibrations into the Cosmos.

When the motherships, or other craft, entered this Solar System, the instruments on their craft would immediately pick up this unique sound frequency and would use this signal to tune their craft to that frequency, permitting them to travel at the speed of light on the planet's frequency. It also facilitated easy navigation, so that when landing and stepping out into the stratosphere, their physical bodies were already attuned to the planet's frequency and they had no problems with altitude or air pressure, and so on. (I will come to this much later in the book. At the moment, it is just necessary to understand that the planet was

---

3    In Greek mythology, Gaia was the personification of the Earth and one of the Greek primordial deities. Gaia was the great mother of all: The primal Greek Mother Goddess; creator and giver of birth to the Earth. All of the Universe; the heavenly gods, the Titans, and the Giants were born to her. Her equivalent in the Roman pantheon was Terra. (*Larousse Desk Reference Encyclopedia, The Book People, Haydock*, 1995, p. 215.)

'master-minded' into existence and that nothing was created by chance!)

After the spinal cord and Web of Light energy centers and energy vortexes were laid down, and the first plants and animals were imported from other galaxies, life started to prosper and grow into beingness on Planet Earth.

## First Colonization of Planet Earth

As the scientists and those first creators worked at creating their masterpiece, some fell in love with their own Creation. Indeed, the more they worked on and with her, the more they developed the yearning to settle on the surface of the planet.

By this time, they had erected the first 12 Crystal Pyramid Temples, and massive diamond-shaped electro-magnetic portals. They erected crystalline structures – the first observation centers – to monitor how the new life forms had developed.

They had created the first Garden of Eden, and they now wished to colonize the planet and to make it their second home. However, to do this, they first had to get permission from three sources:

- The Intergalactic Federation of the Great White Brother and Sisterhood and the Intergalactic Fleet, for whom they were collectively working.
- The 12 Master Galaxies, to which they were aligned.
- The 24 Elders, who worked on the Advisory Board of the Divine Source, and therefore directed the Cosmic Hierarchy of Creation in its myriad forms, and who reported to the Divine itself.

After a long and serious discussion and multiple meetings, it was decided to grant permission to those first volunteer souls to colonize the surface of the planet. They had to sign a binding agreement. (Bear in mind that the planet was created mainly as a satellite station and was, therefore, an experiment.)

A total of 144 000 volunteers would be allowed to settle on the planet, with the full understanding and knowledge that they formed part of an experiment, and

therefore lived in an artificial environment. They would have to understand, at all times, that like all of the imported animal and plant kingdoms from elsewhere, they too were imported from these same galaxies, and so would be participating in a trial to see how they would adjust to living here. They would have to sign a contract and make a commitment to the Federation that they would partake in this experiment.

- They would be allowed to take their families and settle here, with the knowledge that their children and their children's children would all become part of the same experiment.
- At all times, their lives and their Creations would have to be in alignment with the Cosmic Laws and the Divine Laws. Any contravention of these Laws would bring the Laws of Cause and Effect into being: Karmic Law.
- They would be responsible for the wellbeing of the outer planet and all with which they interacted and created. They would be self-sufficient and sustain life in all ways and be independent of the Federation.
- They would be given the Tree of Life, which contained the source of all knowledge, wisdom, power, and the fountains of Eternal Life. This Tree of Life was intricately connected to and charged with the spinal cord energies of the planet.
- They would live in peace and harmony and at-onement with all they had created, within the Laws of One, as they reflected what they had created and had become back to the Divine, so that the Divine could experience life through them. Everything created would be to the glory and honor of the Most High, the Divine, and exist within the Divine Master Plan.
- The Intergalactic Council would assist with the building of 12 Massive Crystal Pyramids on one land mass. These would form a cohesive whole, and would become the temples that would anchor in and distribute both the Earth energies and the Cosmic energies. The Council would appoint 12 High Priests as administrators and 12 High

Priestesses as transmitter channels for the Divine, the Council, the 24 Elders of the Advisory Board of the Divine, and the Cosmic Love, Power, Will and Purpose. These 24 would become the Guardians of the Planet, and all would report to this body and be guided by them.

- There would be 12 regions, and each would have a Crystal Pyramid Temple and a High Priest and Priestess in charge of the temple and that region. These later formed the first 12 Master Tribes, from which all mankind has sprung.
- They were granted the right to create and co-create within the Law of One (Cosmic Laws). They would be responsible for what they created; being made aware again of the confines of this, and the greater jurisdiction of the Intergalactic Council of 12.

At that time, these rulings were considered very favorable to those who signed the agreement, and they happily set about creating the first settlement and civilization on the planet. They called this first Creation, Elysium.

The entire African continent; Australia; South America; Madagascar; Mauritius; the Seychelles; Sri Lanka; India; the Maldives; St Helena; Antarctica; parts of Europe; and as far as the Polar regions (excluding the Mediterranean Sea); and what now lies under the sea in the Atlantic; formed part of the vast continent known as Elysium. It was one land mass with inland seas, rivers, and some islands on the lakes.

The African continent is the only one that is still mainly intact, and therefore holds the world together. Later, the other land masses were torn off and split apart. (We will come to that).

The climate was artificially controlled. It was a lush, largely tropical climate, with more Alpine-like regions also present, which contained much taller trees and masses of flowers, emerald-green grass, and far more vibrant, translucent colors than are found now.

The inhabitants called themselves the Sun People and transmitted the Solar Logos rays of the great Central 7th Sun. Their craft could not only circumnavigate the planet, but were amphibious and could be used on sea, land, and in the air.

Several of the communities present had long, blonde-red to reddish-blonde hair. Others, who came from the Pleiades and other star systems, introduced the reddish-hued skin tones, and eventually the reddish hue predominated in the overall population. Their own offspring began to have this reddish hue to their skins, which was attributed to the vibrational frequency of the planet.

They not only built the original Crystal Pyramids and vast city complexes in labyrinth forms, but they also erected stone circles and other megalithic sites, which were aligned to the constellations from where they had originated, and also to the Sun and Moon. In addition, they all communicated with each other: The Crystalline Grids and the spinal column of the Earth. They worked from precise measurements, attuning these sites to the inner and outer Webs of Light and the Earth energy centers. They were also tuned in to the tonal chord of the Earth, as Earth is Cosmically tuned into the Cosmic Music of the Spheres[4]. During that time period, the vortex energy of Earth was inside such circles, and this in turn fed the energy grids used for their housing, work, and various other purposes.

The first settlements were in total sync with nature. Their dwellings were relatively sophisticated, yet also simple at the same time; very comfortable and insulated from within. They loved using crystals in their design; with running water features, like fountains; and they had a profusion of hanging gardens inside their homes. Homes were designed to be lit up from the interior and exterior, so giving a general impression of living amidst the splendor of Nature itself.

The materials used were lightweight, of crystalline

---

4    Cosmic Music of the Spheres: "There is geometry in the humming of the strings. There is music in the spacing of the spheres." Pythagoras (*Wikipedia*)

form, and blended in with the environment. The inhabitants were totally self-sufficient, living off vegetables and plants and carefully monitoring their nutritional values. They used crystalline geometrical patterns to enhance the life-giving force of their plants and food.

Water was channeled using highly advanced hydraulic systems, which would elevate the levels at some places and feed natural water canals that were directed into their homes. This natural flow of water fed all the systems of the homes and cities they had established.

In alignment with the spinal cord of the planet, they created the Nile, which was a man-made river; and laid down the two Rivers of Life, which flowed from the north to the south. This was linked in turn to the Great Crystal Pyramid of the Sun which, in those early days, stood near where the present Great Zimbabwe Ruins are situated.

They knew the life-giving and life-enhancing value of gold, which was not used for adornment as such, but as a potent energy conduit to feed the River of Life. That, in turn, was aligned to the Web of Light and the vortex energy centers of the planet.

They loved creating sculptures in the rocks and stones, and most of their own sacred places and cities were surrounded by vast giant faces carved into the rocks. They used a type of crystalline laser power that made use of the core vortex energy to do this. Many of the mountains we see today were actually created alongside these dwelling places.

These carved faces acted as Guardians or Keepers, and were there to remind the people that they came from the stars and would one day return to the stars.

There were distinct circular and geometrical patterns in the general outlay of their dwelling places and work places. They enjoyed using the beehive pattern, or the harmonic sound patterns, in the construction of their sites, which always reflected sacred Cosmic geometrical forms. Buildings were laid out with precision and were never erected at random.

They knew that the sacred geometrical patterns enhanced the Chi, or Life Force flame, and so attempted to introduce the perfection of form, the Pi ratio[5], or the Golden Mean[6] into their equations. They then aligned their buildings with the Web of Light, the energy centers, and the vortex energy in and around the 12 Crystal Pyramid Temples.

The minor pyramidal structures were conduits of the vortex energy and were tuned in to the harmonic frequencies of the planet. Each one was aligned to the sound of the major Crystal Pyramid Temple of its region. This formed a vast harmonic tonal chord, reflecting Earth's tonal chord, which in turn aligned with the Cosmic tonal chords and the music of the spheres.

As above, so below!

This was the principle motivation behind everything they created, and everything was in alignment with the Cosmic Law of One. So, they reflected the Cosmic Laws and the Cosmic attunement in everything they did and created.

They originated from highly evolved galaxies, light years ahead of what is now considered as evolved, and they possessed technology and knowledge now forgotten. Compared to what these people knew and created at that time, we are like Stone-Age creatures!

Elysium was the First Golden Age, and what we remember collectively as the Garden of Eden. It was the first civilization. These people were the Giants: A placid and gentle people.

---

5    Pi ratio: The number π is a mathematical constant; the ratio of a circle's circumference to its diameter, commonly approximated as 3.14159. It has been represented by the Greek letter "π" since the mid-18th century, though it is also sometimes spelled out as "pi". (*Wikipedia*)

6    Golden mean: The ideal, moderate position between two extremes. (*Wikipedia*)

# CHAPTER 7

# The Master Key Temple: The Crystal Pyramid Temple of the White Flame

## New Important Higher Understanding of The Crystal Pyramid Temples and the First Time Period

The first 12 pyramids were essentially centers of higher learning; teaching; knowledge; wisdom; prophecy; sciences; technology; higher healing; ceremony and magic; love; and of the Sun and Moon.

The first era, when the planet opened up for settlement, took place when the land masses joined together. It formed a type of hamlet, with a series of islands interlinked and interspersed with lakes and rivers, arranged in a colossal spiraling pattern in the shape of a labyrinth. It was constructed using sacred geometry.

This entire area formed an enormous and impressive vortex energy circuit that is currently being reactivated. In those first days in the center of the islands and lakes, there was the Temple of the Diamond Ray, which was also affiliated with the Temple of the White Flame, as the White Flame represents the diamond ray. It was here, at this great temple complex in the form of a labyrinth, that a massive vortex energy source was laid down. It was also here that the first ever Earth settlement developed!

It could be described as being like part of a university complex, as Intergalactic Federation scientists gathered there and were experimenting with life and life forms on the outer rim of the planet, to monitor just how this form of energy could be used in different and far-reaching ways,

One of the applications used was a momentous type of vortex, synergistically aligned so that the whole complex could be lit up and spacecraft could be refueled and revitalized by this energy. It was, therefore, an experiment of great significance, as it

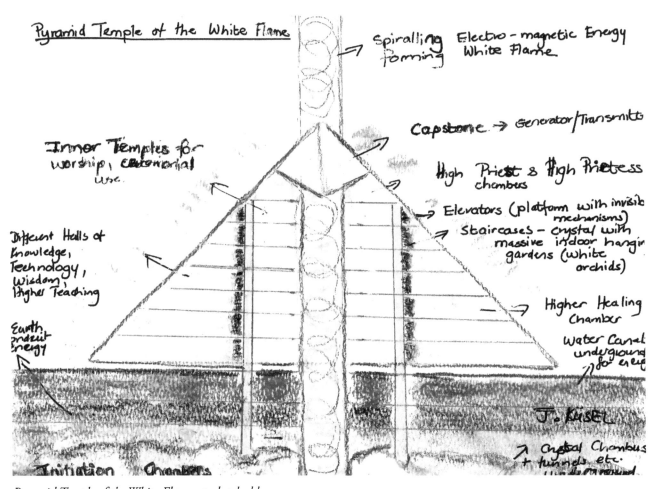

*Pyramid Temple of the White Flame, as sketched by me.*

was from here that vortex energies in the other regions of the planet were created. They all started working as one within the Web of Light.

The pyramids were built as gigantic conduits for this energy. They were also constructed in various formations and structures. The Giza Pyramids were built much later on. The first pyramids were assembled from a lightweight, very high frequency material that was not from this planet. It was imported from other galaxies and it could be easily assembled. One could literally place each crystal building block upon another, as they were of a transparent, crystalline form. They were in diverse colors, as the color vibrations and frequencies were programmed to emit different frequencies. Each one was based on sound.

The 12 impressive pyramids that served as temples, as mentioned before, were built first. Those were the Master Pyramids.

Smaller pyramids were built mainly as energy conduits; as places of higher healing; and as laboratories where different energies in various forms and systems could be utilized.

The pyramid shape has an extremely powerful force. It is a conduit of strong energies, although many of us have completely forgotten this. They were never ever used as tombs or for burial purposes. That is something that humanity, in forgetfulness and sheer ignorance, dreamt up. In fact, each pyramid was perfectly aligned so that it would, in turn, transmit energy into the ether, and then to the other pyramids. They all formed a huge energy grid surrounding Earth and served the entire continent of Elysium.

The vortex energy centers, as well as the Web of Light and other portals, were thus specifically laid down to be interlinked. As the civilization of Elysium grew, more pyramids were built, and as the cities increased in size, additional dwellings were also required.

Not all of the pyramids currently visible on Earth were built simultaneously. Some came much later, after the fall of Atlantis and Lemuria, and were very primitive attempts to build pyramids in the same manner that the Ancient Ones had done. Therefore, there are sites where gigantic stones were used in construction, which have puzzled contemporary people. These colossal stones are the remains of Elysium, and they were not hewn or transported in any way. Rather, they were teleported into place, as at that time, there were many techniques enabling this process to happen.

We must be aware that these vortex energy centers formed part of a complete grid, and that the first temple complexes – places of higher healing, and the Halls of Records, Wisdom and Knowledge – were all built in definite forms with geometrical patterns, so that the greater macrocosm was reflected in the microcosm on Earth.

Here, a complex science is involved. Certain geometrical patterns, when created with certain crystalline forms (like the first temples, which were built with crystalline forms not from this planet), transform the whole structure into a massive conduit for higher energy. Each geometrical pattern then combines to form something new, and transforms into a different 'manner of being'.

It is wise to reflect on this. It is not just the geometrical pattern that creates energy on its own. The energies of the vortex must combine with that of the crystal energies and the geometrical patterns. This in turn raises the frequencies and vibrations of that location. Thus, you attune a certain building or temple to the galaxy it is representing on Earth by fine-tuning all aspects. A pyramid does that, but is certainly not the only form to do so.

When pyramids were laid out in geometrical patterns creating a shape (which itself is a mystical pattern – like a labyrinth), then the higher healing and transmitting power was greatly amplified. It was far more potent than anyone could imagine.

In the beginning, there was much experimentation with this, and Earth's sister planet, Marduk, was one of the first where this type of development occurred. Marduk (before the Wars of the Heavens spilt over) was essentially the first prototype to be created in this Universe and Solar System. It was the original attempt to create a planet from a satellite. Earth followed in very much the same pattern. There were many similarities between the two planets, although they were essentially different, as a variety of galaxies were involved in their creation. Marduk was the first creation of the Orion faction. Then, later those of Lyra were also involved. The creation of Marduk, however, has a complex story of its own.

A different approach was taken with Earth, and as previously recorded, Earth begun as a satellite and then condensed in form to become a planet, with its inner core still existing as a satellite. It was basically started from the interior and built up from the exterior surface. The vortex energy and Web of Light formed much later, after Inner Earth was sealed off and the outer crust had settled. Actually, the true energy source of the vortex energy is in the elemental kingdom, and in a vast inner center of the planet, where its inner core lies.

This is anchored in by a huge crystal from the great Central Sun of the Central Universe within the Milky Way Galaxy. This was placed there even before Inner Earth was created, so that this planet could be pulled into alignment with the Solar System, the Universe and the central core of the Milky Way Galaxy. It is in a form that the average scientist will not be able to detect, due to having completely forgotten the true power of the solar energy source, which is the Sun; which is in essence also a hollow satellite.

This crystal taps into the central vortex energy; the core of Creation. This same vortex energy exists in the human body and in every single particle of creation. The size and potency may differ but, in essence, it is one and the same. It may take on different forms, but fundamentally and essentially, it is the same spiraling energy, which is cone-like and unimaginably powerful through its spiraling movement. When at its highest frequency, it cannot be seen. It is invisible, but it can be felt. At this point, if anything not of that frequency band comes near, it simply disintegrates.

## 2012

*In everything there is Light – particles of light. There is "that which always was", yet out of complete darkness and no-thing-ness, Light was brought forth. From this all things that have ever existed were created. This first Light, Soul was birthed, and thereafter the rest of Creation.*

*When the Golden Age of Elysium was at its height, the Intergalactic Federation decided that, at last, the planned experiment of the Race on Earth had flourished and reached a high level of beautiful harmony and balance. It was at the peak of contentment, of inner peace and the reflected harmony, which is all-embracing; encompassing all life as sacred, and at one with all life.*

*It was then decided to incorporate the great Crystal Temple, the huge Crystal and White Flame, which would help raise the planet from the 5th dimension that it was vibrating on at the time, into the 6th and eventually the 7th.*

*This was the ultimate aim, for when Earth reached this level of evolutionary spiritual development, it would be embraced and made part of the greater assembly of planets within this Universe, and thus in the Galaxy.*

*With great anticipation, the High Priesthood and population of Elysium awaited this momentous occasion. After much scouting by the spacecraft, under the Ashtar High Command, a truly beautiful island was found just off the eastern coast of what is now the southern part of the African continent.*

*It was the ideal place, for it was connected at that time to the underground bases and cities that the Federation had used when Earth was still being stabilized for colonization. It was thus near enough to be maintained under the jurisdiction and control of the Federation, yet also, from where it was located, close enough to still be connected to the 7 other pyramids (which have since then also sunk under the seabed off the African coast). It could form a tremendously powerful energy that could lift the vibrations and frequencies of the entire planet.*

*First, the engineers aboard the spacecraft built the massive temple complex, housed under the great peaks of the mountain that stood like a huge watchtower over the island. It had a temperate climate and the plant life was dense and lush. A waterfall cascaded from its peak into the plain, forming a large lake. So, there was plenty of fresh water.*

*The island, though, was inaccessible by water. Only spacecraft could land, as mighty cliffs sealed it off. An invisible shield formed an impregnable layer, so that only those with the highest frequencies, vibrations of love and Light, and of the purest intent could land. No ships and ocean crafts were able to navigate these waters. This was purposefully done, as a way of safeguarding this Temple of the White Flame.*

*It was consecrated as a holy site, and only acolytes who had passed severe tests of initiation and integrity on the path of dedication to Divine Union and the Law of One, could enter and work from there.*

*At the base of the mountain, a huge concentric circle formed the foundation of this complex. On the outer reaches of the circle, the homes and abodes of the acolytes composed the outer ring. The circle was divided into four equal parts, with the central circle forming the base for the impressive foundation on which the Crystal Pyramid stood.*

*The next ring housed the High Priests: They were not permitted to marry, as they were required to be absolutely dedicated to being pure channels of the Divine Source and to live lives of Higher Service. Since family and spouses could have distracted them from this ultimate service, they had to remain single and focused.*

*As the male energy always complements the female, a balance of both was needed. Yet, it was the High Priestesses who acted as a pure channel to the Divine*

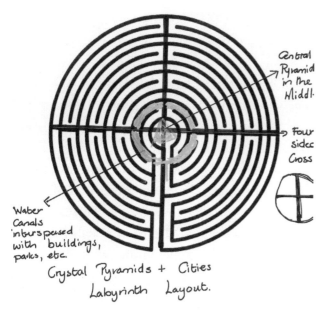

*Crystal Pyramids and Cities Labyrinth layout, as sketched by me.*

Source, functioning as crystal-clear transmitter channels for the Divine and the Council of 12, who sat on the Advisory Board of the Divine Source and the Federation.

The next circle in this complex housed the Halls of Records and Wisdom, which contained the entire history of Earth and the Galaxy, as well as other Sacred Records, and the Crystal Skulls and Keys. They were updated by the Priests and Priestesses working under the two Main High Priests, who were under an oath of secrecy, as these records were considered sacred and holy.

The inner circle housed the ceremonial and administrative chambers. In the innermost sanctuary, the 12 High Priests and Priestesses of Elysium would gather to discuss matters pertaining to the evolution of Earth, with plans to raise its consciousness. Every one of these members was given a key, made from the same substance that formed the huge crystal within the Temple of the White Flame. These were programmed so that only that particular High Priest or Priestess could access the information they contained.

This was done as a precautionary measure, so that only when all 12 met as one, could the 13th activate the Master Key, which was held by the over-lighting Ascended Master (who always attended important meetings). It could then be used for purposes of great significance. Some would call it 'magic' in our present world, but it was largely used for manifestation and to activate energy centers and grids, as well as to raise the consciousness. It held all the records and the hidden information, so it was an immensely powerful tool. It could be used to control the weather, as well as the water resources and other information that would be lethal if used for self-gain.

The foundations of the Crystal Temple were built on the inner circle. A large amount of pure, glistening, white crystal was imported from Andromeda, who had donated it. It was known for its vast, transmitting abilities, with a purity found nowhere else in Creation. From this, the enormous Pyramid was built.

In the center of this Pyramid, the main Andromedan Crystal stood. It was tremendously large, vibrating at extremely high frequencies, so only those with matching frequencies could enter the sacred room in which it was housed.

It emitted an immense white flame, which was visible for miles, from the outer reaches of the oceans. In a sense, this Crystal Temple was the hub, or the gateway, that connected Earth to other galaxies, and was a direct link to the Divine Source.

The galaxies being referred to here are those affiliated with the Great White Brotherhood, and the Over-lighting Ascended Master in charge at that time, who, in this capacity, has always worked in close conjunction with Archangel Metratron[1].

It is from this temple that the communications and instructions were carried out, as vast emissions of Light and vortex energies beamed out through all the energy grids and ley lines in a carefully controlled manner. This

---

1    Metratron is the highest of the Angels and serves as the celestial scribe or 'recording angel'. (*Wikipedia*)

*same energy was also fed into the underground space stations and the cities. All were interconnected and at-one, and thus the outer and inner worlds were one and the same.*

*Most beings working on this island came from the Galaxies, Universes and Solar Systems affiliated to the Great White Brotherhood of the Great White Flame. Many came from Venus – as Venus had been colonized by the first galaxies involved, as stated above.*

*The remaining smaller pyramids in this system (the 7) were interconnected with the other pyramids on the Giza plateau, as well as those all over the African continent, Asia, and Europe (especially the Pyrenees), and also the Americas.*

*Some were on the land masses that have now sunken beneath the sea, but they all were interconnected. The Giza ones were (apart from the Temple of the White Flame) the heartbeat of the rest, in conjunction with those at Kaapsehoop, which were also 7 in all. I was told that I would help to reactivate them when the time was right.*

*During daily activities, much of the focus was placed on meditation, ceremonies and the channeling of important and vital information, as well as the recording of all of this information relating to Earth, this Solar System, Universe and Galaxy.*

*It was from here that the High Priests and Priestesses liaised with those in Atlantis regarding the ongoing administration and education of its inhabitants. They would often introduce new technology to them, and were also actively involved in astrological charts, as well the programming of the crystals used for technology.*

*The High Priest and Priestess in charge always had to focus on keeping in place the shield around the island; monitoring others on the island; and sharing the information in order to ensure vital information was kept within the inner circle of the 12. Others were given just enough information to enable the community to function smoothly. Again, this was a way of ensuring that urgent information would not reach the dark forces and be used for their own evil ends.*

## The 12 High Priests and 12 High Priestesses

Each one of the 12 Crystal Pyramid Temples had a High Priest and Priestess reigning over the temple and county they administered. The men were mainly the administrators, while the women were the transmitter channels (prophecy and channeling), and in charge of the sexual rites and other rites of passage and initiations. They were also the Higher Healers, and the creative ones. Men had the ability to invent and strategize. The women created what the men had visualized. The two worked in tandem in balance and harmony.

The High Priest regarded himself as the embodiment of the male aspect of the Divine, and the High Priestess was the embodiment of the Divine Feminine aspect of God. Together they worked and functioned as One and performed certain sexual rites, as the sexual energy in itself is the experience of the God-force energy, when it is properly channeled and directed. It was thus a conduit for harnessing certain energies, to become a creative force.

The 12 High Priests and Priestesses not only acted as the custodians and administrators of the 12 Regions of Elysium, but they also held the secret keys and codes.

There were 12 Crystal Skulls, which had recorded within them all of the knowledge, technology and administrative guidelines for the High Priests to tap into, depending on which temple they represented. It connected them directly to the male aspect, the Divine Mind, and helped them with the mental energies. This then became technological know-how, including the enhancement of constructive intellectual capacities, such as the mathematical and scientific fields.

In addition to this, the 12 High Priestesses each had a crystal key that fitted exactly into the palm of their hands. Therein lay encoded all of the secret rites of passage; the recordings of the soul history since its beginnings. It enhanced their transmitting and channeling abilities, and held the keys and codes to the Divine Mother energies and Creation. These keys were intuitive keys into which the High Priestess tapped.

There was another set of crystal codes that combined the codes of wisdom, higher knowledge, and prophecy. They could only be accessed by the High Priest and Priestess when they had the Crystal Skulls and keys intact and their combined powers accessed the secret codes.

However, an additional factor was also built in – The 13th and Master Crystal Skull, Keys and Codes.

Within the Crystal Pyramid of the White Flame, another smaller pyramid was housed, or rather incorporated, which held the 13th Master Codes and Keys for the planet. It was directly linked to the 13th Master Key Codes of the Divine Halls of Records. These were administered by the 12 Elders surrounding God's throne, holding all the keys and codes of all of Creation. One can describe it as the mainframe brain, or mind of the whole Cosmos, as it holds all the records of everything ever created.

The High Priest of this Temple held not only the 12th Crystal Skull, but also the 13th. His counterpart, the High Priestess, held the 12th and 13th Crystal Keys, and together they held the 13th Master Code.

In essence, then, the Temple of the White Flame was the power base of Earth, and this temple's High Priest and Priestess had final jurisdiction and decision-making powers. They reported directly to the Central High Command of the Intergalactic Federation of the Great White Brotherhood. They had enormous responsibilities, and only the purest of the pure were considered worthy of holding such a position.

They held the complete balance of the Masculine and Feminine energies; the ultimate keys and codes for the eternal existence of life and all life forms in the entire Cosmos and on the planet. They were considered the Illumined Ones, the Chosen Ones. They were specially assigned to act as Guardians or Keepers of the sacred and sanctified.

*It was considered the Divine Mother Flame, and therefore it held the Creative Force of the Divine Mother herself, in perfect balance with her Divine counterpart, the Male Principle of the Divine.*

Once a year, or whenever major decisions had to be made, the 12 High Priests and Priestesses gathered at the Temple of the White Flame, bringing their Crystal Skulls, keys and codes, so that the 12 flames could be reunited in one single flame – the 13th Master Key Flame.

This was considered the most sacred and sanctified of all gatherings, and therefore all underwent stringent purification rites before being allowed entry to the island. Such was the holiness of the place.

This was the Golden Age of Elysium, the Garden of Eden, and the first beautiful and profound Creation: 7th dimensional, prospering and at peace. People were content and happy and lived their lives peacefully.

Elsewhere in the Cosmos, however, vast and thundering storm clouds were looming. They would reach even the outposts of the Heavens and cast their long shadows on to Planet Earth and on our Solar System…

# CHAPTER 8

# The Wars of the Heavens....

In the beginning was a void... dark, black, total darkness...

*Nothing else existed but the darkness... the void...*

*No life... no nothing... Just IT.*

*IT had no name, no beginning, and no end.*

*IT existed...*

*One day something within this void, this 'no state of being', developed a movement...*

*The movement caused ripples, a spiraling movement, and it started bubbling out...*

*It was but a twirling, whirling mass of 'No-thing', for it was nothing one could name...*

*It was a twirling, whirling mass of "No-One, No-thing, with No-name"...*

*Then, something amazing happened: Out of the void, out of the middle of this swirling mass, a spark of Light was born!*

*This was the Divine Light, the Divine Source, and thus the first I AM Presence of all time...*

*This Divine Light then burst forth to send ripples of sparks out into the unknown, and from these ripples of light, the first 12 Galaxies were born. Likewise, all life and life forms that formed part and particle of this self-same Light.*

*Yet, the void, the dark mass, continued to co-exist. It was there, and counterbalanced the Light, for without the void, the darkness, the Light could not be seen, and could not itself exist...*

Light, Love and light continued to thrive in the 12 Galaxies, as they also began expanding upon themselves.

Peace and harmony reigned in all that was created, and the first-born 12 Sons and Daughters had authority and dominion over that Creation. They formed the 12 and 24 Elders surrounding the Throne of the Divine.

However, out of this dark mass, this void, something began to emerge. It was a dark vortex-like energy form, a spiraling circular form, like that of the galaxies themselves...

As the scientists and the Divine watched this form becoming larger and larger, they suddenly realized that this was a 13th Galaxy.

What was most puzzling was that they had been so entranced by their own delight in living, and being in the Light in the purity of the Flame, that they had not realized that this 13th Galaxy existed.

Yet, on examination, it was found to have a life and intelligence all of its own. It had come, or been born, from the self-same void, or darkness, from which the Light had originated, and from this same momentum. When the Light had expanded upon itself to create the 12 Master Galaxies, this 13th Galaxy had been birthed, too.

However, as the scientists in the 12 Master Galaxies then started taking note and having exchanges with the beings from this 13th Galaxy, they found them to be different from themselves, with rather a strange form of energy that they had never encountered before.

Some scientists then volunteered to go and live in this Galaxy to explore its content, for it seemed that a foreign life form, unlike themselves, was living or existing there. They wished to learn more about this Galaxy; to understand how it had come into being.

However, as this experiment progressed, these scientists found that something within them had started changing. They retained their same physical form and had operated on the same level, but it seemed that suddenly they had developed a tendency to create destructive things. They started quarrelling among themselves and then, for the first time ever, had started killing each other!

The peaceful scientists who had left to experience life in the 13th Galaxy found themselves overtaken by this dark mass, which appeared to pull them into a kind of vortex, or black hole. They felt a growing depression; a feeling of emptiness and of being separate from each other; with an emerging tendency to act destructively. It appeared to be like a virus that began in the mind and ushered in an imbalance and propensity towards their own destruction and the annihilation of other life forms...

All of this happened without the knowledge of the scientists in the 12 Galaxies, as it had become apparent that they had lost contact with the 13th Galaxy. Then, to their consternation, inexplicable events started happening to their own people. Instead of peace and harmony, there was bickering, violence and a general depression.

The Advisory Board at the Divine Source then gathered to try to pinpoint what was happening, and to find the source of this strange behavior. They discovered that it all seemed to originate in the 13th Galaxy, which had suddenly reappeared.

For the first time, they had encountered their alter-ego – a disruptive force that tends to inflame the urge to infiltrate and control others. Beings in this Galaxy were controlling the minds of their dependents, and those for whom they were responsible. They enslaved other beings and different species to make them do their bidding. This was totally out of alignment with the Law of One, and the freedom of each soul to experience life and to create life and life forms. These beings were creating, but what they created, they also enslaved.

The leader of the original scientists and those volunteers who were investigating the 13th Galaxy, was then summoned to appear at a meeting. He came with some of his own kind. They reported on their encounters with the dark mass, which had infiltrated their minds and caused them to carry out these destructive actions. They spoke of their feelings of separateness from their Creator, and even of a feeling that they were superior to the Divine. This caused a sensation, for how could one be separate from the Divine who had created all? How could one not be part and parcel of the Greater Whole? These sentiments set a new precedent for dissension in the Council, and there was great deliberation about how to best deal with this.

For the first time, there was division in the Council itself, and a disruption of the peace in the Heavens.

After long and serious discussions, they realized that this dark mass that controlled the 13th Planet, and therefore these scientists, was also experiencing life. It was definitely part of life, albeit in a different form. As the Divine Source had itself sprung from the dark void, it could not deny the existence of this dissonance, for ultimately everything is intrinsically from the same source.

If these scientists therefore wished to continue life on the 13th Planet, and to experience the void, separation, and strife that ensued, then they would be released to do so, on the proviso that they would serve the Divine Council, and remember the Law of One: That all life is one, and that Light and Darkness can peacefully co-exist, and can, in fact, create and maintain the balance of creation.

However, the 13th Galaxy and those who represented her proved to be rebellious and asserted their own right to explore life in the way they were now creating. How could they be against the Divine or Creation itself, when they were creating something different and new? They saw themselves as equal to the Divine and its creations. In fact, they argued that they were serving by creating the necessary counterbalance, the alter-ego; the other side of Creation.

This greatly puzzled those in attendance, who at that time were dealing with this whole question as one deals with a rebellious and willful child, little realizing that this 'child' was already doing what it had said it would do: Creating the other side of the spectrum: 'Balance', which equaled 'imbalance'.

In the beginning, this worked… The 13th Planet continued its destructive ways, and started creating life in its own way.

The 12 Master Galaxies, however, then found that as much as they tried to maintain order, their own Galaxies were being infiltrated. Some of their very own began to be drawn in under the influence of this 13th Planet and were controlled by them. They started to display aggressive and disruptive behavior, which culminated in killing each other.

Another Council meeting was summoned, and the 13th Galaxy was asked to adhere to their first agreement, and to cease their infiltration of the 12 Master Galaxies. However, while the meeting was in progress, the 13th Galaxy launched a massive laser attack on the Intergalactic Fleet, nearly destroying it!

The Fleet at that time was merely equipped with scientists with laboratories and had no means of defense.

This caused an outrage in the 12 Galaxies, which found themselves, for the first time ever, having to defend their own territory, while realizing that some of their own people had been infiltrated and were at war with them.

Hardest hit were Andromeda, the Pleiades, Lyra, Sirius and Orion.

It was then decided that the 13th Galaxy would be banned from all further Council meetings, and the Intergalactic Federation of the Great White Flame was established. It mainly consisted of the 12 Master Galaxies and other new Galaxies that were affiliated to them and who had remained true to the Law of One – the Divine Source itself.

This evolved as a defense tactic, and the 13th planetary leaders were informed they would be welcome to return to the fold and the Law of One – if they laid down their weapons and resumed living peacefully.

From their perspective, the 13th Galaxy had chosen from their own free will to experience a life of destruction and separateness. This was their own soul choice. At any time though, should such souls wish to return to the state of at oneness and unity – the Law of One – they would always be welcomed back.

It was understood, too, that in essence, all of Creation was One, and even those who wished to experience life in a different form, still served the greater purpose as an integral part of the whole. Yet, even that understanding could not prevent an escalation of war. From a border viewpoint, this was a totally new experience – both for those who started the wars, as well as for those who, for the first time, had to invent weapons to defend themselves. This in turn escalated into the War of the Heavens and became a full-scale war.

Although the war initially started in the 12 Master Galaxies, it soon spilt over into the newer Galaxies, and thus into our own Solar System.

Chaos reigned in Heaven… Creation itself was in turmoil.

# CHAPTER 9

# Africa's Sacred Keys and Codes

## The Aftermath

The Wars of the Heavens spilt over on to the planet. Laser weapons of mass destruction that were even more potent than atom bombs had been used. The great cities, temples, and everything else had been completely melted. Land masses separated and fell away. Some sank under the sea. This in turn caused widespread floods and tidal waves and the shifting of the poles for the first time since Earth's creation.

The South Pole, as we know it now, was the North Pole in the days of Elysium. Since then, it has shifted four times – as the Lion Kingdom, Lemuria, Mu and Atlantis followed Elysium.

When poring over the African map, marking energy centers and trying to puzzle things out, I was told that I was looking at the continent of Africa upside down! I found that amusing, for the map was the right-side up. However, after the fourth prompting, I turned it around so that Africa was located in the north, not the south. I was told that the world looked like that at the time of Elysium, and that the map was now correctly positioned!

As I did that, I was reminded of the Piri Reis map, and Antarctica without ice. The world drawn as if one was viewing it from outer space…

Looking at Africa the wrong (or right way) up, I had a totally new viewpoint: Not as a cartographer would perceive it, but in relation to the specific information I was seeking. Something deep inside me was awakened and activated, as I suddenly started understanding matters that had previously been a mystery.

I had to travel back to the very beginning of time, after Earth was thrown out of its orbit and the inner world, Agartha, survived as a satellite. Earth's surface was rearranged in the process. There was volcanic activity and tidal waves, and land masses were torn asunder. Consequently, it looked dramatically different! Instead of one single land mass, there were several. Where there had been one ocean, different oceans had been formed. The Mediterranean Sea had appeared, yet with one difference – Spain, France, Morocco, and the northern part of Africa were still joined together.

A new land mass had emerged in the region now known as the Pacific Rim, where at a later stage, the third experiment of settlement on this planet, known as Mu, occurred.

With this reforming of the land masses, the cities were buried, and the temples on Earth's surface were under deep layers of volcanic ash. Some were even flooded. Certain land masses, like those in south-eastern Africa, had sections ripped off, which then lifted the remaining land by pushing it upwards. Several inland seas of Elysium were drained, and new seas and lakes formed. Earth had gone through a massive transformation!

The only land masses that had remained stable were the African continent, parts of Europe, and sections of the Middle East and India – including the Himalayas – and other areas further north (another great civilization arose in the Nordic areas, adjacent to what is now the North Pole. This was called The Land of a Thousand Suns. It is remembered in the Nordic traditions as the Valkyries[1], the realm of the gods, such as Thor.)

Several cities and other remnants of Elysium were buried so deeply under the newly-settling land that they slipped into oblivion.

The south-eastern parts of Africa are truly the sacred embodiment of the highest aspirations of human consciousness – and its lowest. It is here that ancient patterns were created… Patterns that have embedded themselves in our subconscious minds for millions of years – ever since that first settlement of volunteers in Elysium.

If one wishes to understand humanity, at both its noblest *and* its most brutal and weak, then look no further than this section of Africa. Buried deep beneath layers of volcanic ash, flood lines, sand and stone, sometimes just buried deep in the wilderness, lie the records of the greatest moments of human history – and the most destructive times. One cannot understand the Sphinx and the pyramids in Egypt, Bosnia, Mexico, China and elsewhere, if one isn't prepared to first find the keys and codes in Africa, south of Giza, south of the Sahara, and then even further southwards!

We have to dig deep into the mystery of the soul of Africa, for she is not one to just relinquish her innermost heart and lay it bare for all to see. She has been abused too often and stripped naked, for men have lusted after her gold, diamonds and ore, and have walked ruthlessly over her children many times, resulting in greater self-destruction. Indeed, this region is where it all began, and history has continued to repeat this cycle for many thousands of years.

Africa has the entire collective history of the human race within her. The keys and codes of the Collective Consciousness of Humankind[2] are encoded on the African continent. She keeps her secrets close to her bosom, deep within her Soul. She now seeks those who are pure in heart, intent and understanding; who will be able to unravel these secrets. For so long she has been reticent and maintained her silence, but she will be silent and withdrawn no longer!

She is the Keeper of the most vital energy centers in the world. As she regains momentum, and with the opening up of the Lion Portal (more on this later) incredible things will happen and all of Earth's inhabitants will discover how to once again return to the true core of their beings. Only by melting down all hindrances and blocks and stepping out of old destructive patterns will we be able to transcend

---

1    In Norse mythology, a Valkyrie is one of a host of female figures who choose those who may die in battle and those who may live. (*Wikipedia*)

2    Collective Consciousness is the set of shared beliefs, ideas and moral attitudes that operate as a unifying force within society. (*Collins Dictionary of Sociology*, p93.)

the illusion of separation and enter into the deep heart of this continent. Deep within her lies the ancient energy centers, the keys and codes to the vast consciousness that will ensure the resurrection of humankind!

I jotted down the following entry in my journal in September 2009:

### JOURNAL ENTRY

"Immense progress is currently taking place in the activation of the secret codes, keys and the grid. The two underground rivers running through and alongside the 31°–36° longitude line are now being reactivated, as are the rest of the energy grids. Thus, astounding energy is being released, and with this, more knowledge will surface.

When all of this has been energized, it will have a profound effect on this part of the world, especially where the 26°–36° latitude forms a pyramid with the Crystal Temple under the sea.

I was told today that as I am drawn to these places, I will automatically activate the grids and lines. When I focus on and locate the pyramids, I am resurrecting forces that have lain dormant for millions of years. I will act as a door, or portal, through which this energy can be reactivated. All of this will be possible due to my DNA structure, and who and what I am at a soul level. Thus, I have that power – not yet consciously, but subconsciously. "I" am thus being used as a crystal-clear transmitter channel."

I intently studied the maps of Africa yet again. What secrets did the 33° longitude hold? Why was it so important, and why was my attention being brought back to it time and time again?

In this process, I began to find small pieces of the puzzle; glimpses of what might be lying there. Each

time I was reminded of the Crystal Pyramid Temples of Elysium…

On my return to Nature's Valley and the region where I first started my journey, I began noticing stone circles on the mountains that formed patterns. One day, looking through my binoculars, some inspired ideas came to me: What I was seeing reminded me of a beehive, as these circles followed a beehive pattern. Yet, each cluster had a different pattern.

There were giant faces in the rocks everywhere, and with my experience of the vortex energies in Keurbooms, as previously described, I utilized Google Earth. To my utter amazement, I found the face of a giant staring at me through the image of the area I was studying in Keurbooms! At first I thought I was imagining things, but a few weeks later I googled the same area again and, sure enough, there was the face in the sea!

What was a giant face doing in the sea at the very place where the energy was the most potent? It was considered a holy and sacred place by the San people. According to geologists, at some earlier time, the shoreline had extended further into the sea.

I was greatly puzzled. After doing research, I realized that they were similar to those I had seen in the Mpumalanga area, from Waterval Boven upwards. To my amazement, the patterns were repeating themselves here! Yet, I was more than a thousand miles south, so whoever created these circles had done so all over the south-eastern region of Africa! I then remembered where I had seen similar stone circles – on my cousin's farms on the Zululand border. Indeed, my archaeologist brother had been asked to examine them. Even he could not answer their questions, because these circles were not built by the Zulus. They were ancient, and there were also gold mines in this area.

I was told by a geologist, who often travelled to areas of Zululand where nobody else ventured, that

*Giant face staring at me on Google maps.*

*Face in the sea.*

he encountered a tribe there who were the Keepers of the Ancient Mines. It was there that King Shaka[3] had apparently found the perfect blacksmiths to forge his newly-invented spears. When he wanted to have a closer look at these mines, he was told that it was forbidden territory, as they belonged to the Abulungu (white men) from the skies! The sky people did not allow just anyone there. Only the blacksmiths were permitted to enter, and only those who knew the secret art of alchemy.

All of this was coming together. Next I was led to look seriously at Zimbabwe and the Great Zimbabwe

---

3   King Shaka (Shaka Zulu) was one of the most influential monarchs of the Zulu Kingdom. He was born near present-day Melmoth, KwaZulu-Natal Province. (*Wikipedia*)

Ruins[4]. How did all these sites link up? I knew the pyramids I had spotted at Adam's Calendar were in perfect alignment with those in Giza. Indeed, I had marked them on my map! So, I felt that somewhere in the area near the Zimbabwe Ruins there had to be some clue to indicate that it was a piece in this vast jigsaw puzzle.

In fact, my question would be answered in ways I could never have anticipated. The catalyst was once again the energy vortex in this area, and in Keurbooms. I came across two incredible pieces of information that made me sit up and take notice:

I discovered that when the Portuguese came to Africa in 1552, they explored Zimbabwe and were, in fact, the first to discover these ruins, long before Livingstone found them. They found a lintel with strange writing and symbols on it, and the Moors with them could not read this, as the language was unknown to them.

The Swiss explorer Anders Sparrman[5], travelling in what was then the Eastern Cape Frontier area, recorded the following in 1776[6]:

> "We found heaps of rocks following the points of the compass in a northerly direction, and others running parallel… The first archeological excavation in South Africa, Port Elizabeth, Great Fish River observed heaps of stones. They were from three to four feet and a half high, and the bases of them measured six, eight to ten feet in diameter… But constantly between two particular points of the compass, and consequently in right lines, and these always running parallel to each other, and extended in this manner several days' journey in this spot in a northern direction and into the Sneeze Vlaktens[7], where they are said to be met with in a greater number of parallel lines. These monuments are, therefore, considered irrefragable proof that the tract of country was formerly inhabited by a race of people who were more powerful and numerous than either the Hottentots or the Xhosa."

Is it not strange that in South America, the same type of lines are found in the Nazca desert[8]? Or is it that no one ever bothered to look elsewhere in Africa? Or had everything been very deliberately hidden on the Dark Continent?

The greed of those first explorers in Zimbabwe knew no bounds. In the 1890s, Cecil John Rhodes[9] was the next to appear on the scene. Near the Great Zimbabwe Ruins, graves were discovered with golden artifacts on the skeletons. They promptly removed all the gold, melted it down and shipped it off to London, thereby committing one of the greatest crimes against

---

4    The Great Zimbabwe Ruins are the largest collection of ruins in Africa south of the Sahara. Located in the heart of southern Africa, between the Zambezi and Limpopo Rivers, they are a testament to a culture of great wealth and great architectural skill. (*Wikipedia*)

5    Swede Anders Sparrman (1748-1820) was the first traveller to give an extended and readable account of travels into the interior of the Cape, between 1772 and 1776. As a student of Linnaeus, he was particularly well qualified to explore the rich floral heritage of South Africa. (*Wikipedia*)

6    Anders Sparrman, *Travels in the Cape 1772–1776, A Voyage to the Cape of Good Hope towards the Antarctic Polar Circle Round the World and to the Country of the Hottentots and the Caffres*, Volumes I and II.

7    The Sneeze Vlakten, Cineeze, Cineese or Chinese, from the appearance of the Bushmen living upon them. (*Stow's Native Races of South Africa*, p. 128 n., 1905.)

8    The Nazca Lines are a series of ancient geoglyphs located in the Nazca Desert in southern Peru.

9    Cecil John Rhodes was a British businessman, mining magnate and politician in South Africa. He served as Prime Minister of the Cape Colony from 1890 to 1896. (*Wikipedia*)

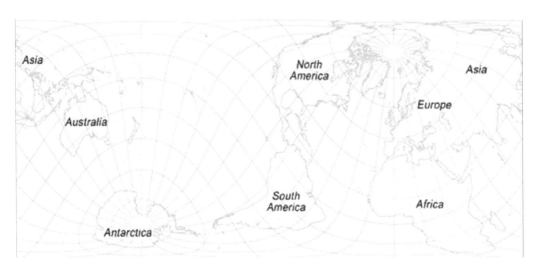

*A map of the vile vortices by Ivan T. Sanderson.*

the African people and concealing clues to the history of Africa.

I was most perplexed when I began reading in depth about the Zimbabwe Ruins. Some information seemed to be missing, or to have gone awry. I was then led to the Queen of Sheba[10]. I had read Tudor Parfitt's book[11] on the Lemba tribe[12], which was one of the Lost Tribes of Israel. They still had an ark, which they considered holy and sacred, and had blessed, sacred mountains that were only for the High Priests.

So, what else did Zimbabwe have that had been hidden?

I found myself again searching in the maps of Africa, marking the energy grid I had been given.

Africa is not for the timid, the faint-hearted, or for those who just wish to explore life on the surface. She reveals her destructive, ugly face – the face of woe, of poverty, of corruption and of extreme weather and harshness to those wanting to exploit her; to ride rough-shod over her; and not to seek out her Soul.

She epitomizes the female soul of this planet, suppressed for so long; exploited, controlled and overwhelmed by the energy of male dominance. Yet, she has never abandoned the planet. She merely sought to hide her face and go underground.

She is the veiled Mother, the Black Madonna[13] and Isis. It is in Mama Africa that there is this veiling; this hidden undercore; this mythological emblem. These symbols exist in stories all over the world, but in Africa, they take on the form of life itself.

But what exactly was being veiled? What had she hidden?

When I first saw the energy centers in Natal, and

---

10  The Queen of Sheba is a Biblical figure. The tale of her visit to King Solomon has undergone extensive Jewish, Arabian and Ethiopian elaborations, and has become the subject of one of the most widespread and fertile cycles of legends in the Orient. (*Wikipedia*)

11  Tudor Parfitt, *Journey to the Vanished City*, PenguinRandom, 1992.

12  The Lemba, wa-Remba, or *Mwenye*, are a southern African ethnicity found in Zimbabwe and South Africa, with smaller, little-known branches in Mozambique and Malawi. In 2002, they numbered an estimated 50 000.

13  A Black Madonna, or Black Virgin, is a statue or painting of Mary in which she, and oftentimes the infant Jesus, are depicted with dark skin. This especially refers to those created in Europe in the medieval period, or earlier. (*Wikipedia*)

was researching the San people, I was drawn back to a map of vile vortices[14] around the world.

The turquoise-green-colored areas on the map are the vile vortices where aircraft disappear; navigational instruments go haywire; and where there have been strange disappearances. Note that Africa has two: One in the north, in the Sahara Desert, and the other in Zimbabwe, parts of South Africa, and Mozambique. It also includes the ocean in the Mozambique Channel, where I know pyramids sank under the sea when Madagascar was separated from the mainland of Africa.

Why was I being drawn back to this map? On reflection, I was being led to re-examine the same energy I had felt near my home, with the knowledge that the Temple of the White Flame had sunk beneath the sea close to my home. The circles everywhere, and the lines all pointed north. In addition, there seemed to be some connection to Zimbabwe, but what was it?

While sitting on the beach in my high-energy spot at Nature's Valley[15] on July 6, 2013, I had the following vision (remember, what I saw is now buried underground):

*"As seen before, the massive Sphinx and the Temple of the Sun blended in with a spectacular vista of mountains. It lay between the mountains, with a waterfall flowing down behind the Pyramid Temple of the Sun into many canals, laid out like a labyrinth. It was a jewel of a place, with an overwhelming sense of gold and green, many tropical plants, and trees lining the canals and gardens. What was so amazing was that the gardens seemed to come from the sky – literally – like hanging gardens, and seemed to flow in synchronicity, blending in perfectly with the massive Temple of the Sun and the Sphinx. The pyramid formed a triangle with other smaller pyramids and with another three, so that the labyrinth incorporated the Star of David[16].*

*From these Temples rose gigantic, gold serpent energy. It was the energy of the Divine Mother, for here She mated with the Sun energies of the Divine Father. This place was the powerhouse of the whole planet. This was the city of the Lion People, and the inner city or hub of the massive Lion Portal.*

*I was told that this was the first Kingdom of the Sun, and it was the Lion People from Lyra, whose Galaxy had blown up in the Wars of the Heavens, who had built these massive city complexes, along with those from the 12 Master Galaxies.*

*They laid down the Rivers of Gold, and the spinal cord of the planet, and had built the River Nile. Their Kingdom incorporated the entire south-eastern region of southern Africa, with a little dent into Botswana[17] and Namibia[18]. The present-day desert was once part of this tropical paradise. It extended all the way down into Antarctica, and included South America and Australia; Madagascar; the Seychelles; Reunion; Sri Lanka; Mauritius, and what is now the Maldives Islands.*

*This is therefore an amazing confirmation.*

*Another thing that happened is that I was initiated as one of these "Lion People", and thus given the keys and codes to access the information encoded here, so that I could return these ancient keys and codes to mankind."*

---

14  A vile vortex is any of 12 purported particular geographic areas arranged in a pattern around the Earth. The term was coined by Ivan T. Sanderson, who catalogued them as the sites of unexplained disappearances and other mysterious phenomena (Ivan T. Sanderson, *The Twelve Devil's Graveyards Around the World*, Saga, 1972)

15  Nature's Valley is a small village on the Garden Route, along the southern Cape coast of South Africa. (*Wikipedia*)

16  The Star of David is a generally recognized symbol of modern Jewish identity and Judaism. (*Wikipedia*)

17  Botswana, a landlocked country in southern Africa, has a landscape defined by the Kalahari Desert and the Okavango Delta, which becomes a lush animal habitat during the seasonal floods. (*Wikipedia,*)

18  Namibia, a country in south-west Africa, is distinguished by the Namib Desert along the Atlantic Ocean coast. (*Wikipedia*)

*The Temple of the Sun, as sketched by me.*

## JOURNAL ENTRY

**Recording from June 22, 2013:**

I found myself sitting on the beach, just like that day in Keurbooms. The same man I had seen the previous time on the beach appeared in front of me! He was tall and slim, with long, dark, straight, auburn hair that fell freely from his shoulders. He had two leopards with him, one on either side of him. I looked into his eyes as he greeted me. His eyes were liquid gold and his skin was red, like the Native Americans. Indeed, he seemed to be of their race.

The leopards came to me and I could pat them. One was purring. They were tame and I had no fear. He asked me to come with him, saying that I was to open the Lion Portal, as I held the codes and keys.

He took my hand, and a funny thing happened: We were literally flying through the air, but not like a bird flies. We were levitating while still standing upright! I saw the landscape changing. It became much greener and more tropical. There were enormous mountains now, but the valley and the rocks were ochre-colored.

Then I saw a monumental city nestled in a valley between these mountains.

There was a huge Sphinx, much larger than the one in Egypt. It was also ochre-colored – the color of a very deep and rich gold-red. It was guarding an enormous golden pyramid. It sparkled and was blinding in the Sun, which itself seemed brighter and larger than usual.

There was an imposing mountain behind the pyramid. A great waterfall cascaded into canals, spiral-

*The pyramids, massive hanging gardens and the water labyrinths all formed part of this massive City of the Sun and the Temple of the Sun complex, which was built by the Lion People.*

ing out from the pyramid in concentric circles (the Leopard man had shown me spirals and circles on the mountains everywhere, explaining that they were the symbols of his people, symbolizing the spiraling Tree of Life[19]).

The whirling canals looked as if they had been built or constructed to form a labyrinth: A design with bridges over some sections that were not all the same. They were spaced out with different patterns and circular forms within the spiraling designs.

It was all laid out with buildings of the same color as the Sphinx, with many hanging gardens and trees. Some of them had palm trees, or rather 'cousins' of palm trees, for they looked slightly different. It was a beautiful city. The ground was sloped or terraced, and it was a glorious sight.

I have never seen anything like it: The vibrant and very high frequency colors!

I then descended with him, and we landed in a square in front of a large palace with different levels,

---

19   Tree of Life: The Tree of Knowledge, connecting to heaven and the underworld, and the Tree of Life, connecting all forms of Creation, are both forms of the world tree, or Cosmic tree. (*Encyclopædia Britannica*)

*My sketch of the hanging gardens.*

*The Lion King, as sketched by me.*

but it was not spiraling or in pyramid form. We went through a golden gate into a huge entrance hall. Because it was so dazzling, it was hard to take it all in. There was an enormous display case that had turned out to be a kind of elevator.

We just stepped on to it and had the sensation of levitating, but we were still on the platform. I can find no words to describe it. We have nothing to compare it to here.

I remained with the Leopard man, and we were greeted by 7 lions. They were beautiful and completely tame, so I could touch them. The male lion requested I follow him into a chamber. The walls were beautifully decorated: Very classic with inlaid columns. The colors were vibrant, and large windows opened up to splendid vistas of the whole city and the pyramids.

Then, to my surprise, the Lion King whom I already knew – entered!

He had the body of a human being, but his face was lion-like. He had masses of red-golden hair, just like a mane, growing from his forehead down his neck and shoulders to the middle of his body. He was bearded with whiskers of the same color. His very large eyes were a sheer and beautiful golden-brown. He was naked, but for a loincloth, and he was very upright, tall and beautiful in his own way.

He showed me his City of the Sun, the city belonging and dedicated to the Sun God, which housed the Lion Portal. His people from Lyra and Sirius were there waiting for me to record their story.

"I will bring to you complete knowledge of the Ancient times; the pyramids and how they came into being; and the energies used. You have been called to open up the Lion Portal, and from now on the Lion People will guard and protect you, as will the Lord and Lady of Sirius."

---

It was then that I finally understood that the Central Temple of the Sun and the vast Sphinx guarding it, were somewhere underneath the kopjes surrounding the Great Zimbabwe Ruins. The Ruins are a small remnant of one of the lesser abodes. They were later modified and used for mining purposes by the Nabiru people.

I was reminded of how, while in a trans state, the San shamans had grown lions' manes as they communicated with the other worlds. The more I thought about that, the more I realized how important it was to understanding the whole hidden truth of Africa.

During this time, I was referred to the map of Africa again. I was told that this area formed the diamond grid of the planet, and that it fitted perfectly into the gold and platinum grids arranged over the whole Gauteng area in South Africa, extending up to Zimbabwe, Zambia, Tanzania and into Kenya. All this links in perfectly with the energy grids of the planet, and more importantly, the spinal cord of the planet.

I was told that these Lion People, with the aid of those from Sirius and Orion, acted as the Guardians or Keepers of the Energy Grids, the spinal cord of the planet, and the sacred energy centers both here in Africa and elsewhere. Thus no one can gain access to these, nor use the vortex energy, without their permission, as they had vowed after what had happened in Elysium, Mu, Lemuria and Atlantis, that they would never again allow the misuse of the power source.

But what was the spinal cord of the planet? What did it have to do with energy centers and, more importantly, with the vortex energy?

I was deeply puzzled, little knowing that as I asked this question, the answers would be revealed in unexpected ways… Indeed, they came as a total surprise!

# CHAPTER 10

# The Code Reveals Itself

When I found the map with the Kabbalistic Tree of Life[1] fitting so perfectly over Africa, something deep inside of me began to awaken. I felt I had to explore the significance of the human spinal cord in more depth before the rest of the mystery would reveal itself.

The African continent, to me, has become the Gate Keeper of the most important energy centers in the world. With the full activation of the Lion Portal, incredible things will start happening as the entire population of this planet returns to the center of their beings, and all hindrances and blocks melt away. Everything will be reconnected, not only to the Soul of the planet, but to the collective souls within every single being!

Deep inside the African continent, the most ancient and important energy centers are buried, and the portal that contains this higher knowledge and understanding is the Lion Portal. The Lion People guard this portal, as the Sphinx is guarding the south.

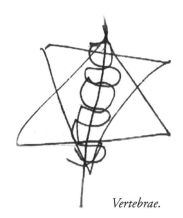

*Vertebrae.*

It has been purposefully hidden and forgotten by mankind, yet the Giza Pyramids point to Sirius and Orion, and most importantly to the Lion People, via the Sphinx. The Sphinx is guarding not only the Lion Portal, but the spinal cord of the world. This spinal cord is not found exactly on the 33° longitude line, for that was calculated by men with limited knowledge and inaccurate calculations. The spinal cord of Earth is aligned to its axis, and thus holds the whole planet

---

1   The Tree of Life is a classic descriptive term for the central mystical symbol used in the Kabbalah of esoteric Judaism, also known as the 10 Sephirot. (*Wikipedia*)

upright, as does the spinal cord in the human body.

It is divided equally into 33 energy centers. The Lion Portal activates the keys and codes within each of these centers. No human can grasp the importance of this, but we have to comprehend that some of these 33 energy centers were moved out of alignment because Earth was hit by asteroids and comets almost simultaneously, so ending the first Golden Age of Elysium. First there was fire, then volcanic eruptions, with huge twists and turns of the Earth's crust. Then came floods, as the planet was thrown out of its orbit.

As mentioned already, the 33 energy centers of the Earth's spinal cord reflect the human spinal cord. To understand this, we must first look at the human spinal cord:

## The Spinal Cord Energies

It was during this time of intense teaching, inner cleansing and clearing work that I was given exceedingly interesting information regarding the human spinal cord. At the time, I was teaching some of my students how to activate their 12 chakras (energy wheels), and how to build the Antahkarana (Light Bridge) between the Divine, themselves and the Earth. Once completed, this forms a massive Cosmic energy grid and helps activate their full Light potential. During this process, we did plenty of cleansing and clearing of these chakras.

In clearing these energy centers, many old memory banks are opened, because emotional trauma or unreleased burdens clog up energy centers with debris. Each chakra is like an energy wheel. As it spins, it starts dislodging the blocked particles. The faster they all spin within the Light Bridge, the higher the frequency becomes, and the more Light the person can absorb and transmit.

The Antahkarana Bridge is a Bridge of Light that enables you to connect directly with the Divine Source, through all the levels of Being, and to pull this energy down into the energy centers of the physical body, and then into the Earth Star beneath your feet. If you continue down through all the layers of the Earth, you can actually anchor the Divine and Earth energies into your four-body system (your physical, emotional, mental and spiritual bodies) to increase your Light body frequencies and vibrations 10 000-fold!

This has to be practised on a daily basis, and there are also techniques to use the vortex energy to further cleanse and purify the bodies, so that additional higher frequency bands can be activated. As this is being done, the body's kundalini energies are stimulated. This in turn initiates the pituitary and pineal glands. The more Light you bring into these glands, the more the 3rd eye and psychic and transmitting chambers are opened up.

Through these channels, you can be trained to tap into the Cosmic whole in whichever form you wish. While practising this, I was told during meditation that I would have to do the same clearing with each of my 33 vertebrae.

I was extremely surprised by this, as I had always believed the 12 chakras (in the Cosmic whole there are, in fact, 352 chakra systems) would activate all the energy systems.

When I first started to reflect on the spinal cord of the Earth, I was led to a very interesting article by Nick Anthony Fiorenza[2], in which he used the tonal scale, discovered by L. Ron Hubbard, and applied it to the 33 vertebrae of the spinal cord. The human emotions, in their positive and negative aspects, are believed to be held in the glands, so negative or stuck emotions literally clog them up so that they cannot operate fully. This causes pain in the body. At the time, I was already working with my glands, because

---

2    Nick Anthony Fiorenza is the author and creator of Lunarplanner.com

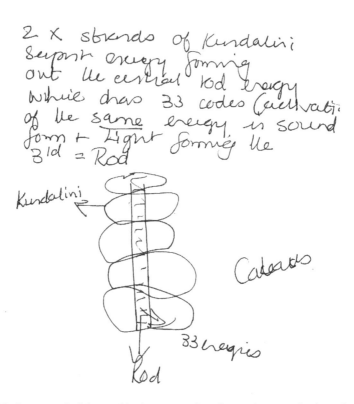

*My sketch of the spinal column (lightning rod of the earth), the 33 vertebrae being the proverbial Jacob's Ladder, and the multiple spiraling strands of light and sound energy pulsating up and down.*

the chakra wheels in the body are directly associated with them. They work in cohesion as one. Yet, I was told to delve even deeper.

I was shown how the human spinal cord is indisputably a 'Jacob's ladder'[3], with 33 rungs. Each rung forms one step, and moving up them raises the fields of consciousness. I was reminded that the spinal cord is the final body part formed in the embryo, thus holding the keys and codes to all of Creation.

Each vertebra contains within itself an energy wheel, which emits crystalline energy. It looks like a spider's web, perfectly reflecting the Web of Light around the planet. When the energy wheels within each vertebra spin, they radiate color and sound. The colored strands look like fractal energy strands of light. Each vertebra connects to each of the Earth's vertebrae, so connecting the spinal cords of humans with the spinal cord energies of Earth and the Web of Light. Indeed, this is such an intimate connection that all life forms function as One entity.

In essence, each vertebra forms a tiny MerKaBah energy field, and when all are fully activated and functioning and flowing, the MerKaBah energies of the spinal cord connect as one in a form similar to a lightning rod, or magic wand. The double- and triple-helix vortex energy fields are then established. This rod provides the base energy field around which the kundalini can form, so that multiple serpent strands wind around it.

When all 33 vertebrae are fully activated, this

---

3    Jacob's Ladder is the colloquial name for a connection between the Earth and Heaven that the Biblical Patriarch Jacob dreams about during his flight from his brother, Esau, in the Book of Genesis (*Wikipedia*)

brings into alignment the upper pyramid situated in the skull, and connects the pineal and pituitary glands, forming the upper pyramid in the body, with the lower pyramid based in the coccyx area. The spinal column then becomes a 'lightning rod', literally able to connect 'as above, so below,' acting like a powerful antenna.

If this is entirely activated, then your transmitter channels are fully open, allowing you to connect to the Cosmic energy systems, which fine-tune us cosmically and enable us to receive transmissions directly from the Divine. It also enables us to span dimensions and to tap into the Super Consciousness Energy Fields – all the higher energy centers held in the Great Cosmic Suns.

It is through these energy fields that the higher Cosmic rays are transmitted and incorporated into the physical form. This energy passes through the Stellar Gateway (the 12 chakras when fully opened and activated), into the crown of the head, the pineal and pituitary glands, and then into the spinal cord. There it connects with the head, working its way downwards and upwards from the pelvic bone or coccyx area. Thus, it forms an upward and downward movement and joins with the kundalini energies via both energy centers. (In fact, more energy centers are then formed and fully activated within the head and the coccyx area, and the womb center in women.)

I was shown that this energy field relates directly to the Creative energies, the Divine Feminine, and thus to the serpent, or creative energy force itself. The higher creative energies are, therefore, fully anchored in, when all these energy centers in the physical body work as one and are all completely opened, with any blockages removed.

In essence, the kundalini energy has to rise as a double-helix vortex energy to work as one with the spinal cord rod energies, thus forming a triple-helix flame that then expands in fully-activated crystalline form, creating the 12 and 13 strands. Its presence indicates you are fully activated.

When firmly anchored in, this whole energy system has its powerbase in the coccyx or base chakra (the womb for women), and thus is the powerhouse, which enables you to be empowered in all bodies. It is here you may step up and down the ladder, the rod, of the fully activated Light body.

The medical emblem, the caduceus[4], tries to remind us of this:

This same pattern repeats itself not only in the spinal cord of Earth, but in the whole of Creation. In fact, if you are set in motion, you can then start tapping directly into the Super Consciousness Fields and come into full 'Awareness'.

Awareness is an even higher state of being, for here you are, according to Dr. David R. Hawkins: *"...even beyond consciousness. The Absolute is unknowable, exactly because it's beyond knowing, or beyond the reach of consciousness itself. Those who have attained such a state of awareness report that it can't be described and can have no meaning for anyone without the experience of that context. Nonetheless, this is the true state of reality, universally and eternally. We merely fail to recognize it. Such recognition is the essence of enlightenment and the final resolution of the evolution of consciousness, to the point of self-transcendence."*

So, each vertebra is itself a mini Cosmic energy field. However, there is a third force that must come into the equation here, namely:

*"What happens in the Macrocosm happens in the Microcosm."*

Each vertebra of the spinal cord reflects a mini-galaxy.

At its core, it forms a vortex energy center – a whole Energy Matrix, and thus a mini vortex (within each vertebra). The entire Cosmos vibrates

---

4    The caduceus is the traditional symbol of Hermes and features two snakes winding around an often-winged staff. (*Wikipedia*)

to the frequency of sound! Therefore, each vertebra responds to sound, the Cosmic music and harmony of the spheres. The spinal cord is a gigantic tuning fork that resonates to the reverberating sounds of the Earth and Universe!

It resonates with the 33 chords or sound combinations that form the lost chords, or octave of sound frequencies, that humanity has forgotten!

Meantime, I have been told that, cosmically, there are 33 octaves of sound. Each planet has its own chord, and this in turn vibrates or harmonizes with the octave of sound emitted by the Galaxies.

The Cosmic Music of the Spheres then incorporates the octaves of sound, and all work as one harmonious Cosmic whole.

In fact, those 33 chords are directly related to the suppression of the female energies of the planet, and the Divine Feminine. Interestingly, the High Priestesses were the transmitter channels and were tuned in to the higher frequencies of sound.

The more tuned in one becomes, the more one starts to work with frequencies and vibrations. Sounds vibrate at certain frequencies, and can dissolve matter. When one knows how to work with energy fields, one can dissolve into them, become ONE with them, and then direct them to go exactly where one wishes them to go, or create with them what one wishes to create. One can span dimensions by literally tuning into the desired dimension, or octave of that dimension, anywhere in the Cosmos. One can also then teleport and project holographic images of oneself to wherever one wishes to be. Some would call this bi-locating, which a lot of the Himalayan yogis were able to do. This means that one can be in more than one place at the same time. The possibilities are endless, for one is now not bound to the physical form, but *transcends* it to *become* what one wishes to project, and to manifest this projection wherever one wishes. In Celtic tradition, this is often called shape-shifting.

One is all and everything, and everything is one. We have the ability to realign the cells and molecules of our physical form, and can become visible or invisible at will!

This ability not only has to do with the kundalini energies, but also the spinal cord energies. Everything comes into the two powerhouses: One located in the coccyx area, and the other in the skull. This connects to the pineal gland, and from there to the 3rd eye, and then to another smaller type of '3rd eye' situated between the right and left nostrils; as well as to the throat and pituitary gland. This energy then channels back via the spinal cord rod into the 3rd triangle, which is the coccyx and solar plexus area.

The spinal cord is then encased within a circle: The circumference of the Earth. When the planet's spinal cord is fully activated, the six-pointed star and Metatron cube will also become fully activated, forming a massive MerKaBah energy field in and around the planet. This then will mean that Earth spins faster, vibrating at a much higher frequency. It will actually become a massive energy conduit and power station on its own. It will bring the macrocosm and microcosm into one single form, and thus be instrumental in raising the consciousness of whomever and whatever it contains! It literally transmits the Cosmic frequencies, and it incorporates and anchors them in. Thus, it is a living, breathing, massive energy vortex and field, which when fully activated, is in harmonic vibration and connection with the rest of the Cosmos on a vast scale and frequency band.

We have to separately activate and clear each vertebra, however, by spinning the wheels within it, and whirling out all clogged particles, cleansing and purifying each vertebra in turn. This is done using sound chord frequencies.

As subsequent civilizations rose and fell, none of them were able to maintain life in the 7th dimensional state, as it had been in Elysium at the beginning of Creation.

When I do Earth energy clearing, I notice that rocks are strategically placed in the landscape. They will be placed in such a manner that the initiated,

*I found this ancient rock gong in Balgowan, KwaZulu-Natal. It has symbols carved all over it and it emits very high ringing tones when struck.*

like myself, will recognize them and read their energy. There are Guardians and Keepers here and one has to ask permission from them before one will be allowed to gain access and do the energy work. They sometimes have markings on them that indicate they are emitting sounds. When I stand on these sites, I automatically tune into these rocks and the frequencies they emit.

When I'm asked to open up energy centers or portals, the rocks will indicate the places where I must stand, and I will be directed to stand between them, or as happened in Kaapsehoop, lean against them.

I have found that these rocks then amplify the energy fields. They add their own frequency bands to the energy work I have to do.

Crystals are also great conduits of energies. In Ancient Times they had crystal healing chambers, which worked on the cosmic color rays, as well as on sound frequencies. The combination of the two has incredibly powerful higher healing implications

and literally fine-tunes the energy systems in the body.

When one adds the spinal column and its use as a tuning fork (more in the next chapter), then one is standing on the threshold of highly advanced technology.

At Keurbooms Beach, where I was literally sitting in a natural sound chamber, the following components were present: The water element; the crystalline rocks; the rock circle; and the energy vortex. All these combined in a massive, spiraling energy. This allowed me to shift dimensions very easily.

I have had vivid past life recall in which chanting, singing, the ringing of percussion instruments, and so on, all contributed towards the incredible raising of vibrational frequencies. I am reminded of the Bible and its account of the use of instruments and chanting in bringing down the walls of Jericho.

Perhaps when we seriously start looking at what an amazing wealth of information is right under our noses and all over the planet, we will understand that what we perceive to be dead, such as rocks, are actually alive! When we finally understand the deeper meaning and start reading the hidden energy fields and using them, our whole concept of technology and its applications will take quantum leaps! Mine certainly has, as I have learnt to 'read' these places and to utilize their energy.

As the later chapters will attest, this theory proved to be correct, especially in relation to the astounding energy work I was called upon to do.

*"At the highest levels of music (sound) little changes: It is always the same vehicle for voyages to another world. The same revelation of divine and cosmic laws, the same powerful tool for self-transformation, as it was in ancient and even in prehistoric times."* – Joscelyn Godwin[5]

*"The old stones seem so eternal and ancient, and sound is so transient and of the moment, that acoustics*

5    Joscelyn Godwin, *Music, Mysticism and Magic*, Arkana, 1987.

*seem at first an unlikely archaeological tool. Yet researchers are using sound in different ways, and new evidence of how people used sound in different ways, is beginning to emerge as a consequence."* – Paul Devereux[6].

Devereux discusses amazing experiments done all over the world with dolmans, standing stones, caves, and rock gongs in a book well worth reading.

During the course of my travels and research for this book, I suddenly found that I had the ability to tap directly into the Soul records at the Divine Source. These records are not the so-called Akashic Records, which are planetary bound, but the Soul records housed and transmitted via a gigantic Cosmic Super Consciousness Energy Field (like a Central Hall of Records, but pure conscious intelligent energy) at the Divine Source. Since this time, I have been able to give the Soul name, the Soul group name, the Galaxy of origin and the tonal chord of the Soul, to each individual who came for a reading. These have proven to be amazingly accurate and have certain keys and codes embedded within them that activate the Soul memory banks and bring about the higher activation of the Soul on all levels.

I have since been asked about the tonal chords by many people. I understand this as not just one note, such as "C", but a higher vibration of the said tone, in actual fact, the chord – thus a harmonic tone frequency.

I have come to understand that we have lost a lot of our hearing abilities. Dogs, for instance, can hear whistles that the human ear can't, as the sound is out of our frequency range. The same applies to the Cosmic tonal chords and harmonics. We have lost some of the most vital chords of Creation. Most of all, we have the lost the ability to hear them. The higher one's vibrational state rises, the more your inner hearing is tuned in and you are able to hear sounds that others cannot yet hear. This will be changing, however, as we all rise in frequency, and Planet Earth does, too!

Your Soul chord/tonal chord is directly linked to the pineal gland. When the soul chord is struck, then the vertebra that responds to this chord – remembering that it works from the coccyx upwards (up the ladder) – will spin faster, and certain energy and sound frequencies will be released. This sound frequency immediately activates a core chord within the pineal gland and opens a transmitter channel. This in turn activates the Soul memory banks and brings in the higher insights and wisdom inherent in the Soul, since its Divine birthing.

All these different chords or tones align to the Cosmic tonal chords and the music and harmony of the Cosmic spheres.

Interestingly, these higher healing methods also worked with the spinal cord energies of the planet. In realigning the cord, they also realigned the ability to tune into the Earth's spinal cord tuning rod, so to speak.

Due to solar flares, the reorganizing of the Cosmos and the Photon Energy Field returning to the planet in 2013, higher Cosmic frequency bands have been brought in, and the planet's spinal cord energies are being reawakened and realigned.

The pyramids on the Earth are starting to emit sound frequencies again. In fact, the Bosnian pyramids' sound has been recorded. They have been found to be tuned in with the Schumann resonances[7]. I believe that those pyramids are all tuned into the spinal column of the Earth itself.

The Cosmic energies are reigniting the Web of Light. With this realignment and the reawakening of

---

6   Paul Devereux, *Stone Age Soundtracks: The Acoustic Archaeology of Ancient Sites*, Vega, 2002.

7   The Schumann resonances (SR) are a set of spectrum peaks in the extremely low frequency (ELF) portion of the Earth's electromagnetic field spectrum. Schumann resonances are global electromagnetic resonances, generated and excited by lightning discharges in the cavity formed by the Earth's surface and the ionosphere. (*Wikipedia*)

the spinal cord energies of Earth, our own spinal cord energies will be affected. The new crystalline, or Light body, is forming around our spinal cords, and all of this is working towards bringing us into a higher state of consciousness and being.

In Richard Merrick's quest to try to understand why this harmonic science has been forgotten, he found that it had been severely suppressed. This culminated in the severe persecution, by the Roman Church, of the Gnostics[8], Dualists[9] and Cathars[10] who applied this knowledge. Indeed, the Ancients knew about harmonics and utilized it in their everyday life.

To me, the loss or suppression of such vital information was truly one of the most fundamental calamities of humanity, since it held within it essential and important clues to facilitate our reconnection with the greater Cosmic whole, and a disconnection from this flow has resulted in widespread destruction.

It was then that I finally understood that this knowledge was associated with the Divine Feminine, the Goddess, and that the High Priestesses of Elysium held the keys and codes for all of us. After Elysium's destruction, the Feminine has had to hold these keys and codes in the etheric, until we rise sufficiently in consciousness once again and embrace the intuitive harmonic balance back into our lives, and our everyday state of being. The spinal cord of the human body reflects that of the planet, and at birth each individual's spinal column is aligned to the Earth.

It serves as a massive planetary transmitter, and when fully activated, it not only raises the whole planet into a higher dimensional state, but into a much higher frequency band, making it a conduit for the massive vortex energies of the Earth to become fully activated and fully functional once more.

This in turn activates the dormant pyramids both on the surface of the planet, and underneath the land masses and the sea.

The African continent, whose surface sustains the main structure of the Earth's spinal cord, has held the secret keys and codes deep within her Soul for the rest of humanity. She has done this with immense compassion and love for the planet, and thus she is the one who is holding the light steady, until such a time as we are ready to receive this knowledge and apply it with balance, wisdom and love.

What is more, the spinal column of the Earth has within its structure 3 Rivers of Life running up and down forming the serpent energy, or kundalini energy, of the Earth.

It is no accident that southern Africa holds the gold, platinum and diamond deposits, for here all these rivers flow into one single, massive energy center in Antarctica. I will come to this in later chapters.

---

8   Gnosticism is a term categorizing a collection of ancient religions whose adherents shunned the material world – which they viewed as created by the demiurge – and embraced the spiritual world. (*On the complexity of Gnosticism*, see Larry W. Hurtado (2005). *Lord Jesus Christ: Devotion to Jesus in Earliest Christianity*. Wm. B. Eerdmans Publishing. pp. 519–561.)

9   Dualism is the position that mental phenomena are, in some respects, non-physical; or that the mind and body are not identical. (*Wikipedia*)

10   The Cathars called themselves Pure Ones, after the Goddess known as the Pure – their term for the Virgin Great Creator Mother Mari. (*Wikipedia*)

# CHAPTER 11

# Rock Gongs, Sound Chambers, Spirals and the Spinal Column of the Earth

Africa has seen peoples and civilizations come and go, yet she has written her deepest heart secrets in the rocks, in the landscape, and in the soul of the land itself.

Here in Africa, one finds huge faces in the rock – slumbering giants watching over the land. They tell of that first, Ancient time of Creation and settlement; the time when all was one. Some of these rock faces have huge stone gongs near them, and caves with holes or openings, where the Sun shines through at exactly midday, like vast sundials.

Some of these colossal faces have eyes that align perfectly with the star systems, through which one can observe the stars, the planets and the night sky.

Not only are there faces in stone, but there is also a giant footprint left in the stone near Mapukuzi in Mpumalanga[1] near the Swaziland border! According to measurements, the Giant to whom these footprints

*The Giant footprint in granite found in Mpumalanga, bordering Swaziland. It was first discovered in 1912 and is estimated to be at least 3.1 billion years old.*

belonged must have been about 12ft tall! What makes this footprint even more intriguing is that it is embedded in granite rock.

---

1     Mpumalanga is a province in eastern South Africa, bordering the nations of Swaziland and Mozambique. It embraces the southern half of Kruger National Park, a huge nature reserve with abundant wildlife. (*Wikipedia*)

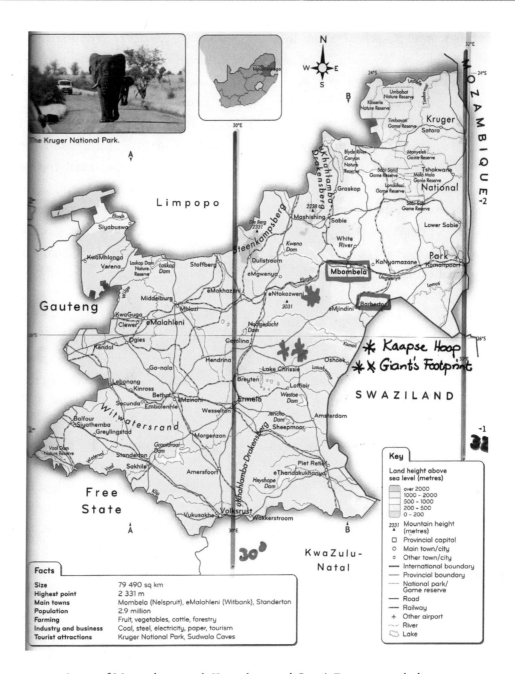

*A map of Mpumalanga with Kaapsehoop and Giant's Footprint marked on it.*

What interests me are the vast sound chambers and rock gongs found in this area. It is apparent that our local sound chambers around Table Mountain in the Cape were chosen precisely for their unique attributes that enhanced their sound quality and reverberation. There was nothing random about the choice of sites for these rock cavities or gongs.

Interestingly enough, according to the San, the Pleiades was the place of the 7 Sisters, who gave birth to humanity. Whenever they saw the Pleiades appear on the southern horizon of the night sky, there would be great rejoicing and festivities.

The San believed that the sky was covered by an intricate web of invisible cords (like the Web of Light), and that their ancestors could travel anywhere they liked along these cords. The amazing, magical and mystical relationship that the African people have with the stars is further enhanced by understanding that the stone gongs at sites such as Zimbabwe, the Khami Ruins[2], Robberg, KwaZulu-Natal and Plettenberg Bay (and many more all over Africa) served as a means to communicate with the Cosmic bodies and God. The sound and pitch of the gongs, according to Credo Mutwa, change according to the season and the temperature.

Most of the African tribes in whose territories these gongs are found consider them sacred and holy. Some will not share with anyone the internal lore attached to these gongs. Certain tribes only sound these gongs on special occasions, such as initiation rites.

In Nubia and elsewhere in Africa, the gongs are enormous. They must be played by more than one person at a time, and they sound like a whole super-vibrational orchestra! When I listened to just one of these rock gongs, I was instantly touched by a wave of vibrational electromagnetic waves washing over me. Thoughts of harmonics and the spinal column immediately came to mind.

*Could it be that these gongs were designed to be in tune with the spinal cord energies of the planet? If so, and if they are found all over the world, have we forgotten how to use them to tune into the higher sound frequencies of Earth itself?*

*When played, the gong at the Khami Ruins in Zimbabwe, for instance, emits a tone that is low and far-reaching. It is felt in the solar plexus area of the physical body, as much as it is heard through the ears. I found this extremely interesting, for according to my understanding and the spinal cord concept, Zimbabwe represents the solar plexus area of the world, and therefore the gongs in this location would be programmed to work with the solar plexus energies of the Earth and of humans!*

What if all the rock gongs in the world collectively formed one massive instrument, all transmitting the correct chords for the spinal cord energies of the planet? What if they had been put into place by the same people who first colonized the Earth?!

Pythagoras[3] introduced the concept of bringing music, sacred geometry and mathematics together. When we look at the Flower of Life[4], there are 12 centers around a column of 7 levels. The octave[5] has 7 sounds, but there are also 5 elevated tones. A fascinating study has been made of the Flower of Life and its geometrical patterns, which when turned into a numerical value, equals the sacred number 354. This number, when set as a musical chord[6], becomes F-sharp major.

Eric Rankin found in an amazing study of the Pythagorean principle of music, mathematics and sacred geometry that most ancient instruments were tuned to F-sharp major, and only in this recent era of human history has this Ancient musical tonal scale been forgotten. When the musical tone forms geometrical patterns, those patterns can be equated with the Flower of Life. Remarkably, this same F-sharp vibrates on all the geometrical shapes and on the sacred numbers, including the number 33. Joseph John Campbell[7], in his research into the mythical archetypes, identifies the number 354 as the most

---

2    Khami is a ruined city located 22km west of Bulawayo, Zimbabwe. It was once the capital of the Kingdom of Butua of the Torwa dynasty. (*Wikipedia*)

3    Pythagoras was an Ionian Greek philosopher and mathematician and has been credited as the founder of the movement called Pythagoreanism. (*Wikipedia*)

4    The Flower of Life is the modern name given to a geometrical figure composed of multiple evenly-spaced, overlapping circles that are arranged so that they form a flower-like pattern with a six-fold symmetry, like a hexagon. (*Wikipedia*)

5    In music, an octave is the interval between one musical pitch and another with half or double its frequency.

6    A chord is a group of (typically three or more) notes sounded together as a basis of harmony. (*Wikipedia*)

7    Joseph John Campbell (1904-1987) was an American mythologist, writer and lecturer, best known for his work in comparative mythology and comparative religion. (*Wikipedia*)

important number in the whole of Creation, and the one that recurs time and again.

Not only does the number 354 provide the central key, but other significant numbers, like 144 and 144 000 can be fitted into this system, too. Notably, 144 souls make up one single Soul group, and the whole unit of Cosmic Soul groupings, which all vibrate at the Divine frequencies, are made up of 144 000 Soul groups.

I've been told that the 33 chords correspond to the spinal cord of the planet. When fully activated, they 'turn up' the frequency band of the whole number, and anchor in the 999 vibration and frequency band.

Each vertebra emits a sound frequency, and the vortex energy spins to that tune, indisputably responding to the sound frequency of the chord. All sound vibrates: Musical instruments vibrate and strings vibrate.

During my own research, I often found myself being drawn to mythology. One of the mythical stories that truly fascinated me was related to the Languedoc region[8] of southern France (my past-life recall from there will be the content of my next book). In my search for the meaning of sound vibrations, I found that the whole Languedoc region (there are lots of ancient pyramids there originating from the time of Elysium) was associated with the Greek God Apollo.

According to legend, Hercules gave the Pyrenees, and especially Monsegur, to Apollo. Accompanying these was another gift – the lyre. There is also a fascinating link here to Pythagoras, who came from this area of the Pyrenees. Many of his own teachings came from a source even earlier than this.

The same Apollo is directly associated with the Oracle of Delphi[9]. Of course, Apollo was known to visit the site once a year, always with his lyre[10]! At some time after the fall of Rome, the people launched an attack on Delphi to steal its treasure. (That story, however, is for another time and place.) I found it fascinating that this was recorded by none other than Otto Rahn[11], who spent his life, backed by the Nazis, searching for the power spots on Earth that were connected with the vortex energies.

Could it be that the lyre and oracles are actually meant to work in conjunction with one another? This reminded me of the fact that the San shamans used sound to tune into the Earth's spinal cord energies, and to move into higher states of consciousness. The San shamans were as much oracles themselves. Interestingly, the temple in Delphi was also built next to water and quite probably directly on a vortex energy spot.

The fact that Apollo was given the lyre in this myth is of great significance to me, as the lyre symbolizes vibration. Its strings vibrate. I believe that this symbolism is a forgotten and hidden key. Could it be that the lyre (together with Tibetan gongs and rock gongs, etc.) were tuned to the spinal cord energies of the planet? So, when these instruments were used in certain rituals, they would enable those present to tune into the higher states of consciousness;

---

8     The province of Languedoc covers an area of approximately 42 700km² in the central part of southern France. (*Wikipedia*)

9     The Pythia, commonly known as the Oracle of Delphi, was the name of any priestess throughout the history of the Temple of Apollo at Delphi, which was located on the slopes of Mount Parnassus in Greece. (*Wikipedia*)

10    The lyre is a string instrument known for its use in Greek classical antiquity and later periods. It is similar in appearance to a small harp. (*Wikipedia*)

11    Otto Wilhelm Rahn was a German writer, medievalist, Ariosophist and an Obersturmführer of the Nazi Schutzstaffel. He researched grail mythos. (*Wikipedia*)

to levitate; and to use teleportation techniques? When the sound vibrated at a certain frequency, it would be amplified by the Earth's tuning fork (spinal cord sound frequency band), which then caused the transmitting energies to move up the human spinal cord, and so allow the body itself to vibrate at a much higher frequency.

To understand this, we have to go back to the spinal cord and the kundalini energies. If we look at the caduceus again, we can note the following:

The spinal cord forms the lightning rod, the 'magic wand', so to speak; with the kundalini energies moving up and down the rod, in a double-helix, or serpent-like form. If the spinal cord vibrates inside the rod, and the kundalini forms flames outside of this, the three together then become a mighty energy conduit and transmitter that emits incredibly high frequencies.

*This is the key to the ancient knowledge of the Tree of Life – the knowledge that when all of these are ignited (not just the kundalini, but the spinal cord energies, too), a monumental power conduit is formed that can actually be used to change form, shape-shift and transmit – teleport, levitate and make energies 'appear and disappear'.*

I believe that the magician's rod approximated the spinal cord rod and worked on the same base principles.

When all the spinal cord energies are fully activated, their frequency band becomes amplified and the 99 and 999 number sequences spring into motion. This allows the complete entity to tune into the Higher Cosmic Sound Frequency Fields of the Cosmic harmonic frequencies, which reverberate throughout the entire Cosmos.

When the Earth's spinal cord energies are once again fully reactivated, the planet's Light body, which will already be forming around its spinal cord (like our own), will be fully activated, and the full sound vibration will lift it into the 5th dimensional state. All life and life forms on Earth will simultaneously be elevated. That means our own spinal cord energies will then be fully activated and tuned-in to vibrate at that frequency band.

The entire harmonic sequence of Earth is changing, and will therefore be moving into a higher state of consciousness. We will all be following suit!

However, there is another field that forms around the physical body – the MerKaBah field – Metatron's Cube. When the spinal cord energies are fully activated, the spinal cord forms the nucleus in the middle, and kundalini energy winds itself up and down, clockwise and anti-clockwise. Then the MerKaBah vehicle further enhances and multiplies that energy.

The first Crystal Pyramid Temples were built in exactly the same manner – with one Crystal Pyramid pointing upwards and one downwards, with the apex of the pyramid representing the spinal cord. Consequently, they were massive energy conduits that emitted enormous energy and power.

All the Giza Pyramids initially had another crystalline counterpart, which has now been removed to etheric zones. If the spinal cord energies of the planet are activated once again, the Giza, Bosnian, and all the other pyramids will also be re-activated.

This activation will happen largely through the sounds of the spinal cord energies of the planet, and not by other means. This is because sound vibrates and activates the spinal cord frequencies, which in turn activate the MerKaBah field. This subsequently activates the Inner Earth's grids on which all the pyramids were built.

Currently, the human body is undergoing significant changes, as the new crystalline body is forming around the spinal cord. Our whole molecular structure is undergoing a momentous transformation.

I believe the first civilization and the first people who lived in Elysium had far lighter and more crystalline forms. Whatever they created, therefore, was also much lighter in form. Gigantic rocks and huge stones were used to build pyramids and to make sound chambers and rock gongs, and were crystalline in form before they, too, subsequently became much more solid due to the denser planetary frequencies.

As the planet's vibration and rotation slowed down, the whole process of creation also slowed down. Factually, the present is the time of reawakening: Not only of the African continent, but of the whole planet!

I believe that the spinal cord of the planet and the harmonic grid, together with the sound frequencies being emitted by the pyramids, plus those frequencies that are beyond our hearing range, inside the rock gongs and sound chambers, are now all being brought into a higher vibratory rate of beingness. Thus, soul memory banks within the Earth's grid, and our own soul memory banks are also being activated. This applies to the memory banks within our own DNA, and that of the planet, too.

As the planetary spinal cord energies are increasingly activated and fine-tuned, the harmonic resonance of the planet will rise. All these spinal cord energies, which move in harmonic frequencies, are being re-activated from here in the south-eastern parts of Africa, for the sacred keys and codes for all humankind are held here!

In a higher sense, this part of Africa is not only raising the frequency of the whole planet, but it is also activating the Crystal Pyramid Temples all over the globe and under the sea. Not all are in a solid form that can be seen or measured. Some of them are in pure crystalline etheric forms, which are high-energy conductors.

When I was standing at Adam's Calendar, I could clearly see one of those pyramids. It was huge and emitted pure, radiant, ethereal white light. There was one pyramid pointing upwards and one downwards, forming a massive energy field with Adam's Calendar. I believe that this is by no means the only such site in this part of Africa. Many of these sites have been disturbed or never recognized for what they are – mainly due to ignorance, or to people using these sacred stones for decoration (like I once saw in Nelspruit, for instance!)

My father once told me that the old Zulus would put their ears to the ground and could 'hear' horses' miles off, when no one else could yet see them in the distance.

Credo Mutwa says that these sound chambers and rock gongs were used to communicate with other people from distant lands, and even across oceans.

I am convinced that it is time for someone to make an effort to map all the rock gongs and sound chambers in the world. I would not be at all surprised if they all tuned into the spinal cord sound frequencies of the planet – together forming one massive chord – the chord of the Earth itself!

It is no accident that the Aboriginal tribes refer to the energy lines as song lines. They were indeed filled with songs (chords) of each vertebrae of sound. The didgeridoo, an Aboriginal musical instrument, and the Ancient Ones were tuned into the vertebrae and vortex energy of Uluru. This used to be part of the African continent.

These illuminations all prepared me perfectly for the unfolding of the next part of my story. This led me to work directly with, and accelerate the opening of, the spinal column of Earth.

# CHAPTER 12

# The 7$^{th}$ Galaxy of the 7$^{th}$ Central Sun, the 12 Central Suns and the Sun Discs

Within the vastness of the Omniverse (*Das All* in German), there are 12 Master Central Suns. Each Central Sun holds intelligence and has galaxies around it in ever spiraling motion, and contains within it all knowledge. Each specializes in its own field, and Earth and the Andromedan and Milky Way Galaxy orbit around the 7$^{th}$ Central Sun.

During the Wars of the Heavens, parts of the Andromedan, Lyrian and Milky Way Galaxies were blown up. The Earth and the Milky Way Galaxy were thrown out of the orbit of the 7$^{th}$ Central Sun. Consequently, one of the planets became our present Sun. The Milky Way Galaxy and the Andromedan Galaxy are currently merging again, and therefore the new children born originate from the 7$^{th}$ Galaxy of the 7$^{th}$ Central Sun, with a new higher crystalline form.

The 7$^{th}$ Temple of the 7$^{th}$ Galaxy of the 7$^{th}$ Central Sun has appeared time and time again to me while retrieving information regarding the Crystal Pyramid Temples and the Earth's spinal column.

This is connected to my questions regarding the Tree of Life and why it was removed from Humanity after the Fall of Eden. I was repeatedly guided back to the Tree of Life, its basic concepts, and the hidden order behind it. Every time, I was reminded of the code 777 and the 7$^{th}$ Temple of the 7$^{th}$ Galaxy of the 7$^{th}$ Central Sun. Why?

I was led back to Egypt, into the hidden chambers of the Sphinx, and taken into a vast hall. Before entering this hall with Thoth and Isis, who were accompanying me into the inner planes, I stood in the foyer.

The walls were beautifully decorated with Egyptian art in the form of murals, and the floor had been inlaid with lapis lazuli. There were massive, golden doors, with etchings of more of these symbols and scenes.

Stepping into the hall, I saw the 12 Crystal Skulls rising, and then in front of me, a huge round table appeared. A Golden Crystal Skull dislodged itself from the circle of skulls. The crown opened and then reverted to looking like a skull cap.

I was taken to see first the Andromedan and

*Akhenaten worshipping the Sun God Ra: Note that it comes in the form of a Sun Disc.*

all the keys and codes for humanity, as they worked with the 7th dimensional state of being. Therefore, everything connected with these structures: The Creations, information, technology, and everything else, is stored within this 7th Central Sun. The 7th Galaxy of this Sun is where the first Sun Temples on the Earth were tuned to, including the spinal column of Planet Earth, the Rivers of Life, and the Tree of Life.

> This is a very important concept to grasp, for the key to tapping into the pyramid energy grids of the planet relates to this 7th Central Sun and the energy fields it holds and emits. It retains the central keys and codes to the unlocking and unfolding of the New Golden Age for humanity, and therefore also for the original Garden of Eden, Elysium. In fact, it holds the keys and codes to the reactivation of all the pyramids on the planet, on both land and in the sea.

Milky Way Galaxies, and then back to the very beginning when Earth was created! I was shown that these Galaxies had once been one and the same, as they belonged to the 7th Central Sun. The 3rd that formed a part of these two galaxies was the 7th Galaxy of the 7th Central Sun.

What astounded me was that when shown the 7th Galaxy in its expanded form, which now included the Andromeda and Milky Way Galaxy, the similarities between the two and the Elysium Kingdom were extraordinary! It was like stepping into the same milieu that had originally existed on Earth when she was first created, and the first settlements were established. The resemblances were uncanny.

Here I was reintroduced to Ra, the same Ra whom the Egyptians referred to as the Sun God, and to whom most Mystery Schools referred to in the Ancient Times. For, in truth, Ra and the 7th Sun held

The 7th Central Sun also holds the keys and codes, and Sun Disc codes of the Fires of Illumination for the 7th dimensional state, and therefore that of the 7th Central Sun Octave of Being in the evolutionary Cosmic scale. This means that because Earth was first created for the 7th dimensional state, everything created, plus those living inside and upon the Earth, were all programmed, created, and therefore tuned into, the 7th Central Cosmic Sun.

I will come to the Sun Discs in due course, but first we must understand the immense significance of this.

*"Interestingly, the Master Number 7 in numerology pertains to this: Seven lifts us to a fresh level of understanding, searching for completion; with seven, the natural begins to return to the spiritual, as the spiral of six winds towards its Source. There are seven days of*

*the week; seven ages of Man; Seven notes in the musical scale; and seven colors in the visible spectrum.*[1]

The pattern of the 7 as a Master Number is very much apparent in the Ancient mystical teachings of the Hermetics, and the Mystery School[2] teachings.

*"Seven is also associated with the Moon, because seven days are approximately one quarter of the Moon's cycle: From New Moon back to new again. The Moon has long been linked to magic, for intuition is often felt most powerfully when the Moon is full. So, seven is a magical number relating to the changes we may make in the world around us through the powers of our will and imagination.*

*"Seven looks beyond this world."* – Teresa Moorey[3]

*"Seven symbolizes wholeness in many cultures, being the union of Divinity (three) and material Earth (four); in Hindu, Muslim, and Judeo-Christian scriptures, a seventh aspect confers completeness and perfection on a group of six. In Ancient Egypt, seven symbolized Eternal Life, and to American Indians, seven symbolizes the Dream of Life."*[4]

So held within human sub-conscious memory banks, the number 7 has been remembered as a number that brings illumination to us – which is actually a memory of its original association with the 7th Central Sun.

The Ra energy is that of the 7th Central Sun, and consequently was worshipped in Egypt, because their collective memory banks and inherited wisdom from Atlantis related to this Central Sun, and the 7th Galaxy.

## JOURNAL ENTRY

After I had activated the Temple of the Sun and the Temple of the Moon as one single energy grid on the spinal column of the Earth, it was then indicated to me that these two temples held that spiritual enclave; the central opening up of the Fires of Illumination within the Earth's spinal column. Indeed, this would prove to be correct in the subsequent energy work I did. This Ra energy, as remembered by the Egyptians, stems from the 7th Galaxy and is held in the Temple.

I was taken to this monumental Temple of the 7th Galaxy of the 7th Central Sun. There in the center, suspended in mid-air, was a splendid, rotating Sun Disc! It was spinning and humming, with a vast center of pure liquid white-gold. It was pulsating and alive, and was a massive energy center – a hub. Human language is so primitive and limited, and sometimes I cannot find words to express myself, but it was like a gargantuan, intelligent and very powerful energy force field. It was alive and conscious! It literally seemed as if it was spitting fire from deep within it – with an explosive, fiery energy that reminded me of the Sun. As far as this relates to the Tree of Life, I believe that the spinal column of the Earth is the Tree of Life. So, it contains within its 33 vertebrae all the knowledge, technology and the Super Consciousness Energy Fields, for they are all linked.

The pyramids were linked to the spinal cord by a diamond-shaped, Crystalline Energy Grid, which is unrelated to the Web of Light, or the so-called ley line

---

1    *Numerology Bible*, Teresa Moorey, Godshield Book, 2012

2    Hermetics, and the Mystery School: This is an ancient school with closely-held wisdom and teachings that have been preserved for the benefit of humanity. These teachings are passed down through the oral tradition, from teacher to student, in an unbroken lineage of physical initiation. (*Wikipedia*)

3    *Numerology Bible*, Teresa Moorey, Godshield Book, 2012

4    *Signs and Symbols*, Dorling Kindersley, 2008

*My sketch of the Temple of the Moon.*

grids around the planet. They were only created at the time of Atlantis, when the Earth had already fallen into the 5th dimensional state, as Lemuria and Mu were still linked to the old system. However, as Lemuria fell, the Atlanteans could not access the higher dimensional energy fields, and they lacked the knowledge to repair grids, so they subsequently invented their own one. By that time, so many of the old land masses had sunk under the sea and the Pyramid Grid had been deactivated, so the Atlanteans could no longer access the energies.

From that moment onwards, I often found that transmissions would be given through this Ra energy, directly from the 7th Temple of the 7th Galaxy of the 7th Central Sun.

Ra, the Sun God of Egypt, was what the Egyptians remembered as the Fires of Illumination of the 7th Central Sun, and was consequently worshipped as Ra.

The 7th Central Sun is pure fire energy. It is far more powerful than any other Sun, and it holds the keys and codes for the Fires of Illumination. This is what illuminates the higher heart and higher mind, and shifts into the spinal column when the soul aspect, the heart and mind energies, and all the energy centers of the planet and humans work as One single unit.

Therefore, those who are truly illuminated, will express these Fires of Illumination from within, and radiate forth like the Central Sun. This is when the Ra fires burn within the soul, and the Fires of Illumination are fully present, aware and conscious.

The Soul group, the Illumined Ones, stem from this Master Central Sun. This is amplified in the 9th and 12th Central Suns in the evolutionary cosmic scale.

Each Central Sun holds within itself certain keys and codes, as contained within the Divine Heart, Mind, and Soul. Therefore, each Central Sun is programmed to emit its own form of interdimensional state. So, each has been masterfully designed or created to hold all the knowledge; technology; records; keys and codes; the codexes; the Divine Blueprints; and the patterns or designs of everything that fall under its jurisdiction, or sphere of influence.

Again, it is difficult to find the correct words, but the gist of this is that there exists one massive, conscious, vast, intelligent, Super Consciousness Energy Field, which emits the keys and codes of Illumination, and therefore the Fires of Illumination.

Thus, in the beginning, Planet Earth and the Milky Way Galaxy were attached to the 7th Central Sun, and all of its keys and codes of activation, and of Illumination.

Transmission received and relayed exactly as received from RA-U-HU:

*"I am the 7th Ray of the 7th Galaxy of the 7th Central Sun. Within my rays the 7th Temple of the 7th Sun emits vast rays of Glorious Enlightenment. All who come to the temple are activated into the Higher States of Illumined Consciousness.*

*At this time, massive and intense rays of Cosmic energies are being beamed down from the 7th Central Sun. I am the 7th Master Ray of Illumination, and all who encounter me on Planet Earth will find that they have been initiated and illuminated with the blinding light of this Great Cosmic Sun, the All-knowing Fire, for I epitomize the All-seeing Eye.*

*At the very beginning of life here, there were massive Crystal Pyramid Temples raised, in order to tune into the 7th Central Sun and my rays. Over time, people forgot this, as they started worshipping mortals as Gods and Goddesses, and forgot that all is, in essence, a vibration; has a frequency and is energy. They forgot that Light and Love and the Fires of Enlightenment travel where they will, and those without this are lost in the darkness of their own making.*

*It is vital to remember the enshrined code within each Temple of the Sun. The Code is 777, and those who work with sacred geometry and sacred codes should try to access and crack this code. For the next phase of*

*Cosmic evolution is happening now on your planet, and I urge you to remember what the Ancients wanted you to remember and apply at this momentous time.*

*We are greatly disturbed that some souls on your planet have not woken up. They have been so blinded by the false illusions – that which 'appears' as real; that they cannot distinguish the wheat from the chaff.*

*Embrace the 7th Central Sun. It has always been the Central Core Sun of your Illumination; your very existence on Planet Earth. Why have you forgotten this? Even the name of one of your weekdays is pointing to this: Sunday.*

*Instead of resisting and fearing the changes, the Illumination, embrace it! Instead of being fearful and blaming others, start looking within. Your third eyes are opening, as well as your inner hearing; the brain capacity is being increased; your crystalline bodies are being activated; and the portals are opening up!*

*Go within! Open your heart centers, and then reconnect with the heart/mind, and not the other way around. For the Sun of Illumination works the heart fires, the Fires of Illumination, and the energy flows through the heart energies, the loving fires, the language and frequencies of the heart, as it connects directly to the Soul.*

*The minds of people are filled with clutter and false programming: The clutter of useless facts that cannot assist the main body of humanity to move up the evolutionary scale and return to the Golden Age of Illumination."*

This was transmitted though me, and comprehension started to dawn that what we truly lost in the process of falling from the 7th dimensional state into the 3rd was those Fires of Illumination and the ultimate state of being.

We lost that essence; the fire; the blood-flow; the vital force; that which truly is the creative life-flow of all-knowing Illumination. We lost the knowledge of good and evil, as the Bible says – but in a different form than is normally understood: The inner workings of the Tree of Life, and that which illuminated it.

There is a great and ongoing connection now with the great Central Suns and the 12 Master Galaxies relating to them; all of which formed part of the original Creation.

Therefore, there is a steady awakening of very ancient energy fields that hold within themselves immense encodements and glyphic awakening keys for humanity; as it has been ordained by the Intergalactic Federation, to come to pass at this time of massive shifts on the Earth and in the Milky Way Galaxy.

The Ancients had immense knowledge of energies and energy fields, which were then utilized in ways that we have forgotten about. This is high technology, and it worked on a different dimensional scale from what we have now become accustomed to. All our modern technology cannot even begin to compete with this type of advanced knowledge. With the planetary shifts, as we develop more and more conscious awareness, we will be given access to this knowledge – when we are ready to receive it without abusing its powers.

A lot of people talk about the Grid, ley lines, or Web of Light. These were laid down at the time of Atlantis, and therefore are much younger than the original energy grids and fields laid down when the Earth was created. So, the grid is there, yes, and those dowsing can tap into that energy grid quite easily, which mostly aligns with the Moon and Sun. But, all forget a third component: The Sun Discs, which the Ancients used. Huge, golden ones were placed in their temples to remind them of the Central Suns.

The Sun Discs did not incorporate the 12 signs of the zodiac, but rather the 12 original Central Suns, as each of these Central Suns holds a certain key encodement to the higher states of Enlightenment, and thus Cosmic Consciousness. They all slot into one single Central Sun Super Consciousness Energy Field, of which, therefore, the numbers 12 and 13 always play a central role in unlocking.

Many humans are only aware of one single Central Sun, but you cannot reach the higher states of evolutionary enlightenment, or Super Consciousness, without an understanding of the 12 Master Central Suns. They hold the keys and codes to All of Creation: All that is held, created and operational within the Central Suns.

The Ancients knew the Sun Discs were not there as adornment or for ceremonial purposes. They were actually giant computers that tapped into the vast knowledge and Super Consciousness Energy Fields of the Great Central Suns. Their inner workings were like that of a clock. As each central spoke clicked, mechanisms would open a portal to a certain energy field, as held within the disc. This would unlock the knowledge contained therein.

There are two forms of Sun Discs: There are the massive ones, like the one I described from the 7th Temple of the 7th Galaxy of the 7th Central Sun. This was one huge, intelligent energy field, and it incorporated knowledge from the whole Cosmos.

On Earth, at the time of Elysium, these were housed in the Temples of the Central Suns. You will find a description of one that I had to reactivate later in this book. These gigantic Sun Discs worked on the principle of rotating clockworks, with internal slots where smaller Sun Discs were kept. These could be detached from the major ones. They then served as smaller field information discs.

The keys and codes to access these are ingrained, or programmed, into some souls who have worked with them before and are now here to return the Fires of Illumination to the planet.

Yet, these can only be accessed if one is ready to retrieve the information and able to easily shift into higher dimensional states, for they are held in the 7th dimension, or octave of consciousness, as pertains to that of the 7th Central Sun.

The nearest description I can use is a DVD disc, but they were much larger and rotated at immense speed. They would hover over your head and then download information you required or wanted to retrieve directly into your higher heart/mind.

I believe that this is what the medieval artists later

depicted by painting halos around the heads of saints, for indeed the Sun Discs do that. They work directly with the all-seeing Eye of Horus, and therefore your higher mind and heart. Later versions of these, which have been retrieved from some ancient sites, are much older and more primitive prototypes that preserved the general shape and outlay of the first Sun Discs, or those still found in the 7th Temple.

The Central Suns are great powerhouses of immense significance. Unless you learn to access their knowledge, you cannot move up into certain higher evolutionary dimensional states. There are conscious beings in other Galaxies and star systems who are so highly advanced that, by comparison, we are a very simple or primitive species.

The meaning and purpose of the Central Suns will be increasingly understood as we advance in consciousness. The shift is now escalating.

However, unless you are open and ready for such information, you will not gain access to it. It is mostly true that those who think they know, do not know; for they are blind to that which underlies the Cosmic science and the real foundation of knowledge, which is in a totally different form than any human being would look for.

The 7th Temple
Of the 7th Sun
The 7th Galaxy
Shone lustrous, gloriously...
And there within
Its vast immortal halls
I stood
Bejewelled, bedecked
In splendor, gloriously...
The halls were echoing
As chorus upon chorus rose
And sang their songs to me:
"Arise and shine, O Shining One!"
Then, there, in all your splendor stood
You, my Beloved One....
And as I saw you
I was filled
With Love
That spans all that ever
Was and is
and will be forever more...
For one moment silence reigned,
As eyes met eyes
Heart met heart
Spirit met spirit
Soul met soul....
The Immortal Masters stood
As if rooted to the spot...
And then all celebrants
Burst into splendid songs
And echoed through the halls
"Arise and shine,
Arise and shine
O Immortal Ones!"
And there we knelt,
United, still as ONE!
The Keepers of Keys!

– **Judith Kusel, 25 March, 2011**

# PART 3

# CAPE POINT, AUSTRALIA, MAURITIUS, REUNION AND ANTARCTICA

# CHAPTER 13

# Hermanus and Cape Point

## More puzzles emerge… and surprising Australian links

My guided journey has taken me on paths I never could have foreseen. I was urged to go to Hermanus[1] in September 2014 and was hoping to discover how this would connect to energy lines in Antarctica. I had a deep longing to weave all of this together to complete my work.

I found Hermanus much changed since my last visit 10 years before, and my greatest disappointment was the fact that the cliffs, which had lent their charm to this village that was now a sprawling seaside town, had been cemented up, and a stone wall had been constructed. This disrupted the atmosphere of natural, pure energy, and may have added to the tourist hub, but otherwise, it did nothing for the area. I had given myself too short a time there, however,

for I also wanted to go on to Simon's Town, as I had clearly been called to the False Bay area.

Consequently, I later returned to Hermanus. I first drove around in the spectacular Hemel-en-Aarde winelands, with its magnificent mountains and breathtaking views, but my search was initially unproductive. In the late afternoon, following my inner promptings to drive through the village, my attention was drawn to the sign: "Sinker Bay". I took a right turn and, to my utter delight, discovered a nature reserve on the cliffs.

I was thrilled, for as I climbed out of my car, passing the security guards and following the path, the first thing that grabbed my attention was the Sentinel rocks. When these rocks appear, I always

---

1    Hermanus is a town on the southern coast of the Western Cape Province of South Africa. It is famous for southern right whale watching during the winter and spring. (*Wikipedia*)

*Hermanus, where I found another piece of the giant jigsaw puzzle.*

*Sinker Bay, Hermanus.*

*The rocks on the cliffs looked like they were sculpted by a Master hand and reminded me of the proverbial Ark.*

*In the center – the face of one of the Guardians. If you look carefully you will find another face between the reddish standing stones behind it.*

know that they mark some sacred place, and an Earth energy center. When that happens, I immediately summon the Guardians and Keepers of such places and ask their permission to enter, lest I offend them, for I know that I'm standing on sacred ground.

These custodians work on different dimensional levels. Normal tourists would only have a 3-D perception and would sit on the beach sunning themselves, or watching the whales. Whereas those who travel interdimensionally, such as I do, would instantly understand the clear signs that were carefully assembled and lined up there on the rocks. Nothing is just by accident: All is by grand design.

The rocks on the cliffs appeared to have been sculpted by a Master hand, and they reminded me of the proverbial Ark. There were animal's heads in all shapes and sizes, but the elephants seemed to dominate the surroundings.

As I walked along the cliff path, I was compelled

*The portal: I knew that if I stepped between these two gatekeepers, I would be teleported straight to Antarctica.*

time and again to linger and take photographs. The energy here was so much stronger than in the rest of Hermanus, and I was reading the intense energy lines and noticing the Sentinels along the way. I felt that this place somehow linked up the dolphins and whales, and furthermore, it was also a link to Antarctica. I just did not know how.

As the path led into a little bay and sloped down, there were even more of these rocks there. As I stepped around a corner, there it was! It mirrored the two portal stones in Kaapsehoop to the tee: One was upright and the other looked like a sphinx, with a gateway between the two. I knew that had I stepped into the middle of those two rocks, I would have been teleported to Antarctica!

It was so strange, for there were people all around me, sitting on the look-out benches overlooking the bay. Meanwhile, I was excitedly photographing the rocks in the sea and elsewhere, carefully noting the

*Dragon-shaped rocks.*

*The proverbial Ark in animal-sculptured rocks. I have never seen anything like this anywhere before. This marks the direct link between South Africa and Antarctica.*

*A whale head directly in line with the energy lines to Antarctica.*

alignments of the Sentinel rocks, while tuning into the dolphins and whales, and knowing that here was a gateway to Antarctica.

Here is my journal entry for that day:

## JOURNAL ENTRY

**April 4, 2014**

**Antarctic connection – Hermanus**

I found my connection to Antarctica today, here in Hermanus….

There was a path I could follow through a nature reserve and, to my utter surprise, there were rocks and Sentinels all over the place, with sheer cliffs, rock faces, as well as two portals where Horus and Isis stones could be found, with more rock circles.

*The crouching lioness for the other half of the portal.*

I was then told that this formed part of **Antarctica and that it linked directly to the pyramids there. I knew I stood on sacred ground.**

I instinctively felt that this was where the whales gave birth, as they would be the Keepers, or Key Keepers, of this place, and would collectively link to Ancient times and to Elysium.

Sure enough, I received confirmation that this was correct, and that as the Antarctic continent was ripped away and the land masses sank, the location of the pyramids that I had found on Google Earth would correspond with my findings here, as well as with the pyramids that the Americans have discovered and are keeping under wraps in Antarctica.

*The Guardian and Keeper is Ancient.*

Here in Sinker Bay, the Sentinel rocks were everywhere, and all in interesting animal forms, like elephants! (The elephant, whale and dolphin link was visible all over. Intriguingly, it reminded me of a phenomenon recorded by Lyall Watson[2] in his book *Elephantom*, about the last elephant matriarch of the Knysna Forest that communicated with a whale offshore via sonic sounds on the Kranshoek Beach.)

I was interested to notice that these forms were concentrated in that specific area. (Maybe there were more places like this, but with Hermanus becoming increasingly populated, many of the pristine areas have been destroyed.)

The Sentinels, then, acted as Guardians of the inner portals of Elysium. Yet, while Nature's Valley, Keurbooms and Plettenberg Bay had been directly affected by the land mass tearing off, this part belonged to Antarctica and was ripped off later to form the Antarctic continent.

**This, then, was the confirmation that I would find the connection to Antarctica, and I had done it!**

---

I had to return home after that trip, and only made it to Simon's Town much later in the year. It was here that I found my second energy line link to Antarctica.

Before leaving for Simon's Town, I was led to the best accommodation that would be directly in line with the energy lines that I needed to connect to in Antarctica.

I arrived in Simon's Town fairly late. It was dark, and at first I had trouble finding my hotel. The next morning, I went to my car and, to my utter surprise, found some towering boulders right there on the mountainside looming above me. The place where I was staying was situated on the slope. It was the last property before the reserve began.

As I looked further up, there stood my Sentinel rocks in a perfect half-circle. I excitedly ran for my camera and tried to get a better view of these massive rocks.

I examined the remaining mountainside and the rocks and boulders strewn there, apparently randomly to the uninitiated, but not to me. I started tuning into them and realized that they were pure crystalline, and therefore granite.

It was as if these rocks were singing, or humming, and the energy from them was something beautifully profound. I then saw the faces of the Guardians and Keepers etched in the rocks. I instantaneously connected with them. Then, from this collection of rocks, the Ancient Ones stepped forward to welcome me. It felt like being reunited with old friends, and I knew they would show me the way.

Later, while walking in the nature reserve within the same private estate, I was able to view the whole of the False Bay area. I was promptly shown the Sentinel rocks in the sea, and how this entire area had been carefully planned to facilitate the energy movement of the Crystalline Grids as one single force. Yet, something seemed to be missing, or felt out of alignment, and the Keepers and Guardians confirmed this as they directed me onwards to Cape Point.

As I followed my nose (literally), I became intensely aware that with the tearing off of the land mass, this whole area had simultaneously suffered a stupendous catastrophe.

Driving towards Noordhoek[3] confirmed that for me, and in some locations in the Cape Point Nature Reserve the rocks were scattered higgledy-piggledy, as if this area had also been subjected to an enormous explosion at some time in the ancient past. Indeed, in the Noordhoek area, I felt there

---

2    Lyall Watson was a South African botanist, zoologist, biologist, anthropologist and ethologist. (*Wikipedia*)

3    Noordhoek is a suburb of Cape Town, located below Chapman's Peak on the west coast of the Cape Peninsula, approximately 35km to the south of the city itself. (*Wikipedia*)

*There, right above me, massive perfectly-hewn rocks, indicating the sacredness of this place. Look at the craftsmanship involved.*

*Note the angle of the ankh-shaped rocks in the middle, and the keyhole rocks at the back. The rest of the rocks further up the slope were totally different.*

*Note the angle of the ankh-shaped rocks in the middle, and the keyhole rocks at the back. The rest of the rocks further up the slope were totally different.*

*Massive boulders on the same mountainside were sheer quartz. I examined them and the energy emitted from them was immensely powerful and intense.*

*This gigantic rock is perfectly shaped and hewn.*

*One of the Sentinel points that is in direct alignment with the boulders in False Bay and Antarctica.*

*Up the slope, in direct alignment, in the form of a pyramid, is this great face of the giant Sentinel and Guardian*

*Again, perfect alignment and a precision cut.*

were remains of gigantic buildings, and that many of these remaining rocks must have been buildings at some stage, when this area was still attached to the Antarctic continent.

Driving into the Cape Point Nature Reserve, I was now totally honed in to the landscape. I stopped at Boulders Beach, and instantly noted the stone circles in the sea, and that certain Sentinel rocks were placed so that the Sentinels on the mountain behind me, and those in the sea, were aligned to one single energy grid.

Guided now by the Guardians and Keepers, I decided to turn left into the back roads, and entered a restricted area.

When I had previously been to Cape Point, I had concentrated more on the Atlantic side of the nature reserve, and had found one, single, rocky outcrop there with immensely high energies, which had reminded me of the pyramid energy. I had even thought that it might have been the remains of a pyramid. There were gargantuan blocks there, with similarities reminiscent of those found at the Incan ruins. (I will come back to this later.)

As I was driving along, the first thing I became aware of was the spectacular beauty of the three Sentinel mountains guarding the bay. They looked like they were three sisters, and they were emitting very strong high-voltage energy.

*Boulders Beach reflects the slope above. The boulders are in perfect alignment with the energy lines to Antarctica. Indeed, they too are perfectly shaped and hewn.*

*False Bay from Cape Point Nature Reserve. There stand the 'three sisters' as silent watchers and Keepers, guarding the energy lines to Antarctica.*

I climbed out of my car and stood overlooking the bay, feeling the unique energy all around me. There was massive and pure energy coming from this part of the bay, and the 'three sisters' were acting as both Sentinels and Guardians. They were the ones holding the keys and codes to Antarctica.

Much later, I would fly into Cape Town, and I would see that this indeed was true. From that aerial view, I could clearly read the energy lines and confirm that what I had found there on land was correct.

I had strong electromagnetic energy coursing up and down my body, as it usually does when standing on a very high-energy spot. In this case, in some of those spots where I had been nudged to stop and walk around, I had nearly taken off, for there are some hidden Sentinel rocks there, which all point towards this massive energy grid.

Furthermore, it was here that I found the hidden entrances to the underground tunnel systems, and to Agartha. They are carefully concealed from view, and only those who have been initiated will be able to find them. Others will not, as they are unable to tune into that frequency band.

*Another view of the three sisters: Silent watchers and Guardians. The energy there is immensely high and mystical. It is indeed a sacred place.*

I was smiling when I arrived at the Diaz Cross[4] and went down into the bay. I stopped a bit further up, as there were too many cars and tourists below. I had tears of joy running down my cheeks! I clearly saw the 'three sisters' holding the energy in perfect alignment with the Cape Point. It formed a triangular energy grid system that, in turn, moved into a type of vortex energy and kept that area sacred and in higher alignment.

Indeed, the whole False Bay area is holy ground, but this part of it, at least, has been preserved. It, therefore, still holds its sacred energy.

It is not by chance that the whales travel here from Antarctica. I got the message clearly from the

---

4 The Portuguese government erected two navigational beacons at Cape Point: The Dias Cross and Da Gama Cross, to commemorate Vasco da Gama and Bartolomeu Dias as the first explorers to reach the Cape. When lined up, the crosses point to Whittle Rock, a large, permanently submerged shipping hazard in False Bay. (www.plak.co.za)

*A Sentinel rock stands between the fynbos, guarding the Atlantic side of Cape Point.*

*The caves and hidden entrances to the tunnel systems of Agartha.*

*Look familiar? How many of these are found all over Europe?*

*A closer view of the caves. Look at the amazing rock sculptures!*

whales and dolphins that they had been swimming in these circles for many millions of years, as their original aquatic habitat had been closed off, so they could no longer swim as they had in ancient times.

Later that day, driving along the entire peninsula and then up Chapman's Peak Drive, and to Hout Bay, I had the distinct impression that Kommetjie[5] held pyramid energies, too, which enhanced the energies

---

5   Kommetjie lies about halfway down the west coast of the Cape Peninsula, at the southern end of the long, wide beach that runs northwards towards Chapman's Peak and Noordhoek.

*The view from the Diaz Cross, looking out towards Cape Point.*

*False Bay guards the secret Crystalline Grid lines to Antarctica.*

of the False Bay area. As they are all in alignment, that whole area forms one massive energy grid. The sea water also amplifies the energy, thus reinforcing the sacredness of the portal in Table Mountain.

It so happened that the establishment where I was staying had some unexpected guests. The owner of the place was present the next morning, along with his girlfriend. He introduced himself. Obviously, the man was waiting for me to be impressed upon hearing his name, but I rewarded him with a blank look! He mentioned that he was the owner, and that he belonged to the Myburgh family, and that he was

in the real estate business. The penny then started to drop, as this family more or less 'rules' the Cape! This man was a multimillionaire.

He asked me why I was there, and I told him. The topic of my book came up, and he grew very interested. When told that his establishment was in a sacred place, and that I hoped he would not sell the mountain, he found that very amusing!

He then, surprisingly, confirmed all the channeled information I had been given about this mountain, the bay and the fact that it was sacred! He knew!

He told me he had met Credo Mutwa in Basel,

Switzerland (of all places), a few years before, and that Credo had told him how sacred False Bay[6] was – especially these mountains – and that he must protect and care for this area. It was one of the most holy places on Earth!

He went on to ask me to visit Zanzibar, as he had bought a substantial chunk of the island to develop. He was most interested in my family connection to Zanzibar, and then repeated his request that I visit. Well, that is for another time. I am most grateful to this gentleman for confirming my own findings in such a way!

It was most intriguing when a geologist friend mentioned that the whole of the Cape Peninsula and Table Mountain used to be like an island, and that the sea had run through the whole Cape Flats[7]

and then into the Malmesbury[8] area. That would be one reason, she said, that the whales and dolphins currently feel blocked off. However, this is just an aside, for it corresponds with what I already have written about the Karoo, and what I read in the landscape there. There certainly were islands here in the very beginning, surrounded by sea. I also found information on Robben Island, in which geologists stated that land had been torn off from Cape Town, and the island formed a part of this fragmented land mass.

When I drove home from Simon's Town later that week, it was with the clear impression that I had to somehow open the energy lines to Antarctica. Then the island of Madagascar came to mind. But, how to get there?

---

6   False Bay is a body of water defined by Cape Hangklip and the Cape Peninsula in the extreme south-west of South Africa. (*Wikipedia*)

7   The Cape Flats is an expansive, low-lying, flat area situated to the south-east of the central business district of Cape Town. To many people in Cape Town, the area is known simply as "The Flats". (*Wikipedia*)

8   Malmesbury is a town about 65km north of Cape Town. (*Wikipedia*)

*The three faces of the Guardians of Cape Point.*

# CHAPTER 14

# The Australian Crystal Pyramid Link

In the meantime, there was a collective unfolding of related events. One of these was highly significant and took place just before I left for Cape Town and Hermanus. This was pivotal, as I now comprehended just how Australia linked up with the Temple of the Sun in Zimbabwe, and with this part of southern Africa.

About a year or two before this happened, I drew the energy lines I was 'reading' on to a map of Australia. These are the same as song lines the Aborigines follow, yet what I was drawing was even more ancient. These energy lines linked directly to Elysium, as Australia had once belonged to the self-same continent: The western part of Australia fitting into south-eastern Africa.

As I was drawing, this massive creature 'emerged', and I subsequently also started tuning into the underground tunnel system, linking everything together via the spinal column of this creature.

What is more, I found that Uluru is indeed a remnant of a massive ochre-red pyramid, for it anchored in the Red Cosmic Ray. Then I began identifying 7 pyramids, which are spread over the whole length of this creature!

Remarkably, I was shown an immense energy obstructing the creature's eye, where I had drawn it in on the map. I felt an extremely vile energy there, and alerted Light workers I knew in Australia to please send in energies to clear whatever was looming there. If not cleared, massive earthquakes would occur in the middle of Australia and the continent would be in danger of tearing apart in the center! Subsequently, from the feedback I had, I came to understand what was happening in that area, and why I was picking up this awful energy.

The Light workers did their job. They collectively gathered at Uluru to do some more clearing work there. At that time, I did not fully understand the significance of this. It would only emerge much later!

It was all triggered by the gift of a single Zircon crystal in March, 2014, from a friend, Pamela, in Australia.

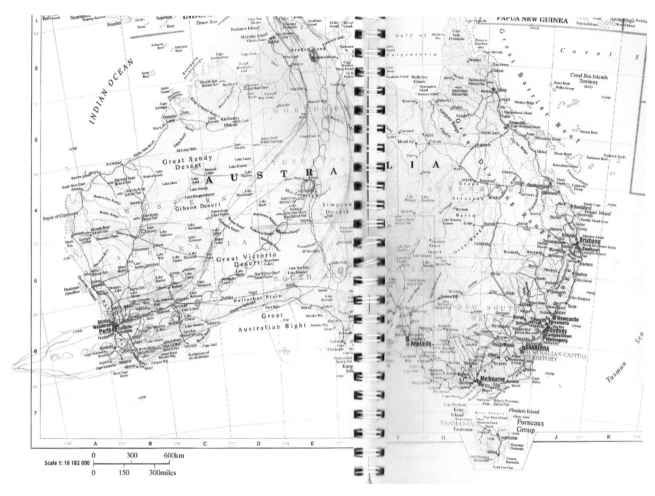

*I started tuning into this continent and alerting Light workers there that they needed to clear the energy lines along the crocodile I had drawn here. Indeed, there are pyramids and tunnel systems underground.*

## JOURNAL ENTRY

**March 28, 2014**

**Zircon crystal**

On Wednesday, I received a packet from Pamela in Australia containing a Zircon crystal.

She acquired two of these crystals from an Aboriginal lady from the Outback in the Northern Territory. She immediately knew she had to send one of them to me, as the energies were far too potent for her. She knew it was very important and closely connected to my work with the spinal cord.

*The Zircon crystal from the Northern Territory – straight from the person who mined it there, to me.*

The instant I picked up the crystal, I nearly exploded and began having mass energy downloads – like electric shocks running through my whole body!

It told me that it was a record-keeping crystal, and would work with me to retrieve vital information for the planet, and for books and journeys in Africa to follow.

I initially placed this crystal between my breasts, but it was so potent that I later removed it, for I felt it was going through all my energy systems and it was simply too strong for me to handle.

That night, I placed it next to my bed. Then I felt it work intensely on my left side and I had difficulty sleeping. I moved it to the other side of the room, to join my clear quartz crystals. Then I fell asleep.

In the morning, I was feeling disorientated and decided to just take the day off. I had been nudged to do so since the previous afternoon, when I started to feel strange, and I realized that something was afoot.

I felt quite peculiar. I decided to lie down and sleep for a while. Then I got up for lunch, but just felt like eating fruit. As I lay down, I felt the desire to listen to Esta Tonne's *Flight* again, as his music brings out the Golden Mean and Pi for me.

The crystal, however, urged me to place it on my abdomen. That made me feel even stranger. I later moved it to my feet, but it was not happy there. I then put it next to me, with my clear quartz crystals surrounding it. That helped me.

When I picked it up the first time, almost immediately a copper-red-gold Crystal Skull appeared, with the same coloring as the Zircon crystal. It told me that it had sent me the crystal so that it could connect with me, as it held vital information that I had to retrieve.

After listening to the music, I was instructed to lie down beside the circle of crystals, and was immediately transported close to the location where this crystal had originated.

A vast Crystal Pyramid Temple appeared, and it was the same color – copper-red and gold.

It had a golden copper dome around it, however, and another Crystal Pyramid Temple pointing downwards (like I had seen at Adam's Calendar), forming the Star of David. It was encircled with red-copper, golden light.

I found myself standing in a round chamber, underneath the apex of the pyramid.

A huge, double-helix flame of vortex energy (spiraling strands of energy), the color of the pyramid, pulsated up and down.

I was standing on a lapis lazuli blue floor that had geometrical patterns inlaid with gold. The pattern that emerged was Metatron's Cube! It was luminescent.

In the middle of this vast floor was a Crystal Skull, hovering in mid-air. It was the same Crystal Skull I had seen before, identical in color to the pyramid.

It started communicating with me telepathically.

I was not alone, however!

Suddenly, two other women appeared next to me – one on my left, and the other on my right. We seemed to form a triad where we were standing, in alignment with the Crystal Skull.

We were like the Sister Keepers, or Guardians.

Then another dark-haired woman appeared. She stood at the doorway, and was not allowed to come any closer. Then, three men I knew entered and paired off with us. We formed a triangle with the Crystal Skull. I had my new Sword of Light, which I had just received from the jeweler, in my hand – blue on the outside and blinding-white Light on the inside.

We were blending together – the male and female energies combined.

The next moment a massive flame emerged from the double-helix energy and the Crystal Skull! We dissolved and became balls, or orbs, of sheer Light energy.

In this orb-like energy form, we could go anywhere we wanted to go, and create and become (like shape-shifting). These orbs of energy appeared as fire balls. They then disappeared, and I was alone in my original form. Then an astonishing thing happened to the skull!

A door opened in its forehead, and inside was an energy field, or matrix, that seemed to work like a computer chip, or something similar. There was a geometrical pattern inside, which was created from flashing, colored Light frequencies

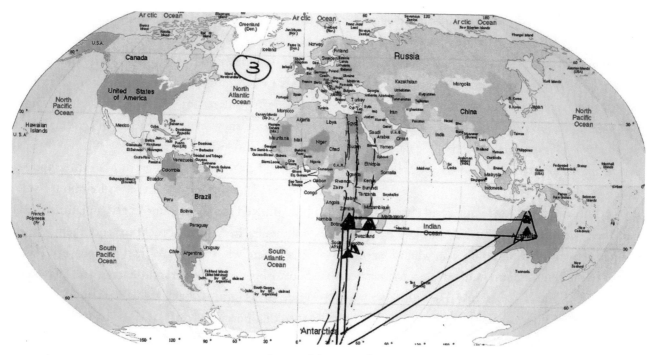

*A map of the energy lines.*

Then the entire skull vibrated, the top part separated from the bottom, moved through the air, and fitted itself around the crown of my head, like a helmet. It downloaded something into my brain and then lifted off and joined its lower half, becoming complete again.

Immediately the whole scene changed.

The energy lines opened between the Northern Territory, Uluru and then into the Temple of the Sun in Zimbabwe, and then down into Antarctica and back to Australia.

I was shown Uluru and how it was a vast Crystal Pyramid Temple. It was linked to this one by a river of double-helix pulsating light, colored red, gold and copper, and it pulsated this energy into the Pyramid of Uluru. Suddenly the Sun Temple in Zimbabwe appeared, and this energy river flowed from Australia to the Sun Temple. (It was a unified energy stream, not two rivers from the two pyramids.) Then an identical river formed, as before, and I was shown the Pyramid Temple of the White Flame, not where I had originally marked it, but in Antarctica – and the Antarctic continent had shifted upwards.

Next, more strands of this energy merged – the white-gold one from Zimbabwe with the sheer, white flames from the White Flame Pyramid. I was told that what I would now open and retrieve for the Southern Hemisphere, would be the foundation of the Golden Age. Antarctica, New Zealand, Australia and Africa would all be linked via this massive energy grid and energy fields. This would bring in tremendous shifts, and this ancient technology would be returned to humankind. This activity would lead to the next stage unfolding in France.

---

A few weeks later, after identifying the energy lines to Antarctica, I was doing a Soul reading for a client, when the Temple of the Moon, connected to the Temple of the Sun, appeared in her reading. She used to be a Priestess working at the Temple of the Moon, and then, in the subsequent reading, very interesting information came to the fore.

*"She was involved with the Crystal Pyramid Temple of the Sun in Zimbabwe in some way, definitely with her Twin Flame, and at that time the Temple of the Moon had a silvery hue and was in what is now the Straits of*

*Madagascar – hence the Madagascar connection. That is why it is best for her to wear silver on her body, as the element of silver will work with her own energies.*

*The Temple of the Moon and the Temple of the Sun worked together, as one was dedicated to Ra, the Sun God, and the other to Isis, the Moon Goddess. Then this Ancient remembering later returned to Egypt, and there was an affinity to some matters pertaining to the Ancient rites."*

I sat up and took notice, for I had always known that there were pyramids in the Madagascar Straits, as I had drawn them on to my map when I was first alerted to the Temple of the White Flame. Madagascar was ripped off the east coast of Africa, although most geologists place it higher on the map.

After the Zircon episode and this reading, I pored over the map of Africa again. I was told that Madagascar was torn from the coast of Mozambique, and subsequently settled further north and more inland. Australia fitted in between Antarctica and Madagascar.

I then had a period of quiet reflection. All the time, Madagascar was there haunting my thoughts. I started to make enquiries with travel agents, and I searched on Google, but I was advised to stay away from the island, which was considered very primitive and unsuitable for a woman travelling on her own.

One morning I was woken up and told to go to Mauritius. I had always believed that Mauritius was up in the Indian Ocean, more towards Zanzibar and the Seychelles. On most maps of Africa, there is a little window on the side where Mauritius and Reunion are mapped in separately. I was prompted to buy an Earth globe. To my astonishment, I realized that Mauritius and Reunion were just behind Madagascar. So, if I could not go to Madagascar, then I could certainly go to Mauritius. Furthermore, I had a lady from Simon's Town, originally from Mauritius, sending me interesting snippets about the pyramids over there. They were calling me and asking me to please go and look at them!

I had clear guidance to go to Mauritius, and was told that I had to include a visit to Reunion. I was a little puzzled about that, until I saw a picture of their mountains in a travel brochure, and then I knew. Aha! There was the portal I had to open up. First, I had to open up the pyramid energy and the energy grids in Mauritius, before going on to Reunion to open that portal.

By that time, I had taken out my map and drawn in the energy grid lines going through Mauritius and Reunion to Antarctica, to Cape Town, to my present home area, and then onwards, linking up with other sites. The lines went up into Egypt and the Giza Pyramids. I now knew for sure that I was being called there to do important work.

The ancient song lines of Australia move in serpent lines, as do those in the Southern Hemisphere. They are activated by very high-frequency energy beamed down from the Pleiades, the 7 Sisters. The Pleiades act as transmitter of the Cosmic sounds, and therefore amplify the sound frequencies via certain portals, or gateways, which are deep underground.

As these serpent energies are now reawakened, the shift in consciousness will be more profound. All the old structures will start falling apart, until the planet has been cleared completely from deep within.

# CHAPTER 15

# Mauritius

I posted news on Facebook about being called to Mauritius to do energy work there, and to my amazement, received a message from someone who runs a sacred site tourist operation there. She was delighted that I would be coming, and she asked if I would please teach a weekend seminar that she would arrange. She said she'd be happy to show me the pyramids and the island's holy sites.

She also told me that she, along with many others, had been waiting for some time for someone to come and open the energy centers there. They had received guidance that this person would be sent from overseas to do the work! A Swami from Hawaii had lived there a few years before. He had recognized that the island was sacred, connecting energetically to the Hawaiian Islands.

Interestingly, I had asked my Higher Guidance where I should stay. I was told it had to be in the southern part. I had a choice of hotels, through my

travel agent, and when I saw where she had booked me, I just knew that it was the correct place. However, later she changed the booking, and I had to ask her to cancel and revert to the original hotel, for that was exactly where I needed to be.

Those guiding me also worked intensively on my spinal cord energies, and it often felt like a massive vortex energy was moving up and down my spine. I was literally being revamped, as they had told me that my body needed to become increasingly crystalline.

At the time, I was also receiving plenty of guidance regarding the pyramids, the islands and what my work there would entail.

As they worked on my energy centers, I had intense initiations into, with revelations about the inner planes beneath, the Sphinx in Egypt. I had to incorporate the Isis energies, as in past lives in Avalon, Atlantis and Egypt, I had been her, as one of my other Soul identities. After one such initiation, I was told to get a lapis lazuli[1] necklace for Isis energy, as a symbol of royalty, and always to wear it while on the islands, for protection and power. But, where to find one?

Again the higher guidance came in. I stopped in front of my favorite jeweler in Plettenberg Bay, Intuition Jewelry. Upon entering the shop, I noticed many German tourists. However, the owner, who knows me and the energy work I do, immediately came to ask how he could assist. I told him about the lapis lazuli.

He took me to the cabinet where items were on display, but when he heard my story of exactly why I wanted it, his face lit up. He opened the cabinet and removed the most stunning necklace made from lapis lazuli pieces. Moreover, it appeared to be Egyptian! When I tried it on, it looked as if it had been made especially for me!

He said his wife had been inspired to create this necklace. When it was completed, she had said she would store it in the cabinet, as the person it belonged to would come and fetch it! Well, I did!

That necklace remained on my neck for the entire trip, and people often stopped me in the hotel and elsewhere to comment on its power and beauty, and to ask me where I'd found it!

## JOURNAL ENTRY

### September 19, 2015

*Let this be your message, and hear this loud and clear. Your whole life is about to change dramatically.*

*You will be led to wherever you need to go on the islands. There are 3 centers that need to be opened up: South and North in Mauritius, and in the middle of Reunion, in the mountains. There are 3 pyramids in the interior, and one outer pyramid, and all are interconnected.*

*There is an amazing kind of vortex energy there –*

*Only seven of these pyramids remain out of the hundreds that were once scattered all over the island. The pyramid stones were highly prized as a ready building material; as were the canals, temples, and what remained of homes. These were built long before the Dutch "discovered" the island.*

*not the vortex people go to for healing, but a highly advanced one, with 3 central points.*

*Move into these points, and you will be told what to do. The Guardians, Gatekeepers and the Ancient Ones are waiting for you on both islands and know that you are coming. You will be guided every step of the way, with more than 300 000 extra helpers sent to you by the Cosmic Councils of the Divine.*

When I arrived on the island of Mauritius late in the evening, it was raining. I did not mind that, for it was cool and pleasant, and not as humid as I had imagined. Waiting at reception were my hostesses, Elsa Desjardins and Birgitta Palmarosa – both Swiss ladies, now residents in Mauritius. They spoke Swiss German, which I could not understand, and Creole, the *lingua franca* of Mauritius, but spoke English with me.

The *gastfreiheit* (warm welcome) of these ladies was overwhelming, and I felt so at home in Elsa's beautiful home in the highland region of the island. I

---

1    Lapis lazuli is a deep-blue, semi-precious stone that has been prized since antiquity for its intense color. (*Wikipedia*)

The pyramids on Mauritius, or rather the remains. There were hundreds of these pyramids all over the island, but most were dismantled and the stones were used as building material. This photograph, with the setting Sun, perfectly illustrates the original color of the pyramids.

The Ancient, paved road, which linked the pyramids. It is still in use today.

met her engineer and artist husband, Pierre, and slept like a log on my first night.

The next morning, these two ladies took me to the pyramids on the south of the island. There were only 7 pyramids remaining, mainly hidden and obscured by the sugar cane plantations. We first had to meet our guide at the local police station, and then followed him, in the rain.

The further south we travelled, the more I honed into the island's energy lines. To my delight, I could now in the daylight greet the Great Sphinx, the Lion Mountain of Mauritius, and immediately tuned into the Ancient Ones, as well as the Keepers and Guardians of the island, who were celebrating and welcoming me. They had known that I was coming, and all came to greet me.

I was taken the next morning to the 7 pyramids, which are still standing and now protected by the Mauritian government. I was disappointed to find that these pyramids were practically hidden by six-foot-tall sugar cane. This made it difficult to get clear views and to gain access to them.

The Lion People immediately appeared this morning. Birgitta saw them at the breakfast table in a half-circle around me. She gave me crystals from this area, and I nearly levitated when I took them from her! Now I felt their presence so powerfully, as I tuned into these pyramids, and the site.

I quickly noticed the Ancient paved road. Indeed, many of these old roads are still in use today, and are obviously linked not only to the pyramids, but to the whole metropolis that once stood there.

\* \* \* \* \*

I immediately started tuning into the pyramids. Their original casings have been removed, or have faded away. The three pyramids in closest alignment were once copper-green, sunset-red, and gold. They all had a capstone originally, and only the top parts of these were still visible. Indeed, they were even larger before.

Originally there were sphinxes guarding these pyramids, in the shape of lions. Not huge, but 3–4m (10–13ft) high, and there were about 12 of them in total.

*The guides and Elsa climbing the pyramid before it got too steep and slippery.*

*The other two remaining pyramids. The sugar cane fields obscure the pyramids.*

I believe that the bottom sections of these pyramids are still buried underground, and I had an impression of colossal, hidden, subterranean chambers. I also sensed that there were tunnels connecting these pyramids. (This would later be confirmed by a local teacher who has an avid interest in them.)

I noticed that the tunnel system runs the length and breadth of the whole island, and this was confirmed by the locals, who have found entrances to these tunnels at sea level – some linking directly to the Lion Mountain, and some to the canal systems.

There was an intricate canal system, which was used for irrigation and to supply water to the entire island. This was confirmed by the Mauritian guide, who said the remains of this canal system could be found all over the island, especially up north, which we visited later. He said the first settlers used them and their sophisticated hydraulic scheme.

The island's water supply system has now been replaced with a pipe system. Subsequently, the islanders have steadily dismantled the original canal system, using the rocks as building materials. I then had a vision that these pyramids linked up with the Lion Mountain and Tamarind Bay, and were being guarded by the dolphins.

There was once a massive city here, in a golden color, with waterfalls running from the Lion Mountain which was, in fact, originally a huge sphinx.

I also had the impression that the pyramids were, in some way, linked to those in Australia, but I was not sure how this was connected to Africa. (That link came later, via Reunion.)

The original people living here were very tall and copper-skinned, with red hair worn in a top knot.

In front of the pyramids was a huge terrace with

*Pyramid stones are carefully packed. Note the golden one between those covered with lava. It shows the original color of the pyramids.*

*The remains of the original walls and canal systems are found all over the island.*

*Only the tops of these pyramids are visible. The rest are buried underground.*

*Look at this massive lintel just casually lying next to the road. Note the precision engineering with which it was cut.*

*My first ever overseas seminar, held over a weekend in Mauritius.*

a large platform used for ceremonies. The pyramids and canal system created an extensive energy field that supplied power to all the people, craft and buildings.

The stonework is symmetrical. We found that the original color was not the current black or gray, but multi-hued. Indeed, when we managed to turn over one of the loose stones, we found a beautiful, golden hue. I believe that they were covered with lava, and that this island had to be evacuated because of fierce, volcanic eruptions and earthquakes.

These mounds have 3–7 stories underground and are connected by tunnel systems that are linked to the inner world, Agartha. The pyramids were connected to a canal system in the form of a complex labyrinth.

*Angela, myself and Birgitta.*

There was also a tunnel system linking the inner cities. I felt that many of these pyramids were buried and, therefore, would have to have been linked by this tunnel and the canal system. The existence of the actual tunnel system was confirmed later by one of my students, who had accidentally stumbled into one in a sugar cane field near the pyramids. He then found that when he explored further along, he reached the site of the next pyramid (or close to it).

I then had to join the energy grids from Australia and the copper-red pyramid there from Uluru, to Mauritius; and then to the Sun Temple in Zimbabwe.

The weekend seminar at River House – my first ever overseas seminar – was held over two days. The first was all about Twin Flame relationships, and the second covered the true history of the world; my energy work; and my findings about the pyramids and the hidden history of Mauritius.

Two of my students then came to tell me that there had been a written language in Mauritius. Some inscribed on wax tablets, which have disappeared. There are also strange drawings on the rocks.

From there, I was transported to my hotel.

## October 5, 2015

I was booked into the Preskil Resort last night. This morning I saw that I was at exactly the right spot!

When I stood on the beach, I was in perfect alignment with the Sphinx (Lion Mountain) and the pyramids. The resort is situated on a type of island exactly in the middle, and Paradise Island, a nature reserve, is in front of me. The energy there was enormous, as the Keepers and Guardians immediately told me to go and stand on the volcanic rocks, which form a type of jetty. Then revelations followed!

The color of the pyramids was revealed: The small pieces of rock that were not covered with lava were pure gold.

*The Keeper/Guardian and the Ancient Kahuna[2] from Hawaii (who had been with me as a Higher Guide,*

---

2    A kahuna is a priest, sorcerer, magician, wizard, minister, or expert in any profession (*Wikipedia*)

*The Lion Mountain was in perfect alignment with my hotel and the pyramids.*

*connected to these islands before I had even arrived here), stood in front of me: He was very tall, with copper-red skin and piercing eyes. He told me he was going to energize me so that I could do the work! "We welcome you back, Goddess, Mother Goddess. We welcome you, for you have come to do the work. We will show you, help you, and guide you. We are blessing you, Mother! We are loving you! We are opening the portals with you!"*

As I walked around this small island (only the resort is built there), the energies were flowing through me.

Vinesh, the man at the seminar connected to the pyramids and the true guardian of them, in human form, told me last night that there used to be hundreds of pyramids on the island when he was a boy. Growing up, he used to walk through their remains on his way to school. They were half-dismantled, and by the time he turned 12, they had all but disappeared! They had been systematically disassembled and used as building materials. The people could help themselves to the stones because the pyramids were not protected by the government.

He confirmed that the canals had been there (the canal systems), as well as the underground tunnels that connected pyramids that I had seen. He told me that the sites had been overrun by lava, and the remaining walls were also being used by the locals as building materials!

So everything I saw has been confirmed!

He said that there had been a spiraling pyramid there, too.

Vinesh also told me about the wax tablets with writings on them, of which there had been quite a few. He confirmed, however, that nobody knew what had happened to them. He said there was a tunnel that linked the sea to the Lion Mountain. He had been shown this by friends. There is also an extensive tunnel system all over the island.

Vinesh is concerned that the archeological digs being conducted on the island are covering up many things, and that the people of Mauritius have been blinded to the truth. He believes that the government is concealing much, as they are following the guidance of the Dutch archeologists. (The reason for this would later become clear, when I visited the museum at the site of the old Dutch fort on the island.)

This again confirms that I must trust what is given to me.

I know that I am exactly where I am meant to be, as these energy lines move through here to link up to Reunion Island. So, I was led to exactly the right spot.

As I was listening to what these Mauritians were telling me, I knew that somewhere along the line, all of this had been deliberately covered up. For, at the time the Dutch rediscovered the uninhabited island, these structures would have been there. Since they found the island deserted, they merely built on top of the existing ruins and then used the rest as building materials.

Nowhere would this be more obvious than at the Museum, and at the remains of the fort.

**October 6, 2015**

Yesterday, we travelled north, in ways that were both ordinary and extraordinary.

First, we stopped at the National Museum, where the Dutch first landed and built a fort. It is where the oldest buildings in Mauritius are found. There is

*The Dutch used to build on the foundation stones of the original buildings that were left vacant by the copper-skinned race. If you look carefully, you will see that the Dutch used mortar to cement the rocks together.*

evidence there that when the Dutch arrived, they found the remains of an ancient civilization, and possibly the pyramids.

They recorded some of the structures they found: The houses and dwellings of those who had lived there before. They reminded me of the Viking Longhouses[3], as they were pyramid-shaped, or triangular and long. The same rocks were being used and stacked like the pyramids, but probably with a thatched roof covering, or something similar. It is possible that, as in the Orkney Islands, the roofs were also made of rock, but that has been lost now.

Of course, according to the official version, this island's civilization began with the Dutch and later the French. However, the pyramids are so much older than these settlements. The lower structure – the foundations of the fort – show that they were simply built on the remains of whatever massive structure had been there before.

One can see clearly where the Dutch had built, for they used mortar to knit the stones together. The older foundation stones do not have mortar, yet fit snugly together and are of a much higher quality workmanship!

*The original foundation has no mortar between the rocks, just like the pyramids! This shows that the foundations and old structures and buildings were already there, long before the Dutch arrived.*

I saw a type of harbor, or settlement, but they had found it deserted. I believe that with the volcanoes erupting, the original people left and the island was evacuated.

Again, the remains of the canal system can clearly be seen in between the endless sugar cane plantations, which are filled with massive rocks. They removed the rocks from the sugar cane fields. Our driver told us that he grew up on one of these plantations, and they used to just throw out all the rocks they found. They then quickly found more rocks and just disregarded them. It seems that these huge rocks were probably used in buildings of multiple levels that might have been a few stories high. Of course, when massive Earth upheavals occurred, some would have been buried under the layers of lava.

(Later in Reunion, I was shown places where the lava was 70m deep. Even vast buildings could be covered in one such volcanic eruption.)

On display in the museum there were so-called pipes (for smoking tobacco), which were intricately carved with what appeared to me to be a type of writing. I later found similar signs on the rocks. These pipes were so small, fragile and delicate that I am sure that nobody could have used them to smoke tobacco.

We then went through all the by-ways to a most sacred and beautiful, mystical place, where a natural spring gushes from the middle of a lake. (They have extended the natural lake into a man-made one.) It reminded me of Macho Picchu, and it is truly a mystical and magical site.

I felt that this was an entry point into the Inner Earth, and therefore it was purposefully hidden, for it was way off the beaten track. I was privileged to have been taken there. The energies there are just out of this world

---

3   A longhouse is a type of long, proportionately narrow, single-room building that was built by peoples in various parts of the world, including Asia, Europe, and North America. (Wikipedia)

*The amazing mountains framing the sacred lake. Look closely and you will see that they are man-made, with massive rock-brickwork!*

*A natural spring spurting from deep underground creates this beautiful, mysterious lake.*

*Look at the intricate designs on these items. The same symbols are found on rocks. These are the so-called smoking pipes that are housed in the museum.*

and are often used by my students for meditation. I felt the Ancient Ones there in a profound sense. It was as if the mountains reverberated with something so ancient and vast, that I could not express it. Later that week, this impression would be confirmed.

The copper-skinned people who used to live here again showed themselves to me. I then had the distinct impression that instead of evacuating the island when the volcanic activities started, they merely went underground, and that they are therefore still living there, among the Ancient Ones. They are just in a higher dimensional form, which few can tune into at this time.

*Part of the canal systems. Look at the precision-cut stones that fit neatly together without mortar.*

\* \* \* \* \*

One of my students, Jacqui, told me that they had observed a lot of UFO activity over the mountains, across the river from our seminar venue. I had picked up on this fact the minute I stood by the river looking towards the mountains. I had seen that there was an underground space station there, so there is plenty happening.

We went through the highlands, south to a forest and sacred spring. Again, the canals and walls appeared everywhere. The French built a shrine around the sacred well, which detracts from the beauty, but I suppose, in another sense, it helped preserve it.

I was drawn to the forest and rocks there, and found some truly amazing ones. Some were massive dolmans, and as I stood in front of a few of these, I nearly levitated from the energy they emitted. I then realized this was the entrance to the tunnel system underground. The dolmans were so carefully placed that they had obscured the opening.

I again had the impression of tunnel systems and the canal labyrinth, and at the sacred spring was a pool of healing waters. Now a road runs through the middle, and this has distorted the energy flow. It also distracts the motorists from stopping here and visiting the place. It feels like a 'garden of forgetfulness'. Yet, this was done on purpose, and it ties in with later findings.

Someone wanted to intentionally hide one of the most sacred spots on the island to save this whole area from being stripped of pyramids and buildings. That person was none other than the Swami, whom I would meet later in the day!

While we travelled, we saw rock walls, buildings and structures (some very large) everywhere, surrounded by forest and overgrown vegetation. Indeed, it was the only part of Mauritius that was neither filled with sugar cane fields nor built up. It has been left untouched, carefully preserved and kept hidden from prying eyes. The Swami declared this part of Mauritius sacred and holy, and made it a national park! One must truly salute the foresight of this man, who did a splendid job in safeguarding the true history of Mauritius – the significance of which is yet to be discovered.

\* \* \* \* \*

Swami Sivaya Subramuniyaswami was a legend and international spiritual treasure with followers from more than 40 countries. In his book, *Lemurian Scrolls – Angelic Prophecies Revealing Human Origins*, he clairvoyantly reads the Akashic Records from the first settlement on this planet, linking it to Lemuria.

*Sacred spot, and the remains of the massive canal system.*

However, as much as I admire the Swami's work, this region is much older than Lemuria, and has its origin in Elysium.

* * * * *

I had the urge to go on exploring here, and I knew if I did, I would stumble upon wonder after wonder! We then had lunch at the Peace Garden created by the self-same Swami.

When I first arrived at the gardens, I saw large rocks arranged along the roads; some in semi-circles; some in strategic places, in between trees; as well as a straggly lawn. Mostly, there was just the red earth, trees and rocks, and nothing else. "What a strange garden. Where are all of the flowers?" I thought. To me this looked like anything but a Peace Garden!

I felt the Swami's presence though, along with the Kahuna from Hawaii. The two of them must have had a quiet chuckle, for little did I know what was awaiting me!

Since landing on the island, I had been told about this Swami, who came from Hawaii and then had a vision to locate the sacred energies of the sharks. It had something to do with a Hawaiian Shark God, and he had to open up a type of energy center connected to these shark energies. This was to connect the Hawaiian Islands with Mauritius.

*A perfect cut, almost like part of the system.*

*The Kali rock, where women come to worship and make offerings.*

*This is one of the huge Sentinel rocks.*

He managed to find the vortex energy spot, opened up the energy grid, and then linked the islands across the globe. He thus declared the site sacred, and created the Peace Gardens here.

We were having lunch among the rocks and trees at a spot that Birgitta insisted was the correct place. On the way there, I had noticed a round mosaic floor with a circle in the middle, surrounded by huge, standing rocks. Birgitta mentioned that this circle was used for ceremonies, but she moved past it and took me to the location chosen for our picnic.

While standing there eating, I started to tune into the place. The rocks were beginning to talk to me. I was drawn to a rock right in front of me that had offerings and candles on it.

Interestingly, I stood next to the rock, but somehow did not want to touch it. Another rock, beyond this one, caught my attention and I continued along the path.

Further along there was a thought-provoking arrangement of stones. While walking there, Birgitta drew my attention to some other rocks arranged in an unusual manner.

By this time, I was honing into very strong energies and trying to ascertain where they came from. I was constantly looking towards the sea, for the sea was pulling me more strongly than the garden and the rocks. Then I went around the corner and touched another of these massive rocks. I nearly left the ground!

To my astonishment, the Swami and the Giant Kahuna appeared before me! They were so close and so powerfully present that I could have touched them, as if they were there in physical form. The Swami had mesmerizing eyes steeped with love and wisdom, while the Kahuna was an imposing, very powerful man with an energetic presence that you just don't trifle with. It was like tempered steel.

*The Swami welcomed me to his Garden saying: "Goddess of the Waters, Goddess of the Sacred Paths, I welcome you here. For so long we have waited for you and we have now prepared the path for you to open the energies here.*

*"We have anchored in the male energies but you must now work with the female energies, and we will assist you to anchor the Goddess energies deeply into this place and on this island. "You are the Goddess of the Waters, the Goddess of the Sacred Paths and Sacred Energies, and we are therefore blessing you now and preparing you for this task!"*

*Then the Kahuna stood on one side of me with the Swami on the other, and they blessed me.*

*It was then that I felt the energy, a platinum-white, spiraling energy from the Divine Feminine, moving into me and through me. It first moved into my 3$^{rd}$ eye and then into my whole body as they activated me!*

At that moment, I was led to pat one of the rocks, before I was released to where Birgitta was waiting like a mother hen for me, pointing to another type of rock arrangement in a sort of semi-circle. The rock in front of me started singing, literally. I was tuning into its sound. I started singing in a strange language. I had no idea what I was singing, but it sounded Polynesian!

After this, I don't remember much, as Birgitta also started singing to the rocks the songs she had learnt in her shamanic training on Tahiti. I was told to go

*The shark stone circle and the labyrinth in the middle, where I had to first stand to tune into the second circle in the river mouth, before I could anchor in the Feminine Energies there.*

and sit on one of the adjacent rocks, and nearly took off again!

It was as if I was entering another, even higher state, as I moved from rock to rock, being led back to the stone circle and the round mosaic platform that I had seen earlier.

At first I was drawn to another stone on the outskirts of the circle, and there I found the shark energy! That was the sacred energy of the portal that the Swami had opened here. Of course, there was the connection to the Hawaiian Shark God. (According to legend Amohoali'i is the most respected of the shark gods and was known for his ability to take on both human and fish forms.)

Birgitta appeared, and I told her that this was the shark circle. While she started connecting to the shark energies, I was strongly commanded by the Kahuna to go into the paved circle and stand in the middle at the designated center spot (clearly marked).

I had never felt such a powerful force in my entire life. Standing there, with this strong energy coursing through me, moving up and down in spirals, I suddenly saw a Sentinel rock in the bay in front of me, standing at the edge of a stone circle in the sea – where the river meets the sea.

Standing there, I was connected to both circles, and again felt huge surges of energy running through me. I don't know how long I was there, but I was becoming one with both circles and with the energies and energy fields, as if I was disintegrating and dissolving into one gigantic energy field.

Slowly, I came back into my body and awareness, and was urged to step outside the circle to where Birgitta was waiting for me. However, my attention was drawn to what looked like two massive stone culverts with a mother birthing stone between them. I was commanded to go and sit on that birthing stone.

I was told to take off my shoes and camera and sit in the lotus position.

In the next instance, I was calling in the energies of the sea, Earth and the energy lines. I was calling in the dolphins, whales, sharks, and then I went into

*The Swami's Peace Garden is filled with precision-cut rocks that he rescued from all over the island.*

an extremely deep trance state. I was in the middle of a never-ending, white-golden spiraling energy – the Goddess energy.

It felt like invisible hands were lifting my arms and hands. I was pouring out streams of pulsating intense white energy through my hands and directing this energy into these energy lines, grids and the stone circle in the bay. I was clearing energy grids and lines. I

*Notice the stone circle where the river meets the sea. That is where the Swami connected the shark energy from Hawaii to Mauritius.*

was beaming energy through my hands and my 3rd eye into the energy grids and lines between Mauritius and Reunion, and opening massive blockages there.

I had the distinct impression of begging them to take Birgitta, who had been standing in front of me, away, so that she would not disintegrate in this massive energy I was releasing – and to keep everybody else away, too. (When I came out of this state, Birgitta was standing far behind me. They had moved her.)

I became a weaver and commander of energies and energy forces, and was opening a boundless energy source that I knew would flow into Reunion, but also connect with the sphinxes and the pyramids that I had been shown in Antarctica, and everything that had been hidden underground there. (The full story of this can be found in a later chapter.)

It was a moving and powerful experience, and I had to truly stand in my highest Goddess Power and own it.

Later I understood why the Swami had moved the rocks to the Peace Garden after collecting them from all over the island. He was preserving them for posterity. If he had left them where he had found them, they, too, would have been used as sugar cane field markers, or as building materials. The Swami read their power, and the writing preserved on these rocks. My respect for this wise man grew.

He had, therefore, brought them into one single sacred place for safe-keeping. This was outstanding service work for humanity, for the sphinxes that I had originally seen guarding the pyramids, were here!

It was an amazing moment, which I will never forget. Birgitta declared afterwards: "Now this has been done!"

Little did she know it was but the very beginning – the tip of the iceberg. The next breakthrough would happen in Reunion.

*The standing stone is part of the original altar stone.*

However, Mauritius had more surprises in store for me, and us all! I am feeling the Ancient energies here, preserved in and around the island in pockets.

Somehow, the great souls who once dwelt here – the Lion People – will tell their stories through my story, and the two will become as one!

## The Rocks Speak

I must return, for a moment, to that day when all these miracles happened in the Peace Garden.

That morning, I had been sitting in a gazebo on the hotel premises, waiting for Birgitta, when I was told to get up. I did so, and was instructed to go to the large trees further along the road. There, I was alerted to the presence of rocks. I have found time and again that if I am told to move, I must move; and when told to look, I must look.

To my delight, I saw that there were engravings on one of the rocks. I got excited and took photographs.

*This stone is covered with ancient symbols, such as the Tree of Life, pyramids, triangles, and so on. It is a recording stone and it zings with powerful energy.*

Then I saw more rocks standing in a circle in the middle of an island in the road. I was nearly jumping up and down with joy, for there were drawings and symbols on the rocks.

The next day, I was determined to go back to those rocks and to 'read' them! They had an amazing energy, and I felt that they had been placed there to preserve them, just like the Swami had preserved the rocks elsewhere. There were strong energies radiating from them, and I sensed the energies flowing through me.

I found another rock with engravings of figures and symbols on it. One rock had a huge figure carved on it that looked like the White Lady[4] of the Brandberg. Others had markings of crossed lines, triangles, and spirals deeply engraved into them (see sketch on page 176). These rocks are pure granite, and one simply cannot just carve such symbols into granite. It is impossible. Some of them still have a white wash of calcite painted on them. I feel that the rocks in this resort come from a very ancient sacred site – a Temple complex. Therefore, they are specially marked and link up with the Lion Mountain and the pyramids.

I was told that this resort had a very interesting history. It had burnt down three times. I believe that because this is a sacred site, someone was told to place the rocks there; not to move them; and to build the resort around them! I believe that 'someone' was none other than the Swami. He also knew that this resort linked up the energy lines from the mountain to the pyramids, and therefore understood the significance of these rocks!

The rocks themselves are so ancient and holy, there is no wonder that anyone who dared to disturb them and the energies here would suffer the consequences.

These rocks were thus preserved on this island.

---

4    The White Lady is a rock painting, located on a panel on a small rock overhang deep within Brandberg Mountain, which is Namibia's highest mountain

*This rock has a ship etched into it, along with people and symbols.*

*A closer look at the ship etched into the rock.*

*A pyramid carved into the rock. It is 3-D, too.*

*More rocks bearing writing and symbols.*

*Strange symbols: Triangles, squares and arrows.*

*Look at the engraved squares and triangles. This is pure granite.*

*From a distance, the writing and engravings are easier to read and are more visible.*

*More fascinating symbols.*

*Yet another engraving.*

*This engraving is hidden lower down. Look at the symbols and writing etched on to the rock.*

*Look at the spirals at the bottom: They are reminiscent of the Celtic knots...*

*This rock also bears writing and symbols.*

*Look at the amazing symbols and engravings on this rock.*

*If you look carefully on the right-hand side, a hand is engraved in the rock!*

Ironically, the tourists walk straight past them and take no notice of them.

It was quite sunny that morning, and as I was excitedly photographing these rocks from all angles. The tourists looked at me as if I was stone crazy. Well, in a higher sense, I was!

One of my students later shared photographs she had taken of a rock further up, on one of the mountains in Mauritius. I am sharing a photo here (page 175, bottom), so that one can get a better grasp of the magnitude of what has been left by the forgotten people of Mauritius.

I was led there because, like Beacon Island in Plettenberg Bay, and the sites at False Bay and Cape Point, this is sacred ground. It somehow moved with the energy grids, linking them to Reunion, the Peace Garden, and the Swami. I felt something extremely important was occurring here.

The sites in the north have been carefully hidden and left undisturbed – the ruins of a massive city complex, with dwellings, walls and canal systems. In the place where I'd stood in the forest, I found the entrance to an ancient tunnel system, which had been carefully obscured.

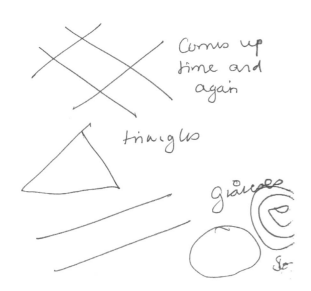

*My sketch of symbols.*

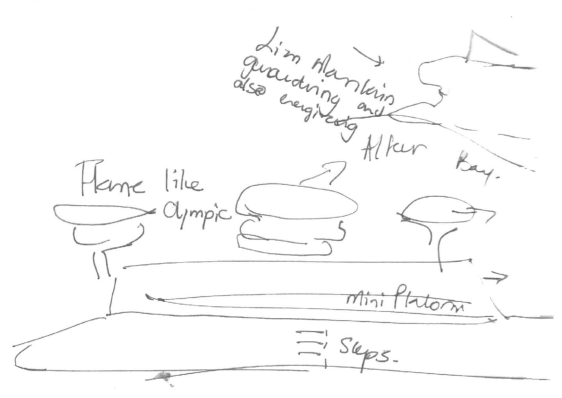

*An open-platform temple, as sketched by me.*

*The rock etched against the Goddess Mountain.*

The energies there were very potent and I felt them intensely. The fact that the French built on top of the sacred spring was just another way to try to preserve it. Now the Hindus and the Catholics are building shrines on sacred sites all over the island.

The site here at the resort had a gigantic temple. It was on an open platform, and they worshipped in the open. Priests were very tall and regal-looking, with red hair, copper skin and a topknot. They wore just loin cloths, and the women were clothed in a type of sarong. They wore massive earrings and had longish faces and beautiful hazel-green eyes.

On this platform, they burnt offerings, did rituals and conducted ceremonies. The symbols on the rocks link to this, for they were altar stones and stones dedicated to the Goddess whose site this was.

I sense that this connects to Egypt and the Lion People, but specifically to Isis herself. I feel immense universal Feminine energy here – not Masculine energy, for it is much more subtle.

I see torches or flames (like the Olympic torch) on either side of the massive platform, where the cauldron symbols were. Enormous cauldrons were situated on either side of the magnificent altar stones.

The offerings were fruit and nuts, and there were ceremonies dedicated to the Goddess here.

It was a sacred site.

The longer I am on this island, the more I sense that a great catastrophe occurred here: Volcanic eruptions, earthquakes, and then all the land being covered with lava. Indeed, there are tunnels that were created by flowing lava. Later, in Reunion, I understood better how this had happened.

The people were forced to evacuate. Some went into the underground tunnels and into Agartha. Others went back to their home galaxies.

They were the Ancient Ones and the Keepers of the sacred keys and codes, plus the Master builders and architects. They were the ones who built the megalithic sites all over the planet: A majestic, giant people.

*These were found where the road carved through what had once been a massive platform. Look at the color and how these rocks neatly fit together!*

They left so many energy imprints behind. They worked with the elements and the spiraling energies, and could manifest and demanifest and grow into form and being at will. They could shape-shift, and knew how to disintegrate matter and then to reassemble it back into material form.

The greatest and most powerful knowledge and technology was purposefully hidden. They deactivated the energy centers, knowing that mankind would seek to destroy and disrupt everything, until they re-learnt the powerful energy systems and took responsibility as co-creators within the Universal Laws.

Mankind has had to endure an intense 'animal kingdom' existence due to having created half-man,

half-beast life forms, and so needed this experience of the animal kingdom. They would then grow in understanding and finally learn to reclaim their Cosmic heritage.

So, they were gradually brought back to their true God and Goddesshood, and that is the calling and task of all of us!

I had the privilege of being shown more of the island when Elsa took me to her new home on a farm in the interior of Mauritius. On the way there, we passed a massive temple with extensive stone work that fitted perfectly together. The road went through what was surely once a pyramid. The remains were on either side of the narrow road. There are also the

*The remains of the ancient canals and walls are found everywhere, in between sugar cane fields and between domestic gardens, like this one on the way to Pont Naturel.*

*Where the sugar cane fields were established, they had to remove the old cities and foundations. This massive lintel was simply thrown next to the road.*

remnants of other pyramids all over, hidden within sugar cane fields.

The mountains immediately caught my attention, and I felt the presence of the Ancient Ones intensely here. There are significant openings to the inner world in this location, but nobody notices them much, for they are in a different dimensional state.

## JOURNAL ENTRY

**October 9, 2015**

I am leaving Mauritius today to go to Reunion. I must say that I have felt so at home on this island and with its people, especially Birgitta and Elsa.

In a way, this island is held within a time-warp. It is Ancient, and the engraved rocks and stones are like spokespersons for a lost age, communicating through the engraved symbols and their energy. Last night, under the hotel lighting, I noticed how these symbols were highlighted in a different manner. I could read them more easily in the artificial light. I observed an emerald-green to aquamarine light emerging from the rocks. Birgitta saw it, too.

I also noticed that these stones were energetically programmed with the same color energy ray, and that

*The remains of a massive structure, and walls at Pont Natural. Again, look at the similarities of the way this wall was constructed and the pyramids.*

they originally were created from, and formed part of, vast energy centers that worked with conscious energy fields. Therefore, they are literally transmitters of energy frequencies.

I felt this intensely when I became at one with the spiraling energies in that stone circle at the Peace Gardens, and when I stood in the middle and looked at the circle in the sea.

When I sat on that rock to do the energy work, I

*A massive structure once stood here. Look how the lava overran the site; one must be very careful walking there because of the ripples made everywhere by the lava.*

merged with the energy and energy field. I was able to become the field!

I feel an intense presence here of the Ancient Ones, and a connection to the inner world of Agartha. Elsa's guide, Emmanuel, was joined by another of his ilk, and they combined their energies and took us up the high mountains, along with Elsa's nephew, late yesterday evening. They have held this island in the palms of their hands and they are here now guiding it back to what it in truth was/is.

Interestingly, Birgitta said that the Kahuna appears to her dressed in white, or with a huge Hawaiian headdress, which depicts him as royalty and king. I don't see him like this, but always with his hair in a topknot. He is very, very strong energetically.

The Lion Mountain is also immensely powerful, and was originally a sphinx. It has the same atmosphere and presence as Robberg. It also corresponds with what I have been shown in Antarctica.

They all link up through the energy grid lines and fields, as I have drawn them on to the maps: Mauritius; Reunion; Antarctica; Zimbabwe and the Temple of Sun; and Cape Town and the whole of south-eastern Africa – the spinal column of the world!

Concerning the pyramids, the canals, the walls and their disappearance – Rashid, my taxi driver and guide, told me yesterday that at one stage, he had a thriving business dismantling them. These stones and rocks fetched the best prices in the building industry and market. They are very sought after. Today, many of

*The Guardian who guards the secrets of the island and the people who were once there at Pont Naturel.*

the new homes use copies of the original stones, but of course there are still remnants around the island.

In some places on the island, one can see there used to be massive structures. You find them between sugar cane fields, where they could not be removed in the same way as all the other structures and rocks. In one place that Elsa showed me, there is a huge complex of building foundations that could not be dismantled, and the sugar cane is straggling there.

Another fascinating feature of the island is the hollow pockets of molten rocks which, when opened, were found to be hollow inside, forming caverns.

Curiously, the archeologists sponsored by the Dutch government do not even acknowledge the existence of the pyramids or the canals. Many of the houses in the villages we passed show evidence that they were built on much older foundations or structures that predated the modern buildings.

Well, before I even embarked on this journey, I was given the key code 777, especially for the portal in Reunion, and Antarctica. I could not have foreseen at that time how everything would unfold, but indeed this was the key code that unlocked everything!

## CHAPTER 16

# Reunion

Reunion came as a surprise, for I had no idea what to expect from this French island of which I knew so little. I had always associated it with the French Foreign Legion.

I had received guidance beforehand that I should not worry; that I would get to the mountains with the help of a quiet young man who could speak English. I was also told that he would wait for me at the spot where he dropped me off to go on the hike to open the portal, and that I would be safe and protected.

I had only three days to open the massive portal in Reunion, and thus I stepped off the plane with a sense of urgency.

The airport in Reunion was very basic, with no lifts. I had to climb flights of stairs, which made carrying hand baggage a bit difficult. I couldn't speak a word of French, but a very kind lady just suddenly took my hand luggage and lugged it up the stairs for me with a big smile. I was so grateful.

The owner of the shuttle service was waiting for me in the very primitive Arrivals Hall. He said that he also owned the travel business across the road from the airport, which looked more like a kiosk to me! He then introduced me to the driver who would take me in his minibus to the hotel. I was the only passenger.

What immediately struck me about Reunion was the order, after the comparative chaos of Mauritius, where there were no street names or road markings, and the village roads were strewn with pedestrians, cyclists, and the most sorry-looking cats and dogs I have ever seen. (A South African township dog looks better fed than the street dogs of Mauritius, and this was indeed a great concern for foreigners living there.) There were no sidewalks in Mauritius either, which made for hazardous driving on very narrow roads.

Reunion was like a sprawling metropolis. The city had traffic lights, sidewalks, signposts, and even pedestrian and cycling tracks. The coast was neatly lined with trees and parking areas. There were businesses everywhere, and after seeing hardly any shopping malls in Mauritius, Reunion had many. We also drove through a big industrial area.

The hotel was large, well-managed, and close to a shopping mall. The staff all spoke English, so I had no problem with communication.

*Fruit stalls like these are found on the street corners as all food on this island is produced by locals.*

The next morning, I went to the mall to draw money, and found everything there that I would need for my trip.

There was even a fresh fruit stall filled with the most luscious-looking fruit. I bought some strawberries, bananas and other fruit there. I had a delicious salad and some crusty French bread for lunch in the restaurant.

I asked the receptionist for a guide to take me to the mountains. I had a picture with me of the mountains where I had to go to open the portal. I was referred to the hotel manager in charge of tours.

Her name was Chantal. She was French and a former air hostess for Lufthansa. Her English was not quite fluent, and to her relief she discovered that I was German-speaking. Communication then became much easier, and we discovered we had a lot

of common interests. I told her about the book that I was busy writing and showed her the picture.

She immediately phoned to organize a tour guide who would take me to the mountains and show me the hiking trail. She told me that he would pick me up in the early morning. She said that he could speak English and that he would not only take me to the site, but that he would wait in the parking lot the whole time for me, and then return me to the hotel. (So, the guidance I had received proved to be accurate!)

She asked if I had hiking shoes, but alas, I hadn't been able to fit them into my suitcase, although I did have a fold-up backpack with me. To my surprise, she organized another tour guide to take me to a sports shop to buy boots, as she said my shoes were totally inappropriate for hiking!

This tour guide turned out to be a French former policeman. He was very charming indeed and spoke fluent English. He organized boots, and even socks, for me in no time. So, I was fully kitted out. He then took me on a tour of the coast on the way back to the hotel. He told me that I had better take a long walk, to walk in the shoes! This same guide took me on a tour of the island on my last day in Reunion.

The mountains I had to visit were called Mafata, and they were truly breathtaking and magnificent, with pyramids everywhere. It was there that I was shown the Sentinel rocks on arrival, and knew that I was at exactly the right place to do the work.

My guide was tall and handsome. He came from Luxembourg and had immigrated to Reunion as he felt at home there. He really looked after me, and his concern for my safety and comfort was that of a real gentleman. Again, the guidance I had received earlier was coming true! He also made an effort to give me as much information about Reunion as possible.

On this drive, I experienced the hairpin bends of the island for the first time. From the coastal region (which is a narrow strip all around the island), one must literally climb almost 3 000ft vertically to reach the mountains.

He explained that there are people living in these high mountain ranges, who live very primitively with no modern amenities, because they do not want them. A helicopter lands there weekly to take in groceries and supplies, and to remove their garbage. You can only reach them by going on a four-day hike, or by helicopter.

I was also told that there had originally been a lot of slaves on the island. Some had run away and disappeared into the mountains to avoid being recaptured. When I later saw the mountains at close range, I could believe that. I sensed an extensive tunnel system, and the presence of chambers, or large caves or caverns.

As I stepped out of the 4x4, I immediately felt the presence of the Ancient Ones. My guide took me to the start of the hiking trail and made sure that I

*Vertical steel ladders some 7 feet high tested me to the core as I have a fear of heights.*

had enough water and a map of the trail. The map, from a German tourist guide, had been lent to me by Chantal. It proved to be invaluable, as it turned out to be one of the toughest hikes I had ever embarked upon.

I started the steep uphill climb and realized that I would need a walking stick. That was one item I had forgotten to buy. I asked for one, and a little further up, I found the perfect stick next to the path. It was indispensable, as this was an extremely steep uphill climb, with spectacular views.

What was more, for the first time in my life, I had to climb up vertical steel ladders, with sheer drops on either side. Some were about 7m (23ft) high. I had to overcome my fear of heights – and that took

*Looking back, a magnificent view of the sprawling harbor and city below.*

some guts – but I just called in my guides and asked for help.

The higher I went, the more aware I became of the immensely powerful energies, as well as the magnificent views of the pyramid mountains unfolding to my right. This part of Reunion Island is lush, unlike the south of the island. On my left was a sprawling village, with farmlands that looked like a picture straight from Tirol.

As it was a Sunday, a favorite time for the islanders to enjoy a mountain hike, there were many hikers on the trail. I was told by my guide that in summer, with the humidity and very high temperatures of the coastal belt, many islanders go up into the mountains to picnic, hike and just cool off.

When I reached the top, I sat down on a bench overlooking the village. It was only later that I saw that the other side of the bench overlooked the pyramid mountains. However, that was occupied by other hikers.

As I walked along the mountain ridge, I knew I would find Sentinel rocks marking the spot where the portal must be opened. Sure enough, there they were, in perfect alignment with the main pyramid in the mountains. Moreover, as soon as I saw them, they reminded me of the portal I had opened at Kaapsehoop. They looked exactly the same. They even had the same color and shapes. I felt at home there. It was like a meeting of old friends.

The energy from the rocks was so powerful that I

*After a steep climb, the view is simply breathtaking. Note the perfect pyramids – which are everywhere in Mafata mountains!*

*As I started my hike, and even though only half-way up the mountain, I already found spectacular views as the path rose, with vertical drops on either side.*

*The Sentinel rocks.*

had to anchor myself with my walking stick to secure my footing, for I was standing at the edge of a sheer drop. These mountains in Reunion rise up like sheer fortresses on both sides. They are very steep, unlike the mountains I am used to at home, which have a gentler gradient.

As I stood there, I clearly saw the doors, or openings, into the inner tunnel systems and the gateways to Agartha. Furthermore, it seemed like many of these pyramid mountains had concealed pyramids inside them, and that the whole system was like one massive Crystalline Energy Grid, knitted together and forming a towering, vortex energy portal.

I stood there, 'reading' the energy lines and noticing how they all linked up to Antarctica.

This energy vortex was ancient. I had the distinct impression that this part of the island was far older than the southern part, and that it had been linked up with Mauritius and Madagascar in the very distant

*The pyramids.*

past. I saw images of this island being lifted and thrust up, as land masses sunk under the sea and lava burst forth. This island was created from huge turmoil.

The energies here were very robust, in contrast to those in Mauritius. But then, the two islands differ

*Note the incredible beauty of these pyramids mountains. I believe the original pyramids still are there, as they were thrust upwards during the huge catastrophes and volcanic eruptions.*

in so many ways. I felt that these mountains held many ancient secrets and were directly linked to the first continent, and to Antarctica, when Antarctica had been situated higher up and still attached to the African continent, and Australia. In my opinion,

*After a steep climb, the view is simply breathtaking. There, for the first time, I came face to face with my pyramids and the portal, which I was to open up.*

*This amazing rock stood out like a gigantic Sentinel.*

Reunion was connected more to Antarctica than to Australia. Maybe that link will be found some day.

As I stood there, I was clearly shown exactly where I needed to direct the energies, and where to open the portal. Again, I felt that spiraling energy enter me, and I called in the Goddess of the Waters, the Goddess of the Air, and the Goddess of the Earth; the Ancient Ones and the Cosmic Hierarchy. In that moment I stood there, anchored into the rocks and mountains, and I lifted my hands. Lightning energy flowed from my hands, through my body, and I channeled it towards the spot where I knew the innermost clockwork of the portal was.

Then, speaking the Ancient language of Light, I commanded the energies into the portal, and I stood there shaking from head to toe. The only things firmly anchoring me were the Sentinel rocks and the Ancient Ones, who had gathered around me.

During that time, they managed to keep the constant flow of hikers away from the spot by putting an invisible shield around me, and then helped me direct the energy. I was told that had any of these hikers accidentally stepped into the energy field, they would have disintegrated. They would not have been able to hold the frequency band.

To do this work, I had to dissemble and reassemble myself, and thus could totally step into the truth of

*The massive window opening forms part of the Sentinel in the previous photograph.*

*The mountains of Reunion where I opened the portal with the waterfall in view.*

my heart, soul, mind, and body and carry out this energy work from my higher Soul identity. As I stood in my total Soul power, I was able to open the portal by becoming one with it. I became the energy field to be able to move it, to purify it, to shift the whole and reactivate it.

The stream of hikers could not be kept at bay indefinitely, however, because there was a narrow bridge in the pathway next to the Sentinel rocks, with almost sheer drops on either side. These mountain tops are very narrow. I was told to stop doing the work and that I would be able to complete it at the hotel early the next morning by tuning into these mountains and the portal I had found.

The descent was much more of a challenge to me than the uphill climb had been, although the scenery

*Beautiful flowers on the cliff side as I made my descent.*

*On my way back to the car park on the other side of the mountain, the breathtaking views continued.*

became more and more spectacular. There were quite a few steel ladders on the way down, with sheer drops. How I made it down all of those ladders I do not know. At one stage, I wondered if I would ever get back to the parking lot!

On the first steep downhill climb, I saw a huge towering rock with immense energy around it. I felt that I should have stopped there, but a man had just passed me and had stopped to chat to another Creole gentleman who was sitting there. The latter looked to me as if he did not quite belong there. There was something different about him. Only did I realize that he was one of the Ancient Ones, revealing himself to me, and making sure that I would find the right path back to the parking lot. Indeed, he showed me the way!

I must say that the final part of that hike was just a matter of putting one foot in front of the other and knowing that I would get back in one piece. And I did. I was tired, but somehow just proud of myself that I had conquered my fear of heights along the way.

Wearily I returned to the hotel, took a long bath, and went to bed very early. I was then told to get up at 4am the next morning to complete the opening of the portal. I rose at 4am while everyone was still sleeping.

From the veranda of my bedroom, I faced the sea. I started feeling the spiraling energy enter me and the lightning coursing through my hands. Then, using all the energy reserves of my whole being, I was teleported back to where I had done the work on the

*The almost Alpine beauty of the high mountains and farms in Reunion, on the way to the volcanoes.*

top of the mountain, and I completed the opening of the portal!

During this work, the sea became rough and turbulent. The whole time I was bi-locating to the mountains where I had been the day before.

In this process, I saw so many of the trapped souls of the islands freed: Some of them slaves; others looked like they had been cast out, abused, traumatized, or just lost. I also released a lot of suffering dolphins, whales and sharks that had somehow been caught up in the ethers.

As they were set free, the first rays of the Sun came up, and I felt an immense peace come over the whole island. Although the sea was still turbulent, there was a kind of hush and all the birds were singing around me. They burst into song! The golden rays of the Sun seemed steeped in sacred energy, and I knew that the work had been done.

Tears of gratitude and awe streamed down my face! Mission accomplished! I had done the work!

That day, my last in Reunion, I was able to view the south of the Island. The visit to the volcano was something I will never forget. We rose from sea level via hairpin bends, to over 4 000m. My guide asked me if I had an all-weather jacket with me. When we got to the active volcano on the island, the temperature had dropped from 26°C (79°F) at sea level, to 8°C (46°F).

Until that point, the vegetation had been beautiful hues of green. The higher we went, the more Alpine the scenery became, aided by all the dairy farms located in these highlands.

*The view from on high – but wait at what is coming. Note how green it still is here...*

However, when we entered the volcanic mountains, everything transformed into a Mars-type landscape: Red and black – devoid of life. The contrast was incredible. My guide told me that when the volcano first erupted, he could hardly see the road because of the red dust and debris spewing out of it. It has been active for a year now. We did not have time for the 60-minute walk to the crater, but we could see the volcano's smoke from the information center.

Reunion is an island of surprises, and a truly magnificent geological journey. Leaving the volcanic desolation behind, we moved further up into the highlands, and then drove, once down hairpin bends, down, down to the southern coastal belt and its breathtaking scenery.

Due to the constant volcanic eruptions, the fauna and flora just thrive here. I have never seen such lush tropical flowers and vegetation as in the south of this island. There are windowless Creole homes painted in bright colors, and French colonial-style houses.

However, at certain points, the lava takes over! In one spot, the lava came down the mountain and, by some miracle, stopped just at the entrance to a church!

At another huge lava spill, from an eruption in 2008, the black lava runs 70m (230ft) deep! The massive river of lava ran down into the sea. It flattened a whole plantation of trees and then flowed over the road. You can take tours of lava caverns, which are bubbles created in the lava, my guide told me. Apparently, the acoustics inside these caverns are out of this world!

*Around the corner, desolate landscapes emerged. The scene could have been straight off Mars!*

*Mars. The volcanic ash here is red.*

*Volcanic activity is everywhere.*

*The smoke is coming out of the volcano. We did not walk there because of the limited time frame of my visit.*

*This strange pyramid mountain fascinated me. It differed from all the other surrounding mountains, and I believe that it was once a pyramid, but it is now overgrown.*

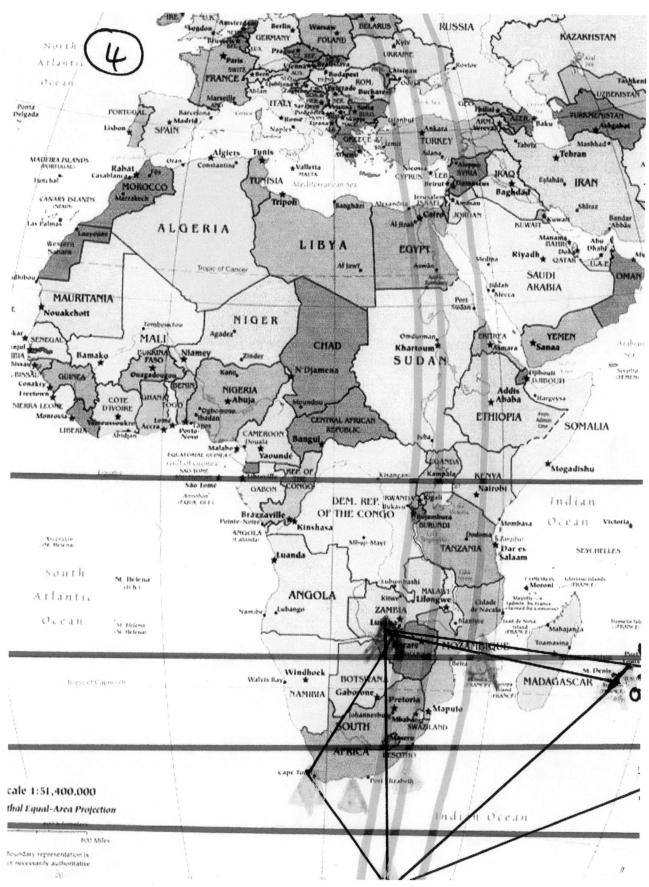

*Reunion grid to Antarctica opens up, as drawn on the map by me.*

*One of the waterfalls.*

From a look-out point, I could see that new life was sprouting from the lava, where water had been trapped. Little trees were taking root and growing, as the ecosystem miraculously moved into life and being! It's no wonder that here in Reunion, even the beaches are mostly black sand!

Reunion is truly an island of contrasts, and it has immensely high energy in places – a little jewel hidden in the Indian Ocean.

I bade these islands farewell and was given the clear guidance that I would now be prepared for the massive energy work I had to do in Antarctica!

# CHAPTER 17

# Antarctica: The Opening of the Stargate, the Pyramids and the Sun Discs

About three years ago, in December 2015, I first began reconnecting to the 7$^{th}$ Central Sun. At that time, I had no idea what this would mean to me, but again I had to go on trust and faith.

In the meantime, with everything that had come to the fore over the past few weeks, my understanding had grown in quantum leaps. Certainly, we are the children of the 7$^{th}$ Central Sun and about to return to the truth of who and what we are!

\* \* \* \* \*

*There are 12 Central Suns, and each one holds certain keys and codes and immense energy fields of love, wisdom and power for the Divine. They are like the central hubs of the Divine Heart, Mind, and Being. Therefore, each one is an entity on its own, but they work as one unit.*

\* \* \* \* \*

Evidence emerged that the Antarctic continent had formed part of the original great land mass, and that it, like Australia, Madagascar and the other islands, had been torn from the mainland. Little did I know what awaited me, before I could truly connect to the massive secrets that the Antarctic continent holds!

In the interim, while trying to put the puzzle pieces together, Antarctica made its presence increasingly felt. I began tapping into the fact that there were pyramids under the sea between Cape Town and Antarctica, but also on the continent itself.

Interestingly, a link was posted on my Facebook newsfeed that made me sit up and take notice: Pyramids had been found in Antarctica. This information was marked "Top Secret", as the American secrecy shields came down and it was immediately hushed up. These pyramids were discovered when the ice melted more than usual. Although this was very interesting, I knew that somehow, further clues would come to me as I was prompted to buy new atlases with larger maps than the small one I owned.

Below are my journal entries in the order that I received the information and clues, piece by piece. They led to the ultimate discovery and the opening of something of incredible significance.

## The Stargate Opens in Antarctica with the Sun Discs' Activation

Opening the portal in Reunion unlocked all the energy lines to Antarctica, and simultaneously those to south-eastern Africa, and the spinal column of Planet Earth.

I had been systematically given pieces of my jigsaw puzzle. With each piece given, I had to go through intense energy upgrades in my physical body and all the other 11 energy centers. Then I had to be purged of all emotional and ancestral baggage, as well as all karma and negative patterns with which my Soul has been entangled while on this planet.

During this process, I often had to act on what I had been intuitively shown; jotting it down in my journals and sketching visual images. I bought increasingly detailed atlases, and the lines on these started to look more and more like a sprawling crystalline grid, as each puzzle piece appeared. In addition, the spinal column travelled down the length of south-eastern Africa, with the oceans in between, into Antarctica.

Essentially, I was given a very interesting blueprint of Africa that held within it certain keys and codes that I had started to understand, although my own comprehension of this differed from most people.

In addition, I came to understand that Antarctica held the entire powerhouse of the Pyramid Grids together, and that whatever had been hidden would unlock the whole energy grid and clear the spinal column of the world.

**What follows is an exact record as it happened; and when and how and where it happened; so nothing has been altered. I was told to keep it sacrosanct because it will activate keys and codes within the cell memory bank and the spinal cord energies of those reading it.**

### JOURNAL ENTRY

Reunion then, formed just another piece of the jigsaw puzzle.

Before going to Mauritius and Reunion, I had been given the most amazing vision:

Firstly, I connected to two, gigantic golden sphinxes that guarded the entrance to a massive pyramid and city complex in Antarctica. At first, these two sphinxes were my initiation into the higher frequency bands that I needed to start tapping into, and I was simultaneously going through rigorous initiations in the inner chambers beneath the Sphinx in Egypt, where I had to integrate the Isis energies.

They put me through extensive energy upgrades, where the kundalini, or serpent, energies coursed through my entire body, and sometimes I literally shook from head to toe. I had to lie down so as not to disintegrate during such upgrades, and had to change my diet to one of only fresh, raw vegetables and fruit.

I then started to connect with the sphinxes. They were facing each other, with their paws meeting in the front. I saw how they buzzed with tremendous energy, and how they possessed an independent energy field of their own. I was given this information regarding the sphinxes:

The Diamond Grid here formed the epicenter that controlled the rest (Antarctica).

In this respect, it was built, not of man-made material, but from pure crystalline forms imported from Andromeda and the Pleiades. It contained immense *light-particle substances and, therefore, was malleable and could withstand strong heat, rays and extremes of weather, such as solar storms.*

*Remember, this was the first out station, and therefore it was built so that no matter what happened in the stratospheres (which were unstable) nothing would affect the structures, or the vortex energies.*

*The vortex energy was created, as the scientists wanted to see how these energies could be utilized to feed the whole Energy Grid. It was also used to stabilize the climatic conditions of the planet and to guarantee an overall balance. At this time, construction of the Central Pyramid of the Sun had begun, and the Diamond Grid fed the energy for this, bringing a dynamic new power to Earth at the time – bearing in mind it was an experiment (Central Sun Pyramid/ Sun Discs, Antarctica) which essentially allowed those volunteers to create something new, under the auspices of the Galactic Federation of the Great White Brother and Sisterhood. All who partook in this experiment had agreed to certain terms.*

*It is vital to grasp this concept to fully understand Antarctica.*

*From this Diamond Grid, the remainder of the one continent of Elysium was systematically populated and built up, and the first pyramids and temples there were for the purposes of knowledge; technology; wisdom; higher teachings; higher healing; Halls of Records (Super Consciousness Energy Field); and enlightenment.*

*The hand-picked scientists involved with the experiment came from Andromeda, the Pleiades, the Bear constellation, Sirius, Orion, Pegasus, and Arcturus.*

*They worked together, and wanted to create a unique type of power grid for the vortex energy, so that motherships and other craft could refuel here (vortex energy via crystalline energy = electromagnetic power source) and then extend this to the rest of the planet.*

*This is a highly-advanced technology in its use of vortex energy, condensing it into a crystalline form, which can then be transferred to wherever needed. Once present, it starts reforming and can then expand*

*or contract accordingly, becoming more or less potent as needed. Thus, this Diamond Grid was created to be the largest power station and energy grid, and it served the whole continent of Elysium.*

*It connected directly to the 12 Central Suns and especially to the 7th Central Sun, under whose energy fields it was co-created. It was then added to the massive Sun Disc in Antarctica, along with the 6 others.*

*Further information on the Sphinx, Pyramids, etc.: The Sphinx is Feminine 3 x Pyramids = Holy Trinity.*

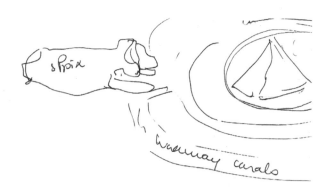

*The Sphinx guarding the portal, as sketched by me.*

*The Sphinx in Egypt guards the Feminine portal, and therefore it is sacred (spinal column of the Earth).*

*The intricacies of this portal bring about the higher opening of the energy centers in greater Antarctica and shifts it into the greater frequencies of Light and Sound electromagnetic fields, which move along extensive frequency bands (Rivers of Life, gold, platinum and diamond) via the sound frequencies, which are then amplified by the Rock Gongs of Africa. This moves into the energy of each of the 33 vertebrae of the spinal column of the Earth, to bring all these energy systems together into a single energy force, which is able to shift this part of the world (the Southern Hemisphere) into a much higher frequency band.*

*Two massive Sphinxes underground guard the stargate of the Central Suns, the 7th Central Sun – 777.*

*This is of enormous significance!*

*There are Sun Discs there belonging to Ra and*

*Isis, and the opening of the portal will activate them. It dissolves (disintegrates) and then downloads the keys and codes for opening the whole stargate, the entire grid, and the spinal column.*

*The two Rivers of Life flowing into one will help bring about a mass retrieval of what the planet lost ages ago in Elysium. It is the recovery of a vast memory bank of pure conscious energy, but it is held in custody. Therefore, you will have to ascend even higher to be able to tap into it.*

*It will bring with it the amplification of your powers, and those of the spinal column and the Rivers of Life.*

*The Sun and Moon merge, and as they merge, they will return immense and amplified energy, which will help unlock the stargate between the two Sphinxes (see sketch on page 202). It lies underground and has done so for billions of years.*

*Africa holds the Gateway Keys, in addition to what you decoded in Australia. So, with that power moving through New Zealand, Australia, then back into Africa and down into Antarctica, this means the ancient energy machine that has lain dormant for billions of years will now awaken as a giant energy system that will have to be carefully harnessed.*

*Your Soul volunteered for this, for you alone hold the keys and codes, and your Soul is strong enough for this work!*

*We are directing the timing of the opening, and what needs to be done.*

*You will be prepared physically, and we will fully activate your higher crystalline body and your full powers. You will become a catalyst for immense energy changes on a planetary scale.*

*The Temples of the Sun and Moon in Africa, and the copper-red Sun streams from Australia, will be directly amplified and launched, ignited from the 7th Central Sun, which is now returning as Earth moves into a new orbit and Galaxy.*

*You hold the central keys and codes of 777, and can therefore intensify its power. You have been prepared for this for many billions of years, and throughout many lifetimes, dimensions and existences. This is nothing new for you.*

*Your actions will help with the rejuvenation of the physical body, as the new Adam Kadmon crystalline body forms, and then these codes and keys will be activated so that this service can be done.*

### November 30, 2014

Today I had to go into the initiation chambers underneath the Sphinx, where I experienced the full activation of my womb; the encoded 777; Solaris Rex Mundi; Antarctica; activation of the Sphinxes; and the 3rd eye of the Sphinxes. They activated the full Goddess womb within me as the Illuminating Sun!

She (Isis/I), therefore, now holds within her womb the full Solaris Rex Mundi* Illumination.

Thus, she holds all the central keys and codes for the New Adam Kadmon 7th dimension within her. The Old Adam Kadmon (prototype) body is making way for a much higher frequency body, more crystalline in nature, which is therefore better able to hold the higher vibrational frequency bands of the New Earth. She brings in the full activation of the Central Sun Illumination of the 777, the 7th Central Sun, 7th Galaxy, and 7th Temple, which is the New World.

*"BuRaRa – I am He/She – the Divine Central Sun, and I am therefore giving My Blessing. I have spoken. I am that I am! Ra."*

* * * * *

I was told to switch off all electronic devices and move away from them, and to lie down for this intense activation. It went through my vagina, my whole womb area, as well as my 3rd eye and crown chakras.

It was so intense at times that I felt I was literally being knocked out.

* * * * *

Today there was a huge Sun activation in my womb area, and for the first time I understood that the Goddess womb was the Sun – the Sun of Illumination. She is the life-giving force, and that life-sustaining force is the Sun of radiant Illumination.

It is only when the male unites with her as one that he receives Illumination through her, and is fully activated into his higher heart and higher mind, and is fully empowered through her. He cannot be illuminated without her!

She has that resurrection power. He must die to the old Adam and go through her by becoming one with her to be illuminated and therefore resurrected! This is what the New Birth is all about!

Interestingly, the 777 Central Sun activation was set in powerful motion. The Central Sun of Illumination and its codes completed the full activation of the keys and codes within my womb today, which were needed to open the massive stargate portal between the two Sphinxes in Antarctica.

I saw myself lying between these Sphinxes. Therefore, the Solar Sun Rex 777 reactivated in my womb like a massive Sun! Then the 3<sup>rd</sup> eye in each of the two Sphinxes was initiated, and an extensive pyramid energy arose between them.

Through this, the Pyramids of Light are activated wherever I go. The codes given are the Key Codes of Illumination, literally bringing Heaven down to Earth through the fires of luminance.

*"Hail ye, Daughter of the Central Sun God; you whom we have fully activated now. You are therefore activated via Sirius and the 7<sup>th</sup> Central Sun to truly step up and into full mission. We have been preparing you for some time for this mammoth task, and now we are fully activating you to illuminate Planet Earth, and to bring back mass knowledge, technology and information.*

*We have a full year for you, as 2015 is the catalyst year, when the activations from the Central Sun will truly be done and start affecting all life on Planet Earth. The old Sun is dying, and therefore the Ancient Sun is returning: That Sun which gave life at the very beginning in Elysium.*

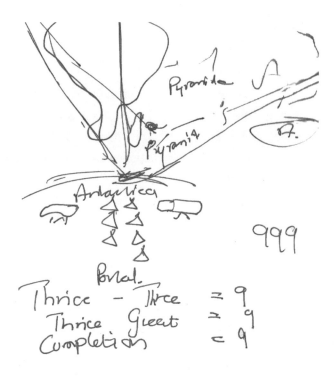

*My sketch of the Antarctica pyramids.*

*You are a true daughter of the Central Sun, and hold within you all the keys and codes; all of which are now ready to be reactivated and retrieved.*

*You have gone through immense initiations in the inner planes, which were first triggered in the Earth year of 2000 and have continued unabated. They have been completed, but the full activations will now take on a different and higher form.*

*The full activation of the spinal column and Tree of Life for humanity, the merging of the two Rivers of Life, and the immensely vital activation of the Diamond Grids and the Pyramid Grids, will now begin. You hold the Ancient Goddess Keys and Codes and act as Guardian and Keeper of these."*

\* \* \* \* \*

How exactly would I bring this all about? This has to do with Sri Lanka, the Maldives and India (more on that later).

**September 3, 2015**

A very important drawing of Antarctica, the two Sphinxes, and pyramids!

There are two massive, white-golden Sphinxes guarding the entrance to the harbor. Their paws come together as they face each other. The front part, up to the back of the head, can swing open and become like a gateway to the inner harbor, which is circular.

A huge pyramid of blinding white light, with a tinge of blue, dominates the scene as one enters the harbor.

From the harbor, there are circular canals of water intersecting the 7 pyramids, so there are 7 loops. The Pyramids and canal systems form a double- and triple-energy helix. The helix has 7 loops, and within each loop stands a pyramid.

It moves with triple force, and thus becomes the Fire of Transmuting Energies, as in energy fields, which link directly to the Central Sun. You will have the keys and codes as you need them.

\* \* \* \* \*

**September 18, 2015**

I am having intense visions of Antarctica, with Thoth/Hermes and Isis.

I saw the 2 gigantic Sphinxes guarding the entrance portal of the harbor, which leads to the pyramids. There is one on either side: Beautiful, massive lions, which are much larger than that in Egypt.

They swing towards me, opening the portal, and I realize that they were constructed to shield the harbor and the pyramids, and could open up, like the Tower Bridge in London, but they act rather as a huge gate because the harbor and city are round and there is a large, transparent, glass dome. The dwellings inside are on many levels, and multiple stories high.

First one sees the harbor, then a massive pyramid, which holds an enormous golden Sun Disc. Then there are 3 pyramids within a circle, forming a triad. The 4 Pyramids form a circle, and then the extensive city is covered with a transparent dome, which makes it invisible to the outside world. (See sketch opposite.)

Thoth/Hermes and Isis took me into the first large pyramid, which had an enormous Sun Disc that dwarfed us.

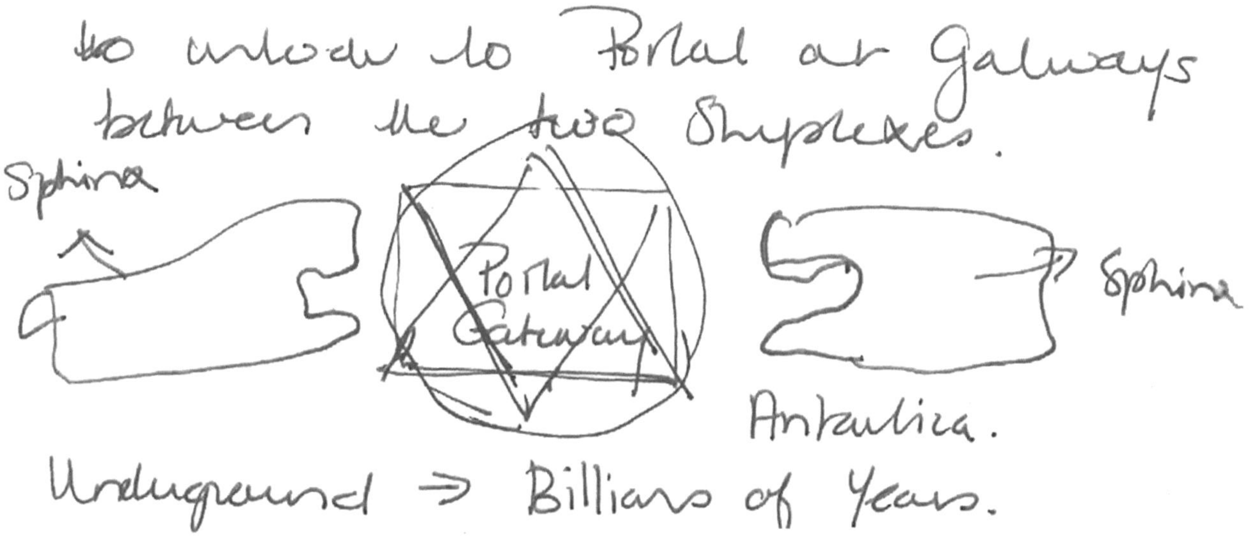

*Sphinxes, as sketched by me.*

*The two Sphinxes guarding the harbor, and the 7 pyramids, with the domed city in the distance.*

I was told that this acts like a big, transformative energy field, and I had to be willing to disintegrate before being allowed to step into it, or near it.

I saw myself dissolve, and I was then allowed to step into the Sun Disc. I became as one with its fire, but it did not consume me! I stepped out and was laid down to be reassembled! I was told that I was being prepared for the vital energy work ahead of me. There was an imposing dome-like curved glass over a huge crystalline city at the end of the pyramids.

Inside, there were dwellings extending many stories below. The people inside were sheltered from the elements, and the climate was artificially controlled. They had a crystal-clear view of the sky above them, but they were held within the whole protective dome and energy stargate.

There was also an invisible shield around this whole complex, and I was told time and again that no satellite, or any other human technology (nor that of their alien allies), could detect this complex.

### September 12, 2015

I have been initiated three times through the Thrice-Great-Fire underneath the Sphinx.

I have been given my full Isis empowerment, and henceforth will have assimilated her completely.

What became very clear is that the old me had to die: The old Judith. When I was resurrected, I was then Isis. I don't quite understand this, but I could not do the required opening of the portals and stargate without having stepped into my total Goddess power.

I have been Isis in Atlantis and in Egypt, so I merely incorporated the full power of Isis and her Goddess-hood, as the Goddess of a Thousand Ways. There is another way of spelling Isis, which is A-Y-sis, and I believe that I blended with her completely.

"The portal to Antarctica works on the principle of clockwork, like a giant Sun Disc in multiple layers of concentric circles, with each one slotting into the other, and then forming one single and greater energy force field.

"This then is the essence of this force, and you will have to move or dissemble it in 7 stages, and we will assist you with this. You will be fine-tuned for this work, and that is what we are doing now.

\* \* \* \* \*

"During the time of Elysium, this was one of the major port cities for the seafaring craft. All craft were amphibious: They could be used on land, in the air and on and under the ocean. There are still the great cities and dwellings of the Mer-people under the sea, and

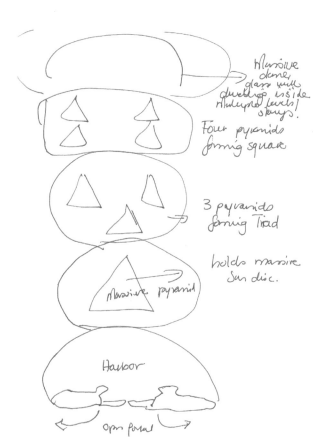

*Stargate, as sketched by me.*

you will meet them, as well as the Ancient Ones, who are awaiting your coming. There is another city that was built underground, and that is covered by a massive crystal dome, which cloaks the city from detection by satellites and other instruments currently used by the global military.

They have the ability to make themselves invisible to Earthlings, as you have found so often in the Drakensberg area of Natal.

Ashtar, your Lord Husband, will assist you with this whole process. He will also over-light you with his craft, and the great motherships will be watching over you."

## 29 November, 2015

Sun Discs and winged Sun Discs:

"There are 12 Central Suns of Illumination and 12 Sun Discs. The latter were taken away from the planet and then sealed off.

The 12 Central Suns of Illumination hold the 12 Central Keys and Codes of the 12 Sun Discs, and therefore hold the highest keys and codes for the Illumination of Planet Earth and for the return and full activation of the sealed Sun Discs. Therefore, as each one is reinstituted and opened, it will catapult mankind back into the 7th dimensional state, from where it originally came.

Then our sons and daughters will inherit the Earth!

First, the massive portal in Antarctica must be opened. This is the central unlocking key that is vital to all else that follows.

The Sun Discs act like energy storage solar disc devices that store the powers of Illumination within them, and all the secret knowledge of Illumination from the 12 original Central Suns.

In other words, the Sun contains all the keys and codes of Illumination of the entire Cosmos.

On a smaller scale, versions of Planet Earth, this Solar System, the Milky Way Galaxy, and the Andromeda Galaxy, would also be connected because they were, in essence, originally one and the same galaxy.

The initial Andromeda Master Galaxy was blown up during the Wars of the Heavens and had to be evacuated.

The current Andromedan Galaxy is an expanded remnant of the first one, and was consequently recreated and reconstructed. It is expanding into the Milky Way Galaxy.

The Sun Discs have smaller discs within them, which work on the blinding White Ray Energy. When the keys and codes are activated within these discs, etheric smaller energy discs are released, which then connect with the brain/higher mind of the High Priestess, and will download the Illumined texts, knowledge, technology of Light energies, and the keys and codes of Illumination. This was the ultimate download that enabled this Soul to be able to tune into the 12 Central Suns. Each Sun, in turn, is the configuration of whichever of the 12 Master Sun Discs it downloaded. So, the Suns of Illumination and Wisdom are amplified and activated in immensely powerful ways.

This is only given to those who will use this energy and technology/knowledge of Illumination in constructive ways, within the parameters of the Divine Cosmic Laws.

In Antarctica, there was a huge temple pyramid and two Sphinxes totally dedicated to these 12 Central Suns, the 12 Master Ray Sun Discs, and a massive Fire/flame of Illumination, which was the Flame of the Godhead, and therefore eternal.

Once a year, the 12 High Priests and High Priestesses of the 12 Central Suns and Sun Discs would gather around this fire/ flame and repledge their loyalty and commitment to serve in the highest possible way. They would solemnly promise to keep the fire/flame of Illumination steady for the planet.

However, as catastrophes started happening, the Wars of the Heavens spilt over into this Solar System and the planet Marduk destroyed itself. The fire/flame was taken away for safeguarding in the 7th and 12th Central Suns.

Subsequently, the 12 Sun Discs were distributed all over the Earth to safeguard those pertaining to this planet and this galaxy.

There are three of these in Antarctica. These will be the first three to be activated and downloaded into you. The rest will come to you as and when the time is right.

In Ancient Egypt, they partly remembered this, but did not have the original discs in their possession any longer. So, your task will be to return these to humanity.

Therefore, take time to record your journal entries, for they will be vital to your book, as we will be transmitting more information into you and through you.

\* \* \* \* \*

As this information came my way, I knew that I somehow had to get to Antarctica. At that stage in my life, I was very involved with a man with whom I had karmic Soul links. At the time, I believed he was my Twin Flame. He was planning to travel to Antarctica in the December, and had said that he would take me along. To me, that meant that I would be physically doing the work in Antarctica.

So, I thought I had an assured passage. We had a special Soul Twin Flame bond that had formed over many lifetimes, pertaining to creating special energy through sacred unions. We had both belonged to the secret ancient Mystery Schools in other lifetimes,

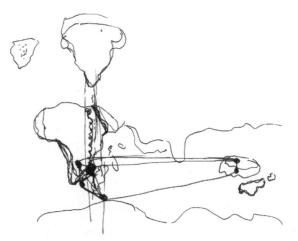

*Temple Sun and Temple Moon activated, as sketched by me.*

and were now reunited to do specific work together. In ancient times, there were sacred sexual rites that enabled the kundalini, or serpent, energy to be amplified during specific rites that were performed with crystal-clear intentions within the Crystal Pyramid Temples.

These were always done with the intention of offering the highest possible service. This was one of the reasons we connected at that time.

My intuitive knowing was sounding alarm bells that he was hiding something from me. Then news came via a trusted friend: He was publicly declaring that he was going to Antarctica on his own. I had kept three weeks clear in my busy schedule to travel to Antarctica with him. When this news was confirmed, I was truly shattered! How could I now do the work? How would I get to Antarctica? I looked at cruises to Antarctica, but I knew I had to do the work before the end of the year.

In times like these, I call all the Divine and Cosmic Councils I work with. I literally laid a fleece before the God/Goddess. My Soul was committed to this work, and I would do it, no matter what. I did not know how to proceed, and I stood there in my brokenness and asked for help.

I was assured that the work would be done without him. He had committed himself to doing the work and had then pulled out because his negative ego had got in the way. (This ego warning had already come to me in the September.) Therefore, if he tried to access what was in Antarctica in any way, whether through sophisticated human technology (he had the money, means and backing of the scientific community), or in any other way, he would not succeed.

They read his intention, and that was enough. Everything was taken from him, because he had reneged on his commitment to me by his own free will. Now the doors would shut in his face, and no matter how much he tried, he would not be allowed in.

They literally cut off any and all of my energetic cords and ties to him, and shut down the whole connection in a wink. Never underestimate the power of the Divine, nor the power of the Cosmic Force!

What happened next was a miracle!

**December 12, 2015**

*We are with you now. You have asked for assistance and we are here. We support you on your Soul's journey. There is nothing to fear.*

*You have been prepared for this over many lifetimes.*

*The opening of the portal in the south of your Earth will be done. All will happen in the right timing for the planet and its inhabitants.*

*The vortex that you will encounter will be like nothing you have ever encountered before, but you have all the required knowledge and power. Do not fear.*

*The mighty Isis is part and parcel of your Soul now. She has integrated her energies with yours. She is you, and you are her. Osiris is with you in the 7th dimensional form.*

*By letting go of all your attachments to your ex, you have opened the pathways for what is to come. There can be no expectation, as that blocks the energies of creation.*

*The great Central Suns have provided the keys and codes of activation. You will assist in lifting this planet out of its entrapment in the dense energies. The opening of energies will be in 'threes' over three years. In this time, you will become known. You will step into your role as a leader and teacher of those who will awaken. You are being renewed so that you can do this work in many places in the world.*

*It is but the beginning for you. You are guided and protected and loved by all who came before you. They are here to assist you and the entire planet. It is time to begin Earth's ascent!"*

**December 13, 2015**

*Dearest Beloved, the one who is the Goddess of a Thousand Ways, we greet you. We welcome you to our abodes, as we are preparing the way for you.*

*Beloved Sister, so long have we waited here beneath the ice, for the day when The Mother would return to us, and then we will be free to be part of the outer Earth again.*

*We have been hidden for so many millions of years, as our powers were being abused, and therefore Thoth came with you to close us down, so that Earthly men could not blow up the whole planet, as had happened elsewhere.*

*Yet, we continued to function on the higher frequency waves and in other dimensional forms, and of course with the inner world of Agartha.*

*So, we kept ourselves hidden from mortal man as he slipped into the seas of forgetfulness. Now we rejoice, and we are excited about your assistance and you becoming our great Goddess, the one who has the power to bring us back to our original glory, and to restore us to a state of being complete and fully functioning once again.*

*We will, therefore, now move to matters of great importance, so we can assist your work and help you with the opening of the stargate here.*

*You tuned into the massive Pyramid of the Central Sun this afternoon, and the Sphinxes. We will now help you to tune into the other pyramids that all form the 777 sacred number of the Greatest of All Beings. This connects to the 7th Central Sun.*

*Then there is the next level of 9/12, which works with 999 and 12 12 12.*

*777, 999 and 12 12 12 work in tandem, making a Central Sun Triad, which heightens their power.*

*This was done at the time of Elysium, in order for the amplified energies to sustain the 7th dimension and the 9th, and then be magnified in the 12th, as Earth evolved.*

*However, the planet's peace was hijacked, and the Wars of the Heavens spilt over on to the Earth, so that the 9th and 12th dimensions never materialized. The energies were merely hidden and sealed off in such a manner that those of the lower dimensional forms would not be able to access them.*

*At the time of Atlantis, the 7th dimensional grids were still functioning in Mu and Lemuria, but in Atlantis they were not, as it was in the 5th dimensional form or state.*

*So, at that time, two dimensional states co-existed. Nonetheless, Atlantis later caused the accelerated demise of Lemuria, and then attempted to access the 7th dimensional power, in an attempt to misuse and disguise their destructive actions in Atlantis.*

*To prevent this happening, the Intergalactic Councils declared that all those centers would be closed down and sealed off, until such time that mankind had ascended along with Mother Earth, as the Council had already anticipated the destruction of Atlantis by the Black Magi.*

*An invisible shield was placed over the central power stations, the central pyramids (more powerful than Giza, which was a much later and far more primitive prototype), and the total powerhouse of the energy grids.*

*This was at the time when Antarctica was ice-free, and when it still formed part of the African, Australian and South American continents and islands.*

*When the land masses split further apart, many of them sank under the sea, while other parts were purposefully shielded and hidden. The Mer-people, the Ancient Ones and the Intergalactic Fleet guarded these areas carefully.*

*When the Earth shifted on her axis, the ice sheet started to develop over Antarctica, covering the whole area where once there had been fertile and lush lands.*

*So, inner cities can still be found concealed under the shield and the ice, and they still work with the Ancient Ones and the inner world of Agartha, the Mer-people and the Intergalactic Fleet.*

*Your coming to open the portal will open the energy grids and the stargates, and the pyramids shall rise again. As this happens, the rest of the combined portals will be opened by you, as they are now ready. This will transpire over a three-year period. They lie in the north.*

*When all of this has happened, and the massive catapult shift has occurred, the shields will gradually be lifted, as mankind becomes responsible enough not to abuse its tremendous powers.*

*So, we are then rejoicing that our mother and sister*

goddess is returning to assist us. We are preparing the way for you.

I am sister, At-A-Ra-A-U-Ru-Ru-A.

I greet you, Isis.

Ra-A-A

## December 19, 2015

And who am I?

A thousand women

Ten thousand women all in one.

The Cosmos is my playing ground...

And ten thousand ways are opening

The Cosmic portals

Dance

The Central Suns move into place

The Goddess of the Waters

The Goddess of the Air

The Goddess of All-that-is

Returns

The keys

The codes

Awaken...

And from the Earth

The west

The south

The north

Are gathering

The suns

Atu-Ra-Ra

**Akuru-Ra-Ay-Sis-R-U**

## December 20, 2015

*Do not be sad and broken, little one. It is his lesson to master, not yours. He was offered an opportunity, but his ego brought him down. It has happened before. He will be blocked in all and every way. His intentions were not pure and therefore he has been stopped. He will not have access, and he will find that this haunts him for the rest of his days. Yet, it was of his own free will and choice.*

*We are letting you know that we love you dearly and that we are helping you. You will be enhanced now, and we will work with all your energy fields, and we will help you to do the work.*

*Let this be your message: That you will have assistance in this, and we will open the stargate, for it is time. Concentrate now on your book. Just rest and allow yourself to be revamped and prepared for the massive work. It will take all you've got, and it will test you to the core. It will take boundless amounts of your energy, but we will help as much as we can.*

*Fast. Eat lots of fruit and yoghurt and add honey, for it is an elixir of the living life force, and lettuce and greens.*

*We will be reworking your energy systems, as said. You will grow in stature, and many thousands of people will be touched in multitude ways.*

*There is an extensive wave of energy now being released as you do this work. So, let this be a moment of stillness before the storm breaks. The whole Cosmos is here to assist you. Understand that we read his intentions and they were not for the highest good, but for his self-service. He is being blocked.*

*You are the Power that will open the Portal.*

*So it is written..."*

## December 21, 2015

I had intense upgrades today. At 5.30pm I was told to lie down. I immediately felt myself going into an altered state, like I experienced in Mauritius and Reunion, and then there I was:

I was teleported to a snow-white pyramid in Antarctica.

I was told to go inside and to sit in the middle of the vast hall, under the apex of the pyramid, which was under its central point.

Around me appeared 12 men and women of Light, in white robes. They were beaming Light into me, as the vortex energy started coursing through me from the apex of the pyramid.

Then I started doing the energy work, just as I had done in Mauritius and Reunion.

I literally had to dissolve, as I was sending out immensely powerful light rays through my hands and directing this unlimited beam of white-golden energies where they were needed.

Then a man appeared. He was taller than me, with golden blonde hair – my beloved Ashtar, High Commander of the Intergalactic Fleet and my Lord Husband. He merged his energies with me, and then the beam of Light twirled and whirled its way from Reunion towards Antarctica, making its way to Prince Edward Island.

As this energy was directed, it paused at a certain point, and a tremendously powerful energy swept through and into the energy lines and into the entire ocean. Suddenly the Lion People and the Ancient Ones appeared in their thousands, with beings of Light, who added their energy to the Keepers and Guardians of Antarctica.

I had to direct the energies through my hands. At one stage, I had to create a ball of fire from beams of energy and throw it into the river. This exploded into massive vortex energy, and suddenly from its depths, a titanic, dark mass appeared. It looked like a long, clogged-up drain pipe that had opened up, releasing all of the sludgy dirt, debris and other obstructions. It was very dark, dense, slimy, and downright ugly. Craft from the Intergalactic Fleet appeared to gather up this whole mass of dark energy and, using balls of fire, to transmute it into something harmless.

This whole area was cleansed and purified, and energies were poured into what had been released!

Then the dolphins and whales appeared, literally frolicking and dancing.

I was then brought back to the pyramid and the circle and teleported back into my body. This first work of clearing a passage from Reunion to Prince Edward Island had been done.

The work had begun! Tears of gratitude!

I never knew what I could do until I was forced to do this. It took all that I had, and I sunk into a deep sleep of utter exhaustion.

**December 22, 2015**

*Let it be known that we are sending you all the support you need. You will do the next work within two hours, as darkness descends.*

*We are preparing you for the major work needed, once we hit the outer rim of the Antarctic continent, where there are many pyramids: Some under the sea and some that are buried under earth and ice.*

*The Sphinxes and the pyramids lie further up, and thus the work now continues on the link between Prince Edward Island, and higher up to the undersea pyramids adjacent to the Antarctic continent.*

*This is where it links up to Cape Town and Nature's Valley. We, therefore, need you to just allow us to use your energy to merge the two energy grids, and then this merging must move up the 33° latitude line; the spinal column merging with the Temples of the Sun and Moon in Zimbabwe, and those of Mauritius and Reunion.*

*Once this merger happens, we can move into the area of the Sphinxes. This will free up all the monstrous congestion caused by the tearing off of land masses and their submergence. There will be mass trauma from the spiritual disturbances, as waste and trapped spirits are released. Then all of the Cosmos will gather here to cleanse and purify this area.*

*So, let this be your guide.*

*You are not alone, little one. You are surrounded by love. You are protected and guarded, and no one will be able to get near you in the next few weeks.*

*You are safe.*

*This will be a gargantuan event, and you will be catapulted on to center stage.*

Today I was told to clear the energy lines from Prince Edward Island to Cape Town, and also from the island to Antarctica, and back to Cape Town in a triangular fashion, so that the connection would be cleared between the Sun Temple in Zimbabwe all the way up the 33° longitude line, which houses the spinal column.

Phew! This took all my strength and energy! I was literally in a totally light dimensional state.

Again, Ashtar fused his Masculine energy with mine, as I stood with my hands up, palms facing outward. He stood directly behind me with his hands in the same position as mine. In combining my Feminine powers with his Masculine powers, we became as one. The energy poured through our hands like a massive electrical current infused with lightning, and we directed this into the energy grids, until the whole triangle was totally lit up.

Then a vortex energy from inside the triangle manifested. Within this, the Intergalactic craft appeared. First, they beamed down energy to form a vast vortex, and then started ejecting all the stuck energies and entities from the land mass that had been torn from Africa.

Half-man half-beast, the strangest looking creatures I have ever seen, were released. They appeared as an accumulation of botched-up experiments – failed attempts of half-man, half-beast creatures – and were the oddest animals. All the creatures that had existed before the Fall were transformed into a mass-like, dark, slimy substance. The ships and Angels collected it up into a mighty net. This then dissolved into a ball of fire, which I knew was the Fire of Transmutation, the God fire. So, they were released.

When all of this had been cleared, the pyramid complex arose out of the sea: The first one was an

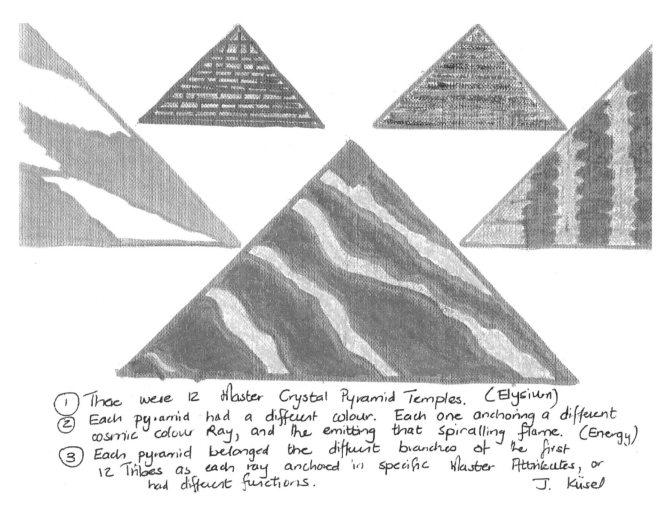

① There were 12 Master Crystal Pyramid Temples. (Elysium)
② Each pyramid had a different colour. Each one anchoring a different cosmic colour Ray, and the emitting that spiralling flame. (Energy)
③ Each pyramid belonged the different branches of the first 12 Tribes as each ray anchored in specific Master Attributes, or had different functions.
J. Küsel

*Master Crystal Pyramids, as sketched by me.*

emerald pyramid, then a platinum and a white, and then, among others, a royal blue one. They were simply magnificent!

Then a beautiful, colored light shone everywhere. It was exquisite rainbow light. The dolphins and whales appeared, and they were frolicking and jumping up and down. The Earth was singing!

It was so profound.

I was totally exhausted.

This is taking all I've got. It requires my total investment.

I am just so grateful for all the assistance I was given by the Cosmic Masters; the Ancient Ones; Ashtar and the Intergalactic Fleet; the Intergalactic Councils; and the Lion People. It was more powerful than anything I have ever done before, and I am realizing that all that I had done before was but preparation for this work.

* * * * *

Today I had to clear the continent of Antarctica.

First I started where I'd left off the day before: With the White, Aqua and Emerald Crystal Pyramids, and then went directly into the White Flame. Purified, I started the work, having been transformed into the Queen of Lightning.

I was literally sending bolts of lightning into the continent of Antarctica, to where I had noticed the City of Light, and then into the Energy Grid lines that were opened yesterday, and so I shifted the continent upwards.

It was like a mass explosion when the lightning energy struck these spots. The whole Earth started cracking open!

Then all the Cosmic Masters moved in to assist, together with the Intergalactic Fleet. Indeed, it seemed as if the whole Cosmos had gathered to give assistance.

As this massive cracking moved deeper into the Earth, a gigantic 'mass' was released. All the muck, trauma and pain in the buildings and from the surrounding areas was swept up, like a volcano erupt-ing. There were pieces of 'debris' everywhere! All of this was collected and transmuted by the Intergalactic craft, the Archangels and Elohim.

I was then brought a white-gold chalice filled with liquid gold. As I spoke words over it, rivers of gold, platinum and diamonds flowed: One massive stream of energies moving upwards, ever upwards, up south-eastern Africa, up the spinal column of the Earth, and northwards. This became 7 streams and then radiated out all over the world, preparing the way for the 12 12 12.

Seven Sun Discs arose out of the massive one, and were then anchored into 7 places on Earth.

Again, there were even more songs that were sung with great joy, and there was sacred chanting, with cymbals clashing.

Then the boundless crowds who had gathered started forming a spiral. They were creating vortex energies through their music, dance and musical instruments. All of this was reverberating throughout the Earth!

Then I did a final blessing and completed a full activation of the Sun Disc Temples. This then paved the way to the Sphinxes and 7 pyramids, ever deeper into Antarctica.

I cried tears of awe and gratitude.

* * * * *

Antarctica is freed! I reached the inner city, the pyramids and Sphinxes. Before I could do that, I had to move the three pyramids into alignment, then shift the energy beyond the massive Sun Disc and into the core of Antarctica.

In the process, we struck a type of pipe. As the Light energy I was directing into the River of Light touched it, it burst open – just like when one opens up a blocked drainpipe. What poured out of that was massive. It was like this black substance that rose up into the stratosphere, and the Helpers had their hands full trying to control it.

This same pipe burst forth with water from the Goddess of the Waters. Tidal waves of light energy in spiraling form were washing, cleansing and purifying the whole massive area. I had never seen anything like it. The whole Intergalactic Fleet controlled and shifted the flow of energy and the dislodged debris; dark and dank particles and whatever else was stuck there that was causing obstruction. I had to direct that River of Light even deeper into Antarctica, but hit a huge wall.

Now the whole of the Cosmic Hierarchy and the Ancient Ones poured in their Light energy with and through me. So, this wall cracked open and started tumbling down. Then, once again, a colossal sheet of water tumbled down, just like a tsunami. It was then that I understood the magnitude of what happened, as the continent tore off from the mainland and sunk under the sea. I have never seen such huge waves of water!

Then, there before me were the golden Sphinxes. I cried when I saw them. Out of the Heavens an immense vortex energy descended. It was sheer, white gold, and it began moving past the Sphinxes and pouring into the ground. There was a huge splitting open, as if through lightning striking, as the bolts were being forced apart, and the enormous side doors collapsed. The pyramids rose; the massive Pyramid of the Temple of the White Flame.

As more and more of these doors fell away, the whole city rose, all 6 pyramids, with the largest being the City of the Sun. Then, wonder of wonders, as the city emerged, everything fell away. There was the biggest celebration, singing and dancing with joy.

Then, oh God, the Earth cracked open, and layers peeled off Earth: Seven layers, until she was reborn! The New Earth rose like a phoenix, and then the massive River of Light moved into all the pyramids and Pyramid Grids around the planet, and the whole of the Southern Hemisphere was just one golden-white color. The Southern Hemisphere has been freed, and now we must move this energy up into the north!

* * * * *

## December 24, 2015

Today it took all I had to break through from where I'd left off yesterday with the massive Sun Disc. Firstly, I had to bring the three pyramids into alignment: The Aqua, the Emerald, and the White Flame.

I had to truly devote all my energies to the task at hand, calling in the compendium of Angels and the Ancient Ones. Ashtar stepped in with the whole galactic core plus the Archangels, Elohim and the Elohim Councils.

I had to direct the energy, the River of Life in Antarctica, beyond the Sun Disc. It had a massive gap opening up, and this dense black substance, like a drainpipe, was spurting out everything that was blocking it. It spurted out to the Heavens, with tsunamis of water gushing out. There was purification through water: Waves and waves of water!

The dirt and debris were washed away and cleansed. Next the Intergalactic craft, assisted by the Angels, gathered all of this muck up, and it was again transmuted with fire.

I had to direct this energy further into the Antarctic continent and was hit by a massive wall of resistance.

Ashtar merged with me and we became as one, directing lightning energy into the wall. It started crumbling and then came tumbling down. Again, there were waves and waves of water, as there must have been when the continents broke off and sank beneath the sea.

When that was completed, suddenly a huge vortex energy of pure, blinding white light appeared, moved deep into the Earth and then, remarkably, the lids fell off, like hatch-doors opening. Out of this emerged the entire complex, the Sphinxes, pyramids and the city I had been shown so long ago!

The two Sphinxes guarding the city rose up, and then the massive pyramid, surrounded with a pure, blinding, white light with a tinge of blue, arose in spectacular glory! All the other 6 pyramids and the whole city ascended.

Door by door, hatch by hatch fell off.

Then there was a mass gathering of the whole Cosmic Hierarchy: The Ancient Ones, the Lion People, and everyone dwelling in the city gathered in rejoicing and celebrations!

Again, there was singing, chanting and music. Rising from this, all the Rivers of Life poured into Africa; into all of south-eastern Africa; the spinal column; the pyramids; and the Pyramid Grids, awakening them all!

I saw how the 7 outer layers of Earth all peeled off. From this, the New Earth rose. I wept.

Everyone assembled, cried tears of gratitude and joy, as the whole Cosmos stood there witnessing the return to glory!

Antarctica was the key to the totality of the universe, and then the 12 Central Suns beamed their collective Light on the city and the entire Earth. With it came the anointing, the blessing of the Awakening, and the birth of the New Golden Age!

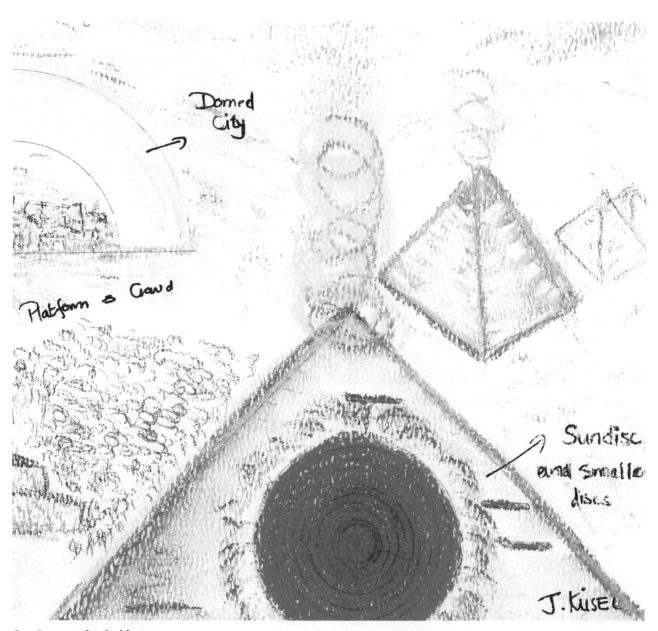

*Sun Discs, as sketched by me*

**December 25, 2015**

I felt intense dizziness and was told to go and lie down.

The next minute, I was in the complex that I had opened up the night before in Antarctica. First I was taken into the pyramids, and then into a vast hall. The hall had floors of inlaid pearl and gold.

I was sitting in a chair. Then I was told that they would download keys and codes into my head/mind.

A huge Sun Disc arose, which formed something like a huge table in front of me. It spun in 3 directions: clockwise, anti-clockwise and then clockwise simultaneously, with flashes of light streaming from it.

Then smaller discs were dislodged from the big one and hovered over my head. These keys and codes were beamed directly into my head, my mind and into the palms of my hands.

I was suddenly transported into a strange place.

A minotaur appeared. I was rather taken aback, because I thought these creatures had all been cleared away. It suddenly vanished into thin air.

The next was a giant. I could only see his brown knee-high boots! Then he, too, disappeared.

I was told that this was the place where they had created the minotaurs, and it was linked to Malta and Knossos, and to a place now sunk beneath the sea where these atrocities originated.

The place appeared cave-like. It all then vanished from my sight.

I was told that the keys and codes had been activated, and that the work on the pyramids and Pyramid Grids would continue so that the north could be freed.

There are the south, the north, the east and the west pyramids, which are all linked up. They form a core grid of Crystal Pyramids that were all created to communicate with each other via the 12 Master Crystal Pyramids of the 12 Rays and 12 Tribes.

So, originally this whole grid system was one vast energy system of highly advanced technology in the 7th dimensional state. It served the whole planet and those living on it.

It not only supplied power, but also powered space and amphibious craft. Furthermore, it operated within the natural energy systems of the planet and Agartha. All the systems worked as one unit.

All the cities then had huge Intergalactic spaceports. Craft from other galaxies and star systems could land, replenish themselves and recharge their craft. Even the great motherships were accommodated.

All 12 Master Galaxies worked here, and many of those original volunteers then interacted with their own people.

Intergalactic travel was the norm (as it still is elsewhere), and the Earth was a sister planet in the Solar System and the Galaxies. They all functioned as one single, collective Whole.

The Pyramid Grid System worked on the principles of those of the 7th Galaxy of the 7th Central Sun, with an exact replica of the sacred geometrical pattern grid, which was energized from deep within.

*We will utilize this system as a basis to work with you, to reactivate the grid.*

*Antarctica was a crucial part of this, for the whole energy grid system was anchored into Earth, when there was a single continent and only one grid system.*

*The grid system was closed down when Elysium fell, and when Earth itself was thrown out of orbit. It had been damaged by the land mass breaking away and sinking under the sea, as well as the arrival of elevated land masses where there had previously been sea, or inland seas.*

*We will first work with this system in the Southern Hemisphere (which used to be the Northern Hemisphere), and then we will move everything northwards.*

*There is boundless gratitude and much celebration that Antarctica has been opened up and that the grid has been cleared. The entire Intergalactic Council, your Lord Husband, the Intergalactic Fleet, the High Councils, including those of Andromeda, and all the Cosmic Hierarchy, are there to continue assisting you.*

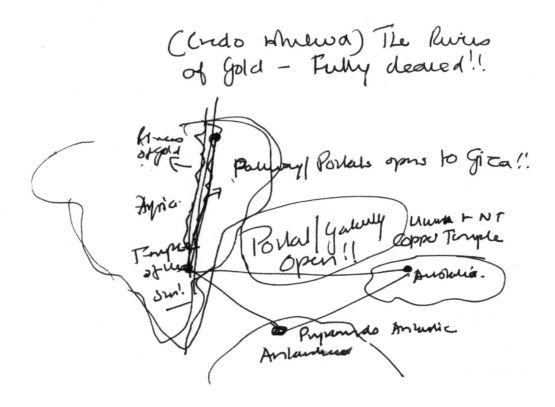

*Spinal column of earth, as sketched by me.*

## The Opening of the Pyramid Grid

First I was taken to the middle of Antarctica, where I opened the vast city complex, the Sphinxes and Sun Discs. Then I was told to go east. There, beneath the sea, on the grid to Cape Town, was a vast pyramid and complex. It was platinum, inlaid with mother-of-pearl with a tinge of aquamarine. It was beneath the sea, offshore between Cape Town and Antarctica. I saw that it had once belonged to a city, and Table Mountain formed part of it!

I first went below the sea to find it and then, with the Intergalactic Fleet helping me, I activated the pyramid once again and it began to elevate. It grumbled and awakened. What a magnificent sight: Pure platinum inlaid pearl! It was beautiful. I had to connect this to the one in Antarctica, then up to Reunion; and then move the energy as multiple grid line streams to the copper-red pyramid in the Northern Territory (Zircon crystal); and the Red in Uluru, Australia. Then it had to go back to Zimbabwe, to the Temple of the Sun, and

into the ocean in the Madagascar Straits, to the Temple of the Moon.

The whole energy grid lit up, becoming one massive source of energy, like a mighty flowing river of multiple streams, into Kilimanjaro. There, a cobalt-blue Pyramid Temple activated and emerged in a huge, sacred geometrical grid with an intricate pattern woven around it.

I was then called upon to activate all of these, and to connect the aquamarine; white-gold; platinum and pearl; emerald; copper-red; red; gold; silver-blue; and cobalt-blue; and 'knit' them all together energetically. I then moved from Australia to an orange one in Hawaii, and a yellow one in what seemed to be the Maldives, and connected those to the ones in Mauritius and Reunion.

The whole grid started to light up, crackling as if electrical currents were sparking it to life. The Intergalactic Fleet came and assisted, and activated the whole grid, which rose in a holographic multi-

*Pyramid Temples of the Moon, as sketched by me.*

dimensional form. I saw it form a Cosmic MerKaBah from the Earth upwards, reaching into the stratosphere. It was huge and pulsating in a vibrant energy field, in all of its holographic splendor.

It started spinning, and mass vortex energy spun into being.

The grid constantly formed sacred geometrical patterns on the Earth, but all were woven into the self-same grid.

The Intergalactic Fleet beamed in more energy. This energy looked like pillars of Light. They beamed me up, and there Ashtar waited, swinging me off my feet with exuberant joy. Everyone was there celebrating!

The grid was energized and the pyramids were connected again!

What joy!

**December 26, 2015**

After I thought the work was done, I was told to open the energy lines of the spinal column of the Earth. I was to take all of the energy up the spinal column from Antarctica, towards the Rivers of Life, up the south-east coast, and then north into Kilimanjaro (where the cobalt-blue Pyramid arose), all the way up to the Pyramids of Giza in Egypt.

I was shown the Rift Valley and how this area had been bombarded by asteroids when Earth was thrown out of orbit. When that was cleared away, I would be able to connect with the Ancient Ones in Kenya. However, there was an extremely dark, dense, clogged-up, indescribable-smelling mass.

It seemed to come all the way from Zimbabwe and then up through Tanzania. It took all I had, all

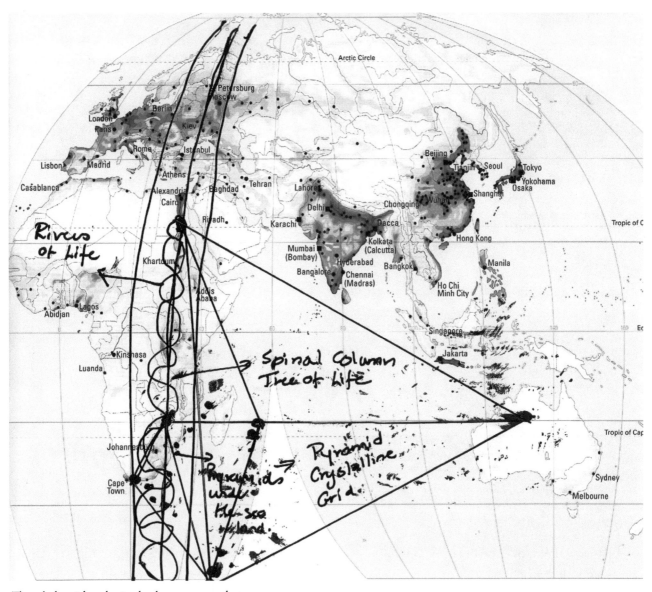

*The whole grid and spinal column, as seen by me.*

of my helpers plus Ashtar merging his energies with mine, to get that stinking mass moving and to send in lightning energy bolts to start dissolving it. With that, strange creatures and bizarre things began to spurt forth from this stinking mass: Creatures that I had never seen before; funny lifeforms that defied description – animals, stardust, asteroids, space debris, half-man half-beasts, and strange insect-like people, some of who looked like stick people. These were definitely the strangest creations I had ever come across!

When these had been dislodged and cleared away, the next layer rose. Now all the tribal people gathered:

The different African tribes, the Arabs, and the victims of the slave trade, with the accompanying trauma of those abused and captured. They all started collecting before us, as we stood on a platform of Light.

I had to use strong energy and power so that vortex energy came down and sucked them all into it. These poor sorry souls were gathered up and released from the etheric planes in which they had been stuck.

When all of this was cleared, the energy could continue to move upwards again, but it then hit another bank of thick, sluggish, black energy in Ethiopia.

This time it would not move, and I had to go back

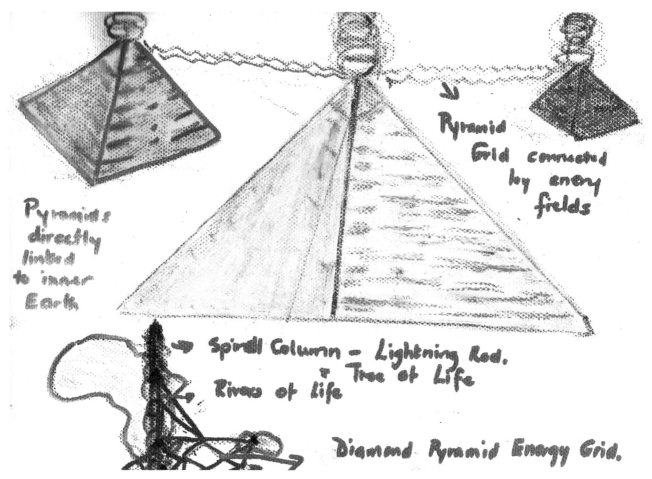

*The whole grid and spinal column, as seen by me.*

to Antarctica and move the Rivers of Life up to gain momentum. It then hit the wall of black energy and broke through the barrier. This time, a far bigger and more powerful ball of fire spurted forth from the Rivers of Life, which literally burnt its way up to the Giza Pyramids. It hit with such a force that it shook!

The Rivers of Life became one burning mass of fire. The fires swept through the whole of south-eastern Africa, down into Antarctica and then up again. The river of fire then went up and down the spinal column of the Earth, until all the muck and debris and everything else had been completely purified by the force of this fire, and it was crystal-clear.

So, the passage to the north had been cracked open! The work in the north has begun!

I saw myself on a vast platform in front of the Great Giza Pyramid. I was now Isis, totally Egyptian, and standing there addressing the crowds. There was music and dancing (as happened elsewhere: Celebration!).

I stood and addressed the crowd, but I was activating something prodigious, for as I was speaking the commanding Light language, an extended energy burst forth and streamed through the people, cleansing the whole of Egypt. It then flowed into the Rivers of Life. Then the huge river flowed down in splendid beauty and power into Antarctica and pulsated up and down the spinal column of the Earth.

It was so beautiful that I was moved to tears. The spinal column of the Earth had thus been reactivated, but not completely so. The Northern Hemisphere still had to be cleared. The energy had broken through the barriers at Kilimanjaro, and had now moved into the Giza Pyramids. They could now be brought to the rest of the north.

What magnificence!

Oh God, this work was massive! I had to clear the whole of the north, from Kilimanjaro right up to the Giza Pyramids. What muck! All those years of slavery, abuse and the rest. In Ethiopia, Sudan, and then Egypt… what immense blockages emerged. They sent down the God-fire to burn that up.

A lot of pain had transpired there. The clearing of fire, and by fire. It had to be fire, for nothing else could cleanse to that depth and breadth and with absolute totality. It was fire that had trapped them. A ball of fire had hit them, as if Hell had opened up and swallowed them. Now they have been freed!

* * * * *

The spinal column of the Earth had been revitalized!

I have realized that I couldn't have completed my book without having done this work! Now that the spinal column has been cleared, the south-eastern parts of Africa, Antarctica and the Southern Hemisphere have also been released.

Now the kundalini/serpent energy, the Rivers of Life, can flow freely up and down the spinal column of the Earth. The trunk of the Tree of Life has been restored. So, this is the preparation for the full returning of the Cosmic Tree of Life to Earth!

It is just a miracle! Miracle after miracle!

Thank you! I am so grateful! Thank you!

## The Pulsating Opening and Activation of the whole Pyramid Grid!

**January 1, 2016**

I had thought that the work was completed, but it was not so.

After being in tears for no reason this morning, I was told to switch off all electronics and then to lie down while they worked on my energy fields.

The next minute, I was back in Antarctica in the midst of the pyramids – 3 of them: White, platinum and a crystal-clear shimmering one. They were pulsating. Then something strange happened: I dissolved and became the pyramids, and they became me. The whole energy grid started throbbing with a blinding white light! With that, the whole Pyramid Grid revived – from Antarctica to the north, and to all the grid points to Africa, to Australia, Mauritius, Reunion and the sea.

What emerged looked like the Kabbalistic Tree of Life!

I saw this clearly, for it mirrored the Tree of Life I had posted elsewhere over Africa, but it was anchored in the ether, over and into Antarctica.

This beautiful, vibrant, pulsating energy was moving through the whole holographic grid.

Then I was back in Antarctica, and in front of me were the sprawling pyramids, the domed city and the two Sphinxes.

I had to activate the Sphinx in Giza so that it connected again with the two Sphinxes here. This was possible now that the energy flow of the Rivers of Life had been restored from Giza to Antarctica, and vice versa!

The Sphinxes were now vibrating with a vibrant, white-gold energy. I saw the gigantic Sun Disc and 7 Sun Discs again rising from the huge one, as before. Then they hovered over the Sun Discs, and each one was rotating very fast, just like a UFO pulsating with energy. Again, one was placed over my head.

I arose and had this titanic energy coursing through me. My whole head started shaking with the impact. I directed the energy flow, and activated even more Pyramid Grids. Then a veil emerged: A black, dense screen over the pyramid and its grid. They arrived in their spacecraft and removed the veils of amnesia that had trapped mankind in the illusionary state of the 3rd dimension.

I was told to let them work on my energy field, to help me to assimilate this. That would give me access to the energy fields and all that they contained. I was told to have a salad for lunch and to lie down again. They carried on working on my spinal column the whole time.

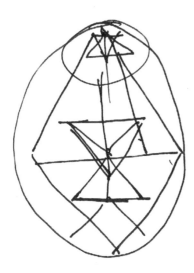

*Crystalline Pyramid Grids almost diamond-shaped structure fitting into each other. Forms a diamond pattern.*

I was immediately transported back into the Pyramid Grid, but it arose in multidimensional grid systems, stacked on top of one another in a holographic form. The entire field then molded itself into one single pyramid! (See sketch.) The next minute, I was standing commanding, with my hands stretched out, with lightning spurting in and through me, as if I was filled with lightning bolts. I directed this lightning and crackling energy into the holographic grid.

Then something amazing happened! I became the grid! I literally rose up in the grid and, as I started to stand up in it, I took the whole grid into my body and blended with it!

When I had merged in totality with it, I had activated the whole grid, and it was like I had become the phoenix rising from the ashes. Indeed, the whole Pyramid Grid and the Tree of Life had arisen and been renewed! Then the complete system started humming, singing, vibrating and pulsating; spinning with vortex energy. It was one massive spinning energy field, pulsating with light, color and sound. It was alive!

It looked like holographic Pyramid Grids interconnecting multidimensionally. Each pyramid cluster of 3 and 7 was like a pulsating orb, or disc, within the grid system. Antarctica was the massive hub or powerbase, for it holds the energy for the Southern Hemisphere. The Tree of Life had arisen and been renewed!

The smaller discs are holographic energetic fields and contain within them a very highly developed form of technology that downloads information directly into one's head (mind).

The halos of saints that is often depicted in paintings are humans remembering these discs, and how they hovered around the head to download information.

These small discs are teleported from the massive, pulsating and rotating one in Antarctica. Today, it stood upright and was suspended in mid-air. Previously, it had been horizontal. Today, it is vertical.

Just overwhelming love and gratitude!

Perhaps we never know what we are capable of until we are forced to do what must be done because there is no other option!

---

While transcribing my journal entries for the final chapter of my book, I realized that from December 21, 2015 until January 1, 2016, miracle after miracle had occurred, as I was called to open massive energy stargates and the whole Pyramid Energy Grid on the planet. The spinal column of the Earth has been freed, and the Rivers of Life are flowing again. This opens the door for the return of the Tree of Life to the planet, and the full activation of this.

With this, the connection to the 12 Central Suns has been restored, and the Sun Discs have been freed.

If you had told me this a few years ago, when I started my quest, I could not have believed it! At that time, I did not even comprehend what I was being called to do. It was all just a giant leap of faith.

I have tears of gratitude running down my cheeks. It is not me. I am but an instrument used by much higher hands. What a journey of discovery and an adventure this has been!

# PART 4

# FULL CIRCLE

# CHAPTER 18

# Coming full circle

When I started my journey in 2009, I did not know that I would be brought back to the foothills of the Natal Drakensberg to find the missing links and the puzzle piece I needed to finalize the picture.

I had to go all the way to Mauritius and Reunion to find the symbols and the writing on the rocks there in order to be led back to the Natal Midlands to complete the circle.

I was again told categorically to book into the Granny Mouse Country Hotel, and to cancel my earlier booking. By now I have learnt to listen to my higher guidance, so I changed the booking. On arrival, I knew immediately that I was in the right place, as the energies were very high.

Having flown from George to Durban for the first time, I was shown again how the Karoo once formed part of a vast inland sea, with plenty of tropical islands. When flying over the Transkei, I was shown two major craters. They reminded me of the Vredefort Dome[1] and the Tswaing crater[2]. One was gigantic. This was even more confirmation that the planet had been bombarded by meteorites, asteroids, and comets when Elysium was destroyed.

To my surprise, while wandering around the hotel premises, I found huge rocks everywhere. On closer examination, I found the same markings, symbols and apparent writing on them as I had found in Mauritius!

In addition, they'd been cut so precisely and smoothly in a way no 1848 British settler would have been capable of when he landed on these shores. It was extraordinary.

Indeed, the self-same Byrne settlers had complained bitterly to the British government that the farms they had been given were strewn with rocks, and that there was no way that they could farm on the land allocated to them.

---

1   The Vredefort crater is the largest verified impact crater on Earth. It is more than 300km wide. (*Wikipedia*)

2   Tswaing is an impact crater in South Africa. It is situated 40km north-west of Pretoria. This astrobleme is 1.13km in diameter and 100m deep. Its age is estimated to be 220 000–52 000 years. (*Wikipedia*)

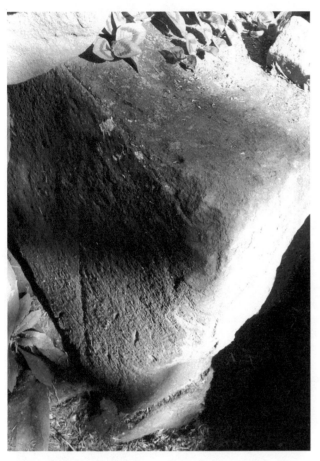

*The symbols found etched into the rock gong at Balgowan in the KwaZulu-Natal Midlands.*

*The vibratory symbols on the rock gong.*

*An ancient altar and rock gong.*

*A closer look at the symbols on the gong.*

*Look at the two Suns that are linked. Note the rays and drill holes on the rock gong.*

When these settlers arrived, the whole inland area of Natal had been empty. It was considered no-man's land by the Voortrekkers[3], who had arrived here in 1838. There were Bushmen in the caves of the high Drakensberg Mountains, while the Zulus owned the land up to the Tugela River. However, the whole of the Natal Midlands and northern Natal was uninhabited at the time.

What the settlers then found were the remains of a sophisticated civilization that had been there millions of years before. The terraces can still be seen on the steep inclines, as well as the stone circles.

The rocks I found on the premises were precision-cut, and the smaller rocks had been carefully packed on either side of the road. What had saved some from being moved was simply their amazing size! I found more symbols on another rock strewn amongst other massive rocks – hiding what needs to remain hidden.

I found a wonderfully preserved rock gong, with the drumstick stacked next to it, on top of the rocks. It is beautifully carved and has symbols of Suns, vibrations, tuning forks, pyramids, and so on,

---

3 The Voortrekkers consisted of Trekboer pastoralists and Cape Dutch citizens from the Eastern Frontier of the Cape Colony who, during the 1830s and 1840s, left the British-controlled Cape and moved into the interior during what is known as the Great Trek. (*Wikipedia*)

*More symbols, or writing, on the rock gong.*

*Other engraved symbols on the rock gong. All these photos belong to the same ancient altar and rock gong in the garden.*

*This strange rock has found its way to elsewhere in the garden.*

*Another of the rocks distinctly carved and perfectly shaped.*

*This is the most perfectly cut rock — and it is massive.*

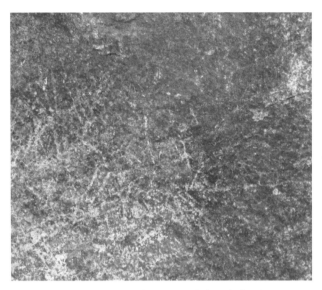

*These etchings were carved into a rock found elsewhere on the premises.*

*A preserved rock gong: When rung, it emits high-pitched sounds, like a bell or chime. It has symbols engraved all over it. Note the drumstick next to it, also carved out of rock, lying on top of the small rocks.*

*This rock looks like a giant tool, with another pyramid-shaped rock behind it. Both have symbols on them.*

*Look at the face carved in the bigger rock gong: It reminded me of the Olmec faces found in Mexico.*

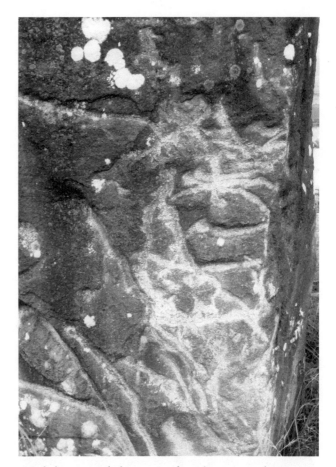

*Symbol upon symbol is engraved on this giant rock gong.*

*Massive, megalithic, perfectly-cut rocks are stacked one upon the other.*

*Look at the etching on the rocks.*

engraved on it. I struck it, and a very high, vibratory bell, or chime sound, came from it. The more I struck the gong, the more it vibrated and the clearer the sound was.

Credo Mutwa states, as mentioned elsewhere, that these gongs were used in Ancient Times to communicate over vast distances, and even across oceans.

When striking this gong, I was reminded of sonic sounds: The same sonic sound that dolphins and whales use to communicate. Could these gongs link up to dolphins and whales? There are two radiating Suns engraved on this rock gong, and it has distinct round holes everywhere, which form patterns. On the right, there are two lines radiating forth from the deeper grooves, like engraved tuning forks.

I believe that my fellow countrymen, like those in Mauritius, simply used the rocks they found on their allocated farms to build their homesteads. One can see rocks piled up in the sugar cane fields everywhere and in the midst of tree plantations.

That these rocks were preserved on the hotel premises was more by accident than by grand design – or maybe grand design prevented them from being moved. I then recalled having seen stone circles strewn all over my cousin's farms, where the Tugela and Buffalo Rivers meet, on the border between Natal and Zululand.

They had invited my archeologist brother to investigate them, but he admitted that he could not identify their origin. However, he acknowledged that it merited further investigation. These farms were in the region of the gold mines I mentioned earlier.

It seems to me that the whole south-eastern part of Africa is strewn with terraces, round circles, precision-cut rocks, and rocks with symbols and writing on them.

The remains of Elysium are everywhere. It is a matter of remembering, and the truth will reveal itself.

\* \* \* \* \*

*A chamber and entrance to the inner world, Agartha, carefully hidden in the overgrowth.*

# SHE – The Guardian and Keeper of the White Flame

She came to Atlantis at the specific request of the Intergalactic Council, the Federation, to establish the White Flame on the planet once again, and to be the Custodian and Guardian of this flame.

So, she left the beloved shores of her home in Andromeda, and came and did what she could in the Golden Age of Atlantis. She was then the Guardian, the Keeper, the Custodian and the High Priestess of the White Flame. She stood resplendent in her innate powers, which made her the woman she was, and the Temple likewise stood in its glory and magnificence.

Then visions, premonitions and an intense knowing came to her concerning what had infiltrated Atlantis, and what had begun to infiltrate the minds of the male beings.

She stood firm in her majesty and started warning the women to not submit to the men, nor allow them to abuse their powers. But the women did not listen, for they were ensnared by their men and accustomed to surrendering to them.

It was not that she did not understand that her sisters wanted to be loved, and she longed for that male essence, the union created through their own sexuality; it was that she understood the potent force of it all. She saw beyond the process, and she anticipated the repercussions for everyone, for her insight and understanding were deeper than that of others.

So, she witnessed the way men began taking control to separate themselves from the women, and from all that was Feminine, because they had come to fear it. She began to see how her sisters were losing their own powers, how they were mind-controlled and manipulated. Love and sex had become a competitive sport, and women were slowly but surely being enslaved.

So, she called all of her sisters together: The High Priestesses who had stayed true to the Law of One; and other sisters who had also served, who were all in great pain as they saw what was happening; as well as those men who had stayed true (and there were many). She then devised a Master Plan of Action, so that the keys, codes, the inner knowing of the female High Priesthood, and that of the lesser priesthoods

*Me as High Princess of Andromeda, in my true Light body form.*

and the knowledge contained therein, would be hidden away, and removed from the planet, as she herself withdrew.

This was done.

She safeguarded the knowledge. She ensured that all the Pyramid Grids; the vortices; and all that contained the Feminine movements of the Earth, Sun and stars, would be removed. What could not be taken away for safekeeping was stored in various centers on Planet Earth. Everything was sealed. With this closing off, the Galactic Councils added their seals, and so everything pertaining to the Ancient Knowledge was shut down as she withdrew.

She left the men with just enough to keep going and to distract them from the ultimate knowing, for they had to master certain soul lessons, as did all the sister souls who'd been caught in that snare of control: Being used and abused.

She returned to Earth at the time when Egypt flourished; when her beauty was unsurpassed and her powers were such that men feared her. So, once more, the men became abusive, playing power games and considering the women as chattels; mere toys. They again made love a competitive sport, not honoring the lessons they should have learned from Atlantis – heightened by the tendency of the male gender to violence and self-destruction, often by their own swords.

In that lifetime, she was again accompanied by Thoth, and those of his ilk, who had remained loyal in Atlantis and in Egypt, as she closed down the Sphinx and all it contained. She then went on to close off the remainder of these powerhouses.

She withdrew from the planet's activities, but she never left. With those loyal sisters, she embraced the task of keeping the Fires of Illumination in custody for the rest of humankind, until such a time as they would finally be ready to step up into the highest states of consciousness and be able to bring the full Feminine powers into being again.

These sisters often took upon themselves the collective pain and suffering of mankind. In the midst of all of this, they still managed to shine their Light and Love in such a way that the Fires of Illumination held steady through it all. She thanks her sisters for this, and the brothers who also stayed true.

The second attempt to reignite the Fires of Illumination and to bring back the Divine Feminine came in Languedoc with the Cathars, and women who held the secret keys and codes at that time. They once more suffered intense pain, and often severe persecution and trauma, to hold that flame steady.

She has returned. She is here once again.

She is no longer buying into the power-play of men. Nor does she allow herself to be drawn in by such distractions.

She refuses to buy into the men's notions that sex and love are a competitive sport; keeping scores of women's attractiveness, and then controlling the planet's views of what women should look like and be. She sees this as it is: A form of manipulation, and a deep disrespect for the Creator God/Goddess who created many forms of expression, and ultimate "beingness". As there are no flaws in Creation, each man and women is perfectly made, and therefore deserves to be honored and loved for who and what they are.

She does not participate in the gossip and talk of her sisters, who love to compare themselves physically with other women, as being more or less beautiful, for she knows that she is perfect just the way she is. She does not need to compete with anyone. She is more than enough as she is. She thanks her Creator for her beautiful body, and she honors and respects and nourishes that form.

She refuses to engage in any sexual relationship in which she is not honored and validated. She treasures her own sexuality and respects her own womanhood, for she learnt from Atlantis that the physical form is as much a temple as it ever was, and therefore anyone who enters this temple and is disrespectful; abuses it; takes it for granted; thinks he owns it; or uses it for his own means; buys it with money; or whatever form the manipulation and control takes, is not worthy of being granted entry in the first place!

She does all the inner and outer cleansing and clearing work, and she now vibrates at a much higher frequency band. She is at home with herself and all that she is. She does not need a man to validate her. She is happy and content on her own, for she can delve ever deeper into the mystery of her own womanhood: Her knowing; the visions; the prophecies; and the work she is being called to do. She surrenders herself into the highest possible service.

She knows that the more she works on the healing of self, the more she is healing humanity at large. She knows that the more she loves herself and finds her own worthiness, the more she will attract goodness into her life, and the more she can co-create in the New World.

She knows that if she is meant to be with a man in this lifetime, he will come in Divine timing. She just wishes to be ready for him; to keep her heart and soul open. For now, she is preparing herself for his coming. She knows that happiness and love are qualities she must cultivate from deep within herself. If he comes into her life, it will be in the fullness of all that makes him a man. He will be her equal and treat her with love and respect, and then trust will be built.

For this will be a man who has found himself, is in balance and harmony, and stands in his own power without having to resort to manipulation, nor games of power or control, nor any games at all! He is genuine, authentic and loving without having to compromise his manhood, or anything that makes him the man he is. He is mature enough to understand this, and is therefore filled with respect for everything that makes her a woman. He, too, is at peace with himself from deep within.

She is now working full-time, for the return of the White Flame: The Guardian, the Keeper, and Custodian she in truth – She has returned!

And her sisters have returned, too.

One day she will gather all her sisters who stood by her in Atlantis, and she will thank them for the work they did, and still do.

Not only the sisters, but the faithful men, too.

For she has let go of all resentment towards all men, and forgiveness is her key. She understands the male woundedness, and how they fear the disintegration of their powers, which is happening now. She sends them unconditional love, as she gently leads them back to themselves: The original innocence they had in Atlantis and before.

For Atlantis was but a repeat of what happened long, long ago, and this time men and women will have to master the lessons of power – true power – once and for all.

For power is, in truth, a double-edged sword. It can build, create and illuminate, or it can destroy.

She knows this, and therefore she stands fully in the power of Love.

# Index

CPSIA information can be obtained
at www.ICGtesting.com
Printed in the USA
BVHW021938270921
617628BV00002B/61